DATE DUE

APR 1 9 2011	
DEC 1 1 2012	

Also by Andrew J. Cherlin

Public and Private Families: An Introduction

The Marriage-Go-Round

The
Marriage-Go-Round

The State of Marriage and the Family

in America Today

Andrew J. Cherlin

Alfred A. Knopf New York 2009

THIS IS A BORZOI BOOK
PUBLISHED BY ALFRED A. KNOPF

www.aaknopf.com

Knopf, Borzoi Books, and the colophon are registered
trademarks of Random House, Inc.

Grateful acknowledgment is made to the following for permission to
reprint previously published material: *Annual Review of Sociology:*
Excerpt from "Stepfamilies in the United States: A Reconsideration" by
Andrew J. Cherlin and Frank F. Furstenberg, Jr. (*Annual Review of Sociology,*
volume 20, August 1994). Reprinted by permission of the *Annual Review
of Sociology.* · Wiley-Blackwell: Excerpts from "The Deinstitutionalization of
American Marriage" by Andrew J. Cherlin (*Journal of Marriage and Family,*
volume 66, November 2004). Reprinted by permission of Wiley-Blackwell.

Library of Congress Cataloging-in-Publication Data

Cherlin, Andrew J., [date]
The marriage-go-round : the state of marriage and the family in America today
/ by Andrew J. Cherlin. — 1st ed.
p. cm.
Includes bibliographical references.
ISBN 978-0-307-26689-7
1. Family—United States—History. I. Title.
HQ535.C416 2009 306.850973—dc22 2008053508

Manufactured in the United States of America
First Edition

To Peach

Contents

Acknowledgments

The idea for this book began with a conversation I had with my British colleague Kathleen Kiernan, of the University of York, about the differences between American families and Western European families. Early on, Nancy Cott and John Gillis took the time to meet with me to discuss my preliminary thoughts on United States history, and Alan Wolfe talked with me about American religion and subsequently read a draft of the manuscript. A conference on marriage and child well-being, hosted by Sara McLanahan at Princeton University, gave me the first opportunity to express some of the arguments in this book. I received valuable comments on early drafts from Larry Bumpass, Frank Furstenberg, and Pamela Smock. I thank Jeffrey Timberlake for providing me with special tabulations on family instability from his work with Patrick Heuveline. I also thank Robert Baller, who at my request constructed a map of high-divorce and low-divorce areas in the United States. Maria Cancian, Myra Marx Ferree, Mary Ann Glendon, and Robin Wilson sent me unpublished papers that were very useful. Gunnar Andersson helped me to interpret his life table estimates from the multinational Fertility and Family Surveys project. In addition, I gratefully acknowledge the John Simon Guggenheim Memorial Foundation for awarding me a fellowship for the academic year 2005–2006 that allowed me to write a first draft. And finally, I thank my editor at Knopf, Victoria Wilson, who saw the promise of the project and helped me transform the drafts into a book.

The Marriage-Go-Round

Introduction

Although I have been writing about American families for three decades, I began to develop the idea for this book only in the past few years. It seemed to me that family life was different in the United States than in the other Western countries—Western Europe and the non-European English-speaking nations of Canada, Australia, and New Zealand—in a way no one really understood. I noticed, first of all, that in none of the other countries has marriage become a social and political battlefield. Nowhere else is the government spending money to promote marriage. In no other Western country would a person walking down the street see the advertisement I have seen on the sides of buses in Baltimore: a smiling couple proclaiming, "Marriage works." Moreover, nowhere else is the debate about same-sex marriage so fierce.

These observations imply that what's different about the United States is the strength of marriage as a cultural ideal. Although that's true, other signs suggested to me that the promarriage ideal is only part of the American difference. I know that in no other Western country is the waiting period for a no-fault divorce so short. I was stunned to read, buried in a footnote in an academic journal, that children living with two married parents in the United States have a higher risk of experiencing a family breakup than do children living with two unmarried parents in Sweden.

Moreover, I reflected on what happened when, in 1997, the Louisiana legislature passed the first law in the United States allowing "covenant marriage" as an option for couples applying for marriage licenses. In a covenant marriage, both spouses agree to restrictions on how quickly and easily they can obtain a divorce. Shortly after the law's enactment I received calls from several reporters seeking my reaction. They assumed that a majority of couples would choose the covenant option. After all, wouldn't people who refused it be telling their partners that they weren't sure they wanted a lifetime commitment? Wouldn't the regular version seem like marriage lite? Despite these arguments, I was skeptical that most people would agree to lock the exit door so tightly. I guessed that maybe a third of all couples would choose covenant marriage. Several years later, it became clear that my guess was wildly high: almost no one had chosen covenant marriage. Less than 2 percent had opted for it in Louisiana and in Arkansas, which introduced it in 2001.

Why did so many newlyweds turn down the opportunity to restrict their ability to divorce? The answer lies in the competing cultural models that Americans hold. Just as the word "marriage" taps a reservoir of positive sentiment in America, so does the phrase "individual freedom." The United States is unique among nations in its strong support for marriage, on one hand, and its postmodern penchant for self-expression and personal growth, on the other hand. You can find other Western countries where marriage is strong, such as Italy, where few children are born outside of marriage and relatively few people live together without marrying, and you can find Western countries with highly individualistic values, such as Sweden, where marriage and cohabitation are virtually indistinguishable. But only in the United States can you find both. Consequently, Americans are conflicted about lifelong marriage: they value the stability and security of marriage, but they tend to believe that individuals who are unhappy with their marriages should be allowed to end them. What Americans want, in other words, is for everyone else to have a covenant marriage.

In fact, the United States has one of the highest levels of both marriage and divorce of any Western nation, and these rates appear to have been higher than in most other Western countries since the early days of the nation. The percentage of people who are projected to marry—close to 90 percent—is higher than elsewhere. Yet the United States has the highest divorce rate in the Western world, higher even than vanguard countries such as Sweden. At current rates, nearly half of all American marriages would end in divorce. In addition, Americans' cohabiting (living-together) relationships end more quickly—either with a breakup or with a marriage—than in other countries.

So while some observers focus on marriage, others on divorce, and others on unmarried parents, I believe that what truly makes American families different is the sum total of these differences—frequent marriage, frequent divorce, more short-term cohabiting relationships. Together these factors create a great turbulence in American family life, a family flux, a coming and going of partners on a scale seen nowhere else. There are more partners in the personal lives of Americans than in the lives of people of any other Western country. The most distinctive characteristic of American family life, then, the trait that most clearly differentiates it from family life in other Western countries, is sheer movement: frequent transitions, shorter relationships. Americans step on and off the carousel of intimate partnerships (by which I mean marriages and cohabiting relationships) more often. Whether an American parent is married or cohabiting or raising children without a partner, she or he is more likely to change living arrangements in the near future than are parents in the rest of the Western world.

This merry-go-round property of American families is more than a statistical curiosity. We should be concerned about it, both as parents and as a nation, because it may increase children's behavioral and emotional problems. Simply put, some children seem to have difficulty adjusting to a series of parents and parents' partners moving in and out of their home. It's not just parental divorces and breakups that are hard for children. Even transitions that bring a new partner or stepparent into the home can be difficult to cope with. Children whose parents have remarried do not have higher levels of well-being than children in lone-parent families, despite the addition of a second parent. (By "lone parent" I mean a parent who is neither married nor living with a partner.) One reason is that new stepparents unavoidably disrupt the existing relationships between lone parents and their children and force family members to construct new relationships—a difficult and demanding task. Children may not have to adjust as much to a short-term live-in boyfriend, but his presence may be disruptive nevertheless. He may not have much commitment to the children's well-being, and he may take some of the mother's time and energy away from child rearing. The children may have to compete for resources with a half sibling or with children from the partner's previous relationships. Children may begin to regard the new partner as a parentlike figure, only to be disappointed when he leaves. Repeated movements of parents and their partners and spouses in and out of the child's household, then, could affect the child's emotional development. Stable households, whether headed by one or two parents, do not require that children adjust repeatedly to the loss of parents and parent figures or to the introduction of cohabiting partners and stepparents and the new children these partnerships sometimes bring.

A close look at this phenomenon will also help us answer the larger question that underlies this book: how to interpret the profound changes in American family life that occurred in the twentieth century, and in particular during the tumultuous past half century. So rapid and radical have these changes been that each generation alive today has experienced them in its own way. Many of today's oldest Americans grew up in the Great Depression and fought in World War II. In the late 1940s and 1950s, exhausted by hard times and war, they turned inward toward home and family. Their early and nearly universal marriages and their large families produced the famous baby boom. Sometimes celebrated as the "greatest generation," they were at least the most distinctive. Neither their own parents before them nor their children after them married as young or had as many children. We sometimes think of the 1950s as the era of the traditional family, perhaps because that's as far back as our collective memory now reaches. But in truth it was the most unusual time for family life in the past century.

When the boomer babies, the large cohort born at midcentury, began to reach adulthood in the 1970s, they changed the nature of family life in ways that puzzled their parents. Sex, living together, and marriage, which had been a package deal in the 1950s, were no longer linked. Young adults no longer needed to get married in order to live openly with a sexual partner. As a card-carrying member of the boomer generation, I can attest to the shock value of these changes. In 1971 I returned home and, during dinner one night, told my parents that I was living with my girlfriend. They were stunned. A year later we married, and the incident was soon forgotten; had we lived together for a longer time, however, my parents would have had a hard time coping with the situation. In addition, my generation witnessed a doubling of the divorce rate from 1960 to 1980. To be sure, the divorce rate has been rising since the Civil War, if not earlier, but the jump in the 1960s and 1970s was especially steep.

By the time my daughter reached young adulthood, at the dawn of the millennium, I would have been surprised had she *not* lived with her boyfriend before marrying him. In her generation, cohabiting before marriage became the norm and premarital sex nearly universal. Having children without marrying—a shameful occurrence in the 1950s— became commonplace. The journey from adolescence to adulthood, so clear at midcentury, is now a long slog filled with choices. Even in midlife, choices continue: *Am I satisfied with my marriage? Should I consider ending it? If I am divorced, should I marry again?* The stakes are high because we place so much emphasis on having a successful personal life, even as the meaning of success becomes less evident.

In some sense, the direction my daughter's generation is taking con- stitutes a return to the way family life was a century ago, when people married at older ages not too different from what we see today. But in other ways today's family patterns are unlike anything that previous generations of Americans have ever seen. While there have always been couples who lived together without a public ceremony or a license, they considered themselves to be married, not merely cohabit- ing. The law referred to them as "common-law marriages." There have always been lone mothers raising children, but most were widowed or were involuntarily separated from their husbands. There have always been births outside of marriage, but in most places at most times, they have been stigmatized.

What we have witnessed over the past half century is, at its core, the unprecedented decline of marriage as the only acceptable arrangement for having sexual relations and for raising children. Marriage is still important, but it is now optional: people can start relationships or have children without it. This transformation reflects deep changes in val- ues, economics, and technology. In the realm of values, Americans place a greater emphasis on personal satisfaction, be it through a career or an intimate partnership. While it's easy to criticize this tendency in others, few Americans are prepared to reject it for themselves—which is why so few young couples have chosen covenant marriage. In economics, the strides of women in the workforce have made them more independent of men. They can wait longer to marry, and they can opt to end a marriage, because they can rely on their earnings more than previous generations of women could. In addition, the economic prospects of young men without a college education have plummeted as globalization and automation have transformed the world economy. As a result, fewer young men make attractive marriage partners, and neither they nor their prospective spouses see them as ready to marry. The big change in technology was the little pill: the medically effective birth control pill became widely available in the 1960s. For the first time in human history, unmarried individuals could have long-term sexual relationships without fear of pregnancy. Better birth control played a key role in the rise of cohabitation.

In the space of a half century, then, we have seen the widest pendulum swing in family life in American history. We have gone from a lockstep pattern of getting married young, then having children, and for the most part staying married, to a bewildering set of alternatives that includes bearing children as a lone parent and perhaps marrying at some later point; living with someone and having children together without marrying; or following the conventional marriage-then-children script, perhaps later divorcing, then probably living with a new partner and maybe remarrying. We have gone from concerns over the costs of conformity—think *The Organization Man*—to troubles over the tyranny of too many choices.

Consequently, we choose and choose again, starting and ending cohabiting relationships and marriages. I will argue that this distinctive pattern of multiple partnerships is related to the central place in American culture of both marriage and a kind of individualism that emphasizes self-expression and personal growth. The term "culture" has many meanings; in the most general sense, it includes everything that makes us human, as opposed to being mere primates. Material culture includes all the tools that humans have invented, from the inclined plane that helped workers haul stones up the sides of the pyramids to the jet plane that hauls passengers up the layers of the atmosphere. Symbolic culture, which I am interested in here, includes our beliefs about what's of value in our world and how we should act toward each other.

Social scientists who think about culture these days claim that people often learn more than one cultural model of the social world and actively choose which one to apply. In other words, they may have different ways of interpreting a given situation—different guidelines about how to act. When waiting with a group of people, I may sometimes line up nicely in single file (as at a bank) and sometimes surge forward (as on a subway platform). Individuals frequently hold more than one way of responding in their heads, flip-flopping from one to another as they go about their lives. My argument is that in American culture, marriage and individualism form a contradictory pair of models. The cultural model of marriage includes a public, formal, lifelong commitment to share your life with another person and, in most cases, to raise children together. Marriage, although optional, remains the most highly valued form of family life in American culture, the most prestigious way to live your life. In fact, marriage is so important to Americans that in the mid-2000s its extension to gay men and lesbians became a major political issue, with President George W. Bush supporting a federal constitutional amendment, and many states amending their own constitutions, to restrict it to heterosexuals.

Yet American culture also contains the model of individualism. What scholars call utilitarian individualism—the self-reliant actor, the rugged individualist, the young man ready to go west at Horace Greeley's suggestion—has long served as an ideal. A second form, expressive individualism, developed during the twentieth century. It is about personal growth, getting in touch with your feelings, and expressing your needs. It emphasizes the continuing development of your sense of self throughout your life. The cultural model of individualism can be found in most Western countries, but its strength is high in the United States.

Family life in America comprises both cultural models—marriage and individualism. Each is part of the cultural tool kit, in sociologist Ann Swidler's phrase, that people use in constructing their personal lives. You can use one set of tools today and another tomorrow. You may cite the prestige and material advantages of marriage to justify marrying your live-in girlfriend or boyfriend. Several years later you may use the language of expressive individualism to justify leaving the marriage because it no longer meets your personal needs. Sometime after that you may employ the model of marriage again. Both cultural models are so ingrained that Americans move from one set of tools to another without necessarily realizing it. The contradictory cultural models of marriage and individualism remain central to American family life in part because religion and law transmit and reinforce both of these models in ways that differ from how it happens in other Western countries.

On one level, then, this book is a consideration of the contradictions of American culture—a set of values found in this peculiar combination nowhere else. To illustrate this, I will compare family life in the United States with family life in other Western countries. I will present information on a broad range of countries when possible. But I will concentrate on Britain and France, two nations with which the United States has long had close relations and which are, in some respects, similar to the United States. Britain is the European nation one would expect to be most like the United States in its family patterns, and in general that is true. We share not only a language with Britain but also a legal heritage: the American colonists retained the British "common law" in matters of family life. We share neither language nor law with the French, and French Catholicism is farther removed from American Protestantism than is the Church of England (and its American relative, the Episcopal Church). We do, however, share the historical experience of a revolution in the late eighteenth century carried out in the name of liberty and equality. Moreover, the founders of the American republic were influenced by the French philosopher Montesquieu, who argued in *The Spirit of the Laws* that marriage was an important component of a successful republic. That's why France provides an interesting case study in potential similarities and differences with the United States and with Britain.

I am interested in these cultural contradictions not in the abstract but rather in how they can help us make sense of the enormous changes in family life. And ultimately I want to confront this question: If experiencing a series of partnerships may hurt children, what should we do about it? Right now, the main message we are giving to young adults and single parents is "Get married." That's the message of government-funded programs to support marriage; that's one of the messages of the 1996 welfare reform law; and that's the message of civic groups such as the ones that have plastered promarriage posters on Baltimore buses. I will suggest, however, that we spend less effort promoting marriage and more effort promoting stable family lives for children. These two goals are not the same. It makes sense to encourage two parents who have just had a child together to get married and stay married if their relationship is good. We know that married biological or adoptive parents who get along well can provide an excellent, stable environment for raising children. (So that I don't have to repeat the phrase "biological or adoptive" throughout the book or invent a new term, please take the category "biological parent" to include both genetic and adoptive parents.) It makes less sense, however, to encourage a lone mother who has long since ended her relationship with the father of her children to get married. (To simplify my prose, I will refer to "lone mothers" and "nonresident fathers" even though there are a modest number of lone fathers with children.) If she were to marry anyone, it would almost always be someone other than the father. The resulting stepfamily would not, on average, improve her children's well-being. And a child whose mother moves in with and then soon separates from a new partner may be worse off than a child whose mother remains unpartnered. In other words, the well-being of the children of lone parents may be improved not by urging their parents to quickly bring a stepparent into the household but rather by urging them to search longer and more carefully for a partner, or to remain single if they choose. The stable home a single parent can provide to her children may be more beneficial than a quick repartnering or remarriage.

Consequently, to the current chorus of "Get married," I would sound a counterpoint: "Slow down." If you are a lone parent, take your time finding a new live-in partner. See the traffic light of singlehood as yellow rather than green. Don't move in with someone, and don't remarry, until you are sure the relationship will be a lasting one that will benefit your children. I grant that if lone parents were to follow this advice, they might take longer to marry, and some might never marry. So be it. Although marriage is important, slowing down the process of partnering would, I am convinced, be in the best interests of American children. We should make stable families a policy priority regardless of how many parents are present in the home.

I am not writing this book to suggest a return to some bygone golden era of family life. I am not nostalgic for the 1950s. The increase in individual rights since then is in many ways an advance. No one wants to go back to a time when husbands could beat their wives with little fear of prosecution, when children born outside of marriage had no right to expect support from their fathers, or when married couples who agreed to split up had to concoct a sham story about which one of them was at fault in order to get a divorce. Yet those archaic circumstances held a half century ago. Moreover, many adults value the opportunity to grow and develop during adulthood, much as they may belittle the similar desires of others.

But along with its advantages, greater individualism also brings problems. One is the instability of family life and its consequences for children. This is not a catastrophic problem; a majority of children probably can cope with their parents' series of partnerships without serious difficulties. But it's likely that a series of partnerships raises the risk that children will experience problems such as being disobedient at school or at home or becoming pregnant as teenagers. If it were your child, you might not want to raise that risk, even if you knew that your child was still unlikely to experience serious problems. That's why we need to understand the American pattern of partnering and its consequences and to determine whether there is anything we can do as a society to mitigate the difficulties it seems to cause. And that's the goal of this book.

How American Family Life Is Different

On Valentine's Day in 2005, Governor Mike Huckabee of Arkansas, who would gain recognition in 2008 as a candidate for the Republican presidential nomination, and his wife, Janet, converted their marriage to a covenant marriage in front of a crowd of 6,400 at an arena in North Little Rock. The governor was aware that few Arkansas couples were choosing the covenant option—of the first hundred thousand or so marriages that had begun since it was introduced in 2001, about six hundred couples had chosen it. In Louisiana and Arizona, the other states that offered covenant marriages, the take-up rate wasn't much better. Advocates for covenant marriage claimed that many couples were unaware of it and that the laws had been poorly implemented. Even so, the numbers were far smaller than anyone expected. Those who chose Arkansas's option agreed to undergo premarital counseling. They also agreed that if either spouse ever requested a divorce, they would attend marital counseling before splitting up. And they agreed that neither spouse could obtain a quick divorce based on "no-fault" grounds such as incompatibility. Only if the other spouse had committed a serious transgression such as adultery or physical or sexual abuse could a covenant-married person ask for an immediate divorce. Otherwise, the person who wanted out had to wait at least two years for a divorce.

In order to breathe life into this moribund option, the governor had announced his intention to enter into a covenant marriage and invited others to join him. "This law allows couples to choose to be held to a higher level of marital commitment," he said in a radio address promoting his rally. At the event, thousands of married couples, many bused by their churches, filed into the arena as love songs played on the public address system. After the governor and his wife exchanged vows, they asked the couples in the audience to stand and face each other, and they led a mass recitation of vows. Only the Huckabees' ceremony legally counted as a covenant marriage, however, because couples who are already married must submit an affidavit to the county clerk in order to convert their marriages, and according to news reports the logistics had proven too complicated for the churches that were supporting the rally. Nevertheless, the governor, a former Baptist pastor, had made his point: there was too much divorce in Arkansas and people's commitment to their marriages needed to be strengthened.

Governor Huckabee's concern about the divorce rate in Arkansas, which led him to sponsor the Valentine's Day covenant marriage rally, was well-taken. In 2004, for instance, Arkansas had the second-highest number of divorces per person of any state (after Nevada, a divorce destination that does a brisk business with out-of-state visitors). But Governor Huckabee may not have known that Arkansas also had a large number of weddings. In 2004, it had the third-highest per capita rate of marriage (after Nevada and Hawaii, two popular wedding destinations). With much divorce *and* much marriage, Arkansas exemplifies the American pattern.

That a state in the Bible Belt—Arkansas is well above average in church membership—has a high rate of marriage may seem unremarkable; by contrast, its high divorce rate may seem odd. Yet six of the ten states with the highest divorce rates are in the South, and the other four are in the West. George W. Bush carried all ten states in the 2004 presidential election, which suggests that having a socially conservative electorate does not insulate a state from divorce. It is true that people who are religious are less likely to divorce, but religious Americans still have high divorce rates by international standards. Moreover, people in high-divorce states tend to have less education, to marry earlier, and not to be Catholic—all of which are risk factors for divorce. That's why Arkansas stands out: it has one of the lowest percentages of high school graduates and of Catholics, and one of the lowest median ages at marriage, of any state.

Both marriage and divorce contribute to the larger picture of a country in which people partner, unpartner, and repartner faster than do people in any other Western nation. They form cohabiting relationships easily, but they end them after a shorter time than people in other nations. They tend to marry at younger ages. After a divorce, they tend to find a new partner more quickly. In other words, having several partnerships is more common in the United States not just because people exit intimate partnerships faster but also because they *enter* them faster and after a breakup *reenter* them faster. We know these facts from the work of demographers using the Fertility and Family Surveys, a remarkable set of surveys conducted between 1989 and 1997 in European countries, Canada, New Zealand, and the United States (as well as from other surveys in Great Britain and Australia, two countries that were not included). In each nation researchers asked a large, random sample of individuals comparable questions about their marriages, divorces, and cohabiting relationships.

Why, you might ask, did researchers go to the expense and trouble of conducting these surveys throughout Western Europe and non-European English-speaking countries? The answer is that enormous changes have occurred in family life not only in the United States but also throughout the Western world in the past half century (and in much of the rest of the world, too, for that matter). People everywhere are concerned about the future of the family as they know it. In the Scandinavian countries and in France, cohabitation is even more common than in the United States, and a large proportion of all births occur to cohabiting couples—more than half of first births in Sweden. Divorce rates have increased, too, although not to the height seen in the United States. Yet what drives European concern is not the decline of marriage but rather the decline in births. It's hard for Americans to understand this concern because we don't share it. American women have enough children to maintain the size of our population, even ignoring immigration. In many European countries, in contrast, women are having fewer births. Countries such as France and Germany have long been concerned with keeping their populations up so that they can field armies large enough to defend themselves. More recently, they have been concerned about having enough working-age adults to care for their growing elderly populations.

In the United States, however, the concern is about marriage, and the Fertility and Family Surveys have much to say about it. To compare, say, current divorce rates across countries, ideally we would interview a sample of people who get married this year in each country, follow them for the next several decades, and see how many become divorced. But no mere mortal has the time to wait that long. Instead, demographers use the "life table" method, so called because one of its first uses was to estimate how long people would live so that insurance companies could determine how much to charge them for life insurance policies. It can be used to estimate the expected "survival" time of marriages, cohabiting relationships, or periods of singlehood. Its estimates will be inaccurate if conditions change greatly in the future. Essentially, the life table answers this question: If conditions stay the same as they have been recently, how long would we expect a marriage, a cohabiting relationship, or a spell of being single to last?

The American Difference

Here are some comparisons that can be made between women in the United States (the American survey did not include men) and in other Western nations in the mid-1990s, when most of the surveys were conducted:

- *Americans marry and cohabit for the first time sooner than people in most other Western nations.* Half of all first marriages occurred by age twenty-five in the United States, compared to age twenty-nine in Italy, thirty in France, thirty-one in Sweden, and thirty-two in the former West Germany. In part, ages of marriage are older in Europe because in some countries more young adults cohabit prior to marrying. Yet even if we consider the age at which half of all first partnerships of either kind (marital or cohabiting) occur, American women were relatively young: age twenty-two, compared to twenty-one in Sweden, age twenty-three in France, twenty-six in West Germany, and twenty-eight in Italy.
- *A higher proportion of Americans marry at some point in their lives than in most other Western nations: 84 percent of American women*

are predicted to marry by age forty. In contrast, the forecast drops to 70 percent in Sweden and 68 percent in France. (For technical reasons, all of these forecasts are likely to be somewhat lower than the actual percentages who will ever marry.) If we consider both marital and cohabiting relationships, however, over 90 percent of women in nearly all countries will eventually begin an intimate partnership.

So Americans begin to have partners at a relatively young age, whereas many Europeans wait longer. And Americans turn those partnerships into marriages—or marry without living together beforehand—much more quickly. In France and the Nordic countries, in contrast, young adults tend to live with partners for several years before marrying, if they marry at all. In some southern European countries, such as Spain and Italy, living together prior to marrying is less common, and many young adults live with their parents well into their twenties before marrying. Other English-speaking countries are more similar to the United States, but people there still marry at somewhat older ages and are less likely to ever marry over their lifetimes.

- *Marriages and cohabiting relationships in the United States are far more fragile than elsewhere.* After only five years, more than one-fifth of Americans who married had separated or divorced, compared to half that many or even fewer in other Western nations. And among Americans who began a cohabiting relationship, over half had broken up five years later (as opposed to remaining together, whether they subsequently married or not), which is a substantially higher figure than in other nations. Whether they started a partnership by marrying or by living together, Americans were less likely to be living with that partner five years later.
- *Because of these fragile partnerships, American children born to married or cohabiting parents are more likely to see their parents' partnership break up than are children in most other countries.* Forty percent experienced a breakup by age fifteen. About the same percentage experienced a breakup in New Zealand. In Sweden, the country with the next-highest rate, the comparable figure was 30 percent; it was in the high twenties in western Germany and Canada, and the low twenties in France and Australia. Children born to cohabiting

parents in the United States and New Zealand faced exceptionally high risks of experiencing a breakup: about three-fourths no longer lived with both parents at age fifteen. But even if we look just at children born to married couples, American children were more likely to see their parents break up. In fact, children born to *married* parents in the United States were more likely to experience their parents' breakup than were children born to *cohabiting* parents in Sweden.

Without doubt, then, there are more breakups of married and cohabiting couples in the United States than in any other Western country with the possible exception of New Zealand. So not only do Americans marry more, they also divorce more. Further, they end their cohabiting relationships more quickly. So they start and end partnerships with a speed that is virtually unmatched.

- *After their breakups, American parents are more likely to repartner. Consequently, children in the United States who have seen their parents' partnership end are more likely to have another adult partner (cohabiting or married) enter their household than are children living elsewhere.* In the United States, nearly half of children who had experienced the breakup of their parents' marriage or cohabiting relationship saw the entry of another partner into their household within three years, a much higher proportion than in Sweden (where one-third see a new partner within three years), West Germany (29 percent), France (23 percent), or Italy (8 percent). In fact, American children spent more of their childhoods in stepfamilies than did children in continental Europe, Canada, or New Zealand. As a result, American children experienced not only more breakups but also more new adults moving in with the biological parent who cared for them.
- *American women become parents at an earlier age and are much more likely to spend time as lone parents in their teens or twenties than are women in Western Europe.* By age thirty, one-third of American women had spent time as lone mothers; in European countries such as France, Sweden, and the western part of Germany, the comparable percentages were half as large or even less. But children born to

lone parents in the United States are also more likely to experience a parent's new partner moving into the household than in some other countries, including France, Sweden, and Germany. So more lone-parent families started, and more ended.

What all these statistics mean is that family life in the United States involves more transitions than anywhere else. There is more marriage but also more divorce. There are more lone parents but also more repartnering. Cohabiting relationships are shorter. Over the course of people's adult lives, there is more movement into and out of marriages and cohabiting relationships than in other countries. The sheer number of partners people experience during their lives is greater. Jeffrey Timberlake has estimated the percentage of women in each country who had three or more live-in partners (married or cohabiting) by age thirty-five. These were women who may have lived with a man and then perhaps married him and had children, divorced him, lived with another man (partner number two), ended that relationship, and then lived with or married yet another man (partner number three). In most countries, the percentage of women who accomplished this feat by age thirty-five is negligible: almost no one in Italy or Spain, less than 2 percent in France or Canada, and 3 percent in Germany. The highest figures elsewhere were 4.5 percent in Sweden and 4 percent in New Zealand. But in the United States, 10 percent of women had three or more husbands or live-in partners by age thirty-five, more than twice the percentage in Sweden and New Zealand and several times the percentage anywhere else.

The Impact

From a child's perspective, experiencing three or more parental partnerships would imply a scenario such as being born to a lone mother who later marries the child's father, then divorces him and starts a cohabiting relationship, then ends that relationship and lives with someone else. The percentage of children who experienced three or more mother's partners by age fifteen in the mid-1990s was less than

2 percent in every other country except for Sweden, where it was 3 percent. But in the United States, it was 8 percent. So about one out of
twelve American children saw at least this many transitions in their living arrangements. The number of children who experienced exactly
two parental partnerships (but not three) is considerably higher, and
again the United States led with 21 percent, compared to 16 percent in
Sweden, 11 percent in Canada, and 8 percent in France. Nowhere else
did children see so many adults come and go.

Children who experience a series of transitions appear to have more
difficulties than children raised in stable two-parent families and perhaps even more than children raised in stable lone-parent families. For
instance, they tend to have sexual intercourse at an earlier age and are
more likely to have a first child outside of marriage, even after taking
into account how much time they have spent in lone-parent families.
Studies in other countries have produced similar results. In Australia,
children whose mothers changed partners had more behavior problems than both children whose mothers remained married and children whose mothers remained single. In Britain, children who had
experienced more than one divorce reported lower levels of happiness.
In New Zealand, the more parental separations, divorces, remarriages,
deaths, or reconciliations a girl had experienced, the more likely she
was to become pregnant by age twenty.

A group of American researchers followed more than a thousand
children from nine states from birth until first grade. They found that
the more family transitions the children experienced, the more likely
they were to show behavior problems in first grade. For instance, they
were more likely to be disruptive with teachers and not to comply with
teachers' requests, whether they had been born to married parents or
not. You might expect that children born to single parents would be
doing better in first grade if their mothers had found new partners. But
just the opposite occurred: children who had been born to single parents showed fewer problems in first grade if their parents had remained
single than if their parents had started (and sometimes ended) new
partnerships.

Still, we cannot be sure that experiencing parents and partners moving in and out of the house actually *causes* the difficulties researchers

have found in children. Some aspects of the parents' personalities or abilities could affect both the stability of their partnerships and their children's behavior. We know, for example, that some of the seeming effects of divorce are visible even before the parents separate, which suggests that they might have appeared even if the parents had stayed together. It's possible that parents and their children might share a genetic trait—a susceptibility to depression, for example—that could cause parents' marriages to fail and their children's emotional problems to be worse. A way to test this possibility is to compare the adjustment of biological children, who share their parents' genes, with adopted children, who do not. If having genes in common is the root cause of the difficulties we see in families of divorce, we would expect that biological children of divorced parents would show more problems after a parental divorce than would adopted children. But that's not what researchers find. Rather, emotional problems increase comparably for both groups, suggesting that the problems children show after a breakup are not just the consequence of inherited traits.

Why do the comings and goings of parents' partners affect some children's well-being? We know the most about what happens after married parents separate and divorce. The breakup of a marriage usually produces a short-term crisis during which children are upset and parents experience diminished parenting skills. But gradually lone parents and their children establish agreed-upon rules and new daily schedules. They work out ways of relating to each other that may differ from prebreakup days. A daughter may become a special confidante to her mother, or a son may assume new responsibilities, such as taking out the garbage, washing the car, and performing other tasks his father used to do. Put another way, lone parents and children create a new family system. Then into that system, with its shared history, intensive relationships, and agreed-upon roles, walks a parent's new live-in partner.

When Frank Furstenberg and I began to study stepfamilies a quarter century ago, we thought that remarriage would improve the overall well-being of children whose parents had divorced. For one thing, when a lone mother remarries, her household income usually rises dramatically because men's wages are so much higher, on average, than women's wages. Consequently, if a decline in the standard of living hurts the well-being of children in lone-parent families, an increase after the mother remarries should improve it. In addition, the stepparent adds a second adult to the home. He or she can provide support to the biological parent and back up that parent's monitoring and control of the children's behavior. A stepparent can also provide an adult role model for a child of the same gender.

But children whose parents have remarried do not have higher levels of well-being than children in lone-parent families. Their levels of behavior problems, for example, are similar to those of children in lone-parent families and higher than those of children in two-biological-parent families. While many explanations have been suggested, the most common is that the addition of a stepparent increases stress in the family system at least temporarily, as families adjust to new routines, as the biological parent focuses attention on the new partnership, or as stepchildren come into conflict with the stepparent. This increased stress could cause children to have more emotional problems or to perform worse in school, which could counterbalance the positive effects of having a second adult and a second income in the household.

Today, a majority of stepfamilies begin as cohabiting relationships. We know little about what the addition of a cohabiting partner does to the well-being of children. But in some respects, such as school achievement, children living with a cohabiting mother appear to fare less well than children living with lone mothers or remarried mothers. Lone mothers may be willing to live with a partner whom they wouldn't necessarily marry. After all, letting someone move in is a decision that can be reversed more easily than getting married. So lone parents may begin cohabiting with partners whom they like but whom they don't see as marriage material. Their partners, in turn, may not be interested in becoming permanent family members or in developing parentlike relationships with their children. Consequently, even if they make life better for the parent, cohabiting partners may not do as much for the children. They could even be a net drain on children's resources if the parent becomes preoccupied with the intimate relationship. Children living with a mother and her cohabiting partner tend to get poorer grades in school, skip school more often, and have more trouble getting their homework done than do children with a mother and a married stepfather or, sometimes, than children living with a lone mother who remains single.

Moreover, cohabiting partnerships tend to be short-lived, and the departure of a cohabiting partner could once again produce more stress in the household. If the cohabiting stepfamily has established family routines, these would be disrupted again, and the biological parent and the children would have to adjust to the loss. In addition, if the mother and the stepfather have had a child together before he leaves, he may remain part of the family's web of kin after his departure. In this way, a series of short-term cohabiting relationships can create complex kin networks that require time and effort for mothers to manage, reducing the energy they have left for their children.

The 8 percent of American children who experienced three parental partnerships had to adjust to the arrival of two or three new adults, depending on whether they had been born to lone or married parents. They might also have had to adjust to the presence of new half siblings or stepsiblings. The intricate family ties produced by children from recent partnerships could decrease the resources going to the older children. Repeated movements of parents and their partners and spouses in and out of the child's household could produce a series of disruptions of the child's family system that could undermine a child's sense of security and trust. This series of events, in turn, could affect the child's emotional development.

Not all changes in the household are bad for children. If children are being raised by parents who have chronic open conflict, substance abuse problems, or other very serious difficulties, they may be better off if the parents separate. In families with less severe difficulties, however, it's not at all clear that children benefit if their parents break up (and, unfortunately, no one can say for sure just how much conflict is too much). In any case, it's hard to envision how experiencing a series of transitions could be beneficial to children, except as relief from a series of conflicted relationships. At best, the transitions might do little harm to children. For adults, however, having a series of partners could sometimes be positive. At least one partner chooses to initiate the breakup of a relationship, and that partner may be better off for it.

In addition, people increasingly value marriage and intimate relationships for emotional gratification and the opportunity for personal
growth. Living with a series of partners, while not a style of life that all
Americans would approve of, could nevertheless be a twenty-first-
century means for adults to find, through successive approximations,
highly fulfilling relationships.

The Contradictions of American Culture

There are many similarities, of course, between the United States and
other Western nations. All have industrialized in similar ways, and all
are making the transition from factory work to office work. All are
being affected by the globalizing economy. Moreover, all of the Western nations are democracies, and they share a common cultural heritage. The United States has even more in common with Great Britain
than with the rest of Europe, including a language, a legal system, and
a colonial past. All of these similarities reflect important characteristics
of Western societies, but they won't help us to explain distinctive
American family patterns. To do that, we have to look for differences,
not similarities, between the United States and other countries.

One difference lies in the realm of culture: the contradictory em-
phases on marriage and individualism found only in the United States.
People tend to think of a nation's culture as consistent and unified—
a set of values and expectations that fit together to create a coherent
whole. We learn this culture in childhood, it is commonly thought,
from parents, teachers, and the media, and each of us applies it the
same way as adults. But this understanding is simplistic. Culture often
contains multiple, inconsistent ways of viewing the same reality, and
individuals choose, sometimes without even realizing it, which view
to adopt. We have more culture in our heads than we use, in other
words, and not all of it coheres. To use Swidler's metaphor, culture
is a vast tool kit, and people reach into this kit to select the tools
they need to organize their lives. In the kit are sets of tools I will call
cultural models—frameworks for interpreting common situations we

encounter. Cultural models are habits of thought, taken-for-granted ways of interpreting the world that we draw upon in everyday life. But sometimes there is more than one cultural model—more than one set of tools—that we can apply to a given situation. That is the case with intimate partnerships, where Americans can draw upon both a cultural model of marriage and a cultural model of individualism.

In a similar vein, Karla B. Hackstaff wrote a book about the "contesting ideologies" of a marriage culture and a divorce culture in contemporary American society. The marriage culture, she maintained, has three bases. First, marriage is a given: you have to marry, it's something everyone does, it's the only proper way to live your adult life. Second, marriage is forever. Third, divorce is a last resort. I think that fifty or sixty years ago marriage was indeed a given in American culture. But I don't think it's a given anymore. You can choose not to marry and still live a socially acceptable life. Nevertheless, marriage continues to be the most desired and most prestigious way to have a family.

Consequently, I would amend Hackstaff's definition to say that marriage is no longer a given but is still the preferred way to live one's personal life. I agree with her that people still think of marriage as lasting forever and of divorce as a last resort. Everyone, of course, is aware that these days marriages often end in separation or divorce. Yet most people still think that marriage *should* last forever and that divorce should be avoided. For instance, Americans were asked in a national survey whether they agreed or disagreed with this statement: "Marriage is a lifetime relationship that should never be ended except under extreme circumstances." Seventy-six percent agreed, 13 percent said they neither agreed nor disagreed, and only 11 percent said they disagreed. Moreover, when people marry, almost all of them intend for their own marriage to last forever. When a journalist interviewed sixty people whose marriages had ended within five years, she found that every one of them expected at first that their marriages would last forever. Nor are these expectations limited to the middle class. Low-income, unmarried mothers in the Philadelphia area told two sociologists that they would marry only if they were sure the relationship would last forever. A twenty-year-old Puerto Rican mother said, "If I get married, I wanna be with this person for the rest of my life. I don't wanna just get married and then our relationship goes wrong, and then I have to go and get a *divorce*!"

This tendency to draw a line between other people's families (lots of marriages fail these days) and your own (my marriage will last forever) can be seen in other opinions about family life. For instance, in another national survey, people were asked, "In general, do you think that because of such things as divorce, more working mothers, or single parents, etc., family ties in the U.S. are breaking down—or don't you think so?" Seventy-six percent responded that they thought family ties were breaking down. Yet their responses were very different to the follow-up question "What about your own family? Are family ties breaking down, or not?" Eighty-two percent said that their own family ties were *not* breaking down. Some may call it denial, but people think their own family is in good shape even though they think the family in general is in decline. Similarly, they are optimistic that their own marriage will last forever—at least when they start it—although they know that many other marriages will not.

Americans also believe that spouses should be sexually faithful to each other. In fact, over the past few decades, people have become *more* disapproving of extramarital sex. The number of Americans who answered "always wrong" to the question "What is your opinion about a married person having sexual relations with someone other than the marriage partner—is it always wrong, almost always wrong, wrong only sometimes, or not wrong at all?" increased from 70 percent in 1973 to 82 percent in 2004. This trend is all the more notable since, during the same period, people have become much more tolerant of sex before marriage, with close to a majority now saying that premarital sex is not wrong at all.

Overall, then, I would suggest that the American cultural model of marriage contains the following elements today:

- Marriage is the best way to live one's family life.
- A marriage should be a permanent, loving relationship.
- A marriage should be a sexually exclusive partnership.
- Divorce should be a last resort.

There may be other elements, but these are the ones that matter for the argument I am making. Despite the decline in the percentage of people who ever marry, the rise of cohabitation, and the increase in divorce, Americans still have this set of tools in their kit.

The cultural model of marriage is stronger in the United States than in most other Western countries. In 2006, the U.S. Congress debated the wisdom of a federal constitutional amendment stating, in part, "Marriage in the United States shall consist only of the union of a man and a woman." In his weekly radio address two days before the senatorial debate, President George W. Bush, a supporter of the amendment, told the nation, "Marriage cannot be cut off from its cultural, religious, and natural roots without weakening this good influence on society." No political observers expected this amendment to be approved by Congress, because a two-thirds majority is required, and indeed it was defeated. But a simple majority of senators and representatives voted for it.

In another sign of support for heterosexual marriage, Congress, in early 2006, enacted a law providing $150 million per year for research and demonstration projects that promote "healthy marriage and responsible fatherhood." These funds can be used for activities such as relationship skills training for young couples who want to marry or married couples who want to avoid divorce, public advertising campaigns on the value of marriage, and education programs in high school that promote marriage. The advertisements that I saw on the sides of buses in Baltimore saying "Marriage works" were privately funded, but they were a prototype of what the healthy marriage funds may support.

These government interventions on behalf of marriage have no counterpart in other Western nations, because nowhere else is the meaning and function of marriage such a contested issue. No other government provides funds for promoting marriage. Just north of the border in 2004, Paul Martin, the prime minister of Canada, announced plans to introduce legislation that would legalize same-sex marriage. He told reporters he expected the measure to pass because "I've always thought Canada is the most postmodern country," an assertion one cannot imagine an American president making. By 2005 Canada and a few other Western countries (Belgium, the Netherlands, Spain) allowed same-sex marriage. Many European countries, including Britain and France, had enacted national, civil union–like statuses for same-sex partners. A British legal scholar, John Eekelaar, wrote, "The Civil Partnership Act of 2004 has cleverly created an institution for England and Wales for same-sex partners that is equivalent to marriage with hardly a murmur of protest." Such a measure in the United States would cause a cacophony of protest. Only in the United States is marriage so central a value that conservatives and liberals battle fiercely over its definition and over providing government support.

How Americans' beliefs about marriage compare to other nations can also be seen in the World Values Surveys, conducted in more than sixty countries, including all members of the European Union, Canada, and the United States, between 1999 and 2002. Adults in each country were asked whether they agreed or disagreed with the statement "Marriage is an outdated institution." Fewer Americans agreed (10 percent)—that is, fewer endorsed the idea that marriage is outdated—than in any other Western country, including Italy (17 percent), Sweden (20 percent), Canada (22 percent), Great Britain (26 percent), or France (36 percent). Americans are more likely to think that marriage is still appropriate for the times.

There's not much written about the strength of the cultural model of marriage because many observers mistakenly think that marriage is fading away. But the literature on the cultural model of individualism today is vast. The rise of individualism, historians and social commentators have argued, has been one of the master trends in the development of Western society over the past few centuries. And most would agree that an individualistic outlook on family and personal life has become more important since the mid-twentieth century. Robert Bellah and his colleagues, in an influential book on individualism and commitment in American life, distinguished between two types of individualism. They called the older form "utilitarian individualism." Think of the utilitarian individualist as the self-reliant, independent entrepreneur pursuing material success, such as a high position in a corporation or a senior partnership in a law firm. The great German social theorist Max Weber, in a classic book, suggested that there is a link between a similar concept, which he called "the Protestant ethic," and the economic development of the West. He noted that Calvinists (including the group that became known as the Puritans in England and America) believed that some individuals had been predestined by God for earthly success. This doctrine encouraged people to work hard so that they could prove to others (and themselves) that they were among the elect. Weber used the writings of Benjamin Franklin, a prototype of the utilitarian individualist, to illustrate this spirit of industriousness. "Early to bed and early to rise," Franklin advised in one of his famous aphorisms, "makes a man healthy, wealthy, and wise."

The newer form of individualism, which Bellah and his colleagues called "expressive individualism," germinated in the late nineteenth and early twentieth centuries and flowered in the second half of the twentieth. It is a view of life that emphasizes the development of one's sense of self, the pursuit of emotional satisfaction, and the expression of one's feelings. Until the past half century, individuals moved through a series of roles (student, spouse, parent, housewife or breadwinner) in a way that seemed more or less natural. Choices were constrained. In mill towns, two or three generations of kin might work at the same factory. Getting married was the only acceptable way to have children, except perhaps among the poor. Young people often chose their spouses from among a pool of acquaintances in their neighborhood, church, or school. But now you can't get a job in the factory where your father and grandfather worked because overseas competition has forced it to close, so you must choose another career. You get little help from relatives in finding a partner, so you sign on to an Internet dating service and review hundreds of personal profiles. As other lifestyles become more acceptable, you must choose whether to get married and whether to have children. You develop your own sense of self by continually examining your situation, reflecting on it, and deciding whether to alter your behavior as a result. People pay attention to their experiences and make changes in their lives if they are not satisfied. They want to continue to grow and change throughout adulthood.

This kind of expressive individualism has flourished as prosperity has given more Americans the time and money to develop their senses of self—to cultivate their own emotional gardens, as it were. It suggests a view of intimate partnerships as continually changing as the partners' inner selves develop. It encourages people to view the success of their partnerships in individualistic terms. And it suggests that commitments to spouses and partners are personal choices that can be, and perhaps should be, ended if they become unsatisfying.

The World Values Surveys asked about expressive individualism using a cluster of questions that contrast "survival versus self-expression" values. The answers to these questions suggest that the level of expressive individualism among Americans is high but not out of line for a wealthy Western nation: a little below that in Sweden and the Netherlands, comparable to the levels in Norway and West Germany, and greater than in Britain, Canada, or France. One question in this cluster asked people to place themselves on a scale of 1 to 10, where 1 means that they think the actions they take have no real effect on what happens to them (which indicates survival values) and 10 means they think they have completely free choice and control over their lives (self-expression values). More Americans placed themselves at the free choice end than did people in any other Western country, but some of the other countries were close: 82 percent of Americans chose 7, 8, 9, or 10, compared to 77 percent of Canadians, 74 percent of Swedes, and 73 percent of Germans.

The cultural model of individualism, then, holds that self-development and personal satisfaction are the key rewards of an intimate partnership. Your partnership must provide you with the opportunity to develop your sense of who you are and to express that sense through your relations with your partner. If it does not, then you should end it.

Cohabiting relationships, especially those without children, come closest to this kind of partnership. They are held together solely by the voluntary commitments of the partners, and should either party become dissatisfied with the relationship, it is expected that she or he will end it. The rise of cohabitation reflects the growing influence of the cultural model of individualism on personal and family life. Living together provides a way of obtaining the emotional rewards of a partnership while minimizing the commitment to it.

Even among married couples, we have seen the rise of what Barbara

Whitehead calls "expressive divorce." Beginning in the 1960s people began to judge the success of their marriages not by their material standard of living or how well they raised children but rather by whether they felt their personal needs and desires were being fulfilled. They turned inward and examined whether their marriages restricted their personal development. They were more likely to turn to psychotherapists for help in seeking out the causes of their unhappiness with their marriages. And if they perceived that their marriages were personally unfulfilling, they considered leaving. According to this logic, if a person finds that he or she has changed since marriage in a direction different from the one his or her spouse has taken, then that person is justified in leaving the marriage in order to express this newer, fuller sense of self. It's too bad, the feeling goes, especially if the couple is raising children, but to stay in a marriage that constrains the partners' sense of who they are would be worse.

Concerning family life, then, the cultural model of individualism in the United States today emphasizes these elements:

- One's primary obligation is to oneself rather than to one's partner and children.
- Individuals must make choices over the life course about the kinds of intimate lives they wish to lead.
- A variety of living arrangements are acceptable.
- People who are personally dissatisfied with marriages and other intimate partnerships are justified in ending them.

As a twenty-first-century individual, you must choose your style of personal life. You are allowed to—in fact, you almost required to—continually monitor your sense of self and to look inward to see how well your inner life fits with your married (or cohabiting) life. If the fit deteriorates, you are almost required to leave. For according to the cultural model of individualism, a relationship that no longer fits your needs is inauthentic and hollow. It limits the personal rewards that you, and perhaps your partner, can achieve. In this event, a breakup is unfortunate, but you will, and must, move on.

In practice, few Americans use just the cultural tools of the marriage model or just the tools of the individualism model. Rather, most Americans draw upon both. As a result, our actual marriages and cohabiting relationships typically combine them. People may rely on both sets of tools at the same time, or they may move from one to the other over time as their assessment of their personal lives changes. Moreover, they may not realize that they are combining two inconsistent models.

For instance, let's return to the national survey in which people were asked whether they thought marriage was a lifetime relationship that shouldn't be ended except under extreme circumstances. You'll recall that 76 percent agreed. The great majority, then, answered in a way consistent with the cultural model of marriage. Just a few pages farther along in the questionnaire they were asked whether they agreed or disagreed with this statement: "When a marriage is troubled and unhappy, it is generally better for the children if the couple stays together." It, too, reflects the marriage model, because the troubled and unhappy individual, by staying in the marriage, subordinates his or her personal satisfaction to the greater goal of raising the children well. It would seem logical, therefore, that most of the people who agreed that marriage is for life would also agree that it's better if the couple stays together. But they don't. Only 25 percent of the people who said marriage is for life also said that the couple should stay together. Forty percent disagreed and 35 percent said they neither agreed nor disagreed. How can it be that a few minutes after they all agreed that marriage is for life, only one-fourth agreed that unhappy people should stay in marriages for the sake of the children? These respondents, like many Americans, are drawing from two different cultural models simultaneously. When people think about the way marriage should be, they tend to say that it should be for life. But when people think about individual satisfaction, they tend to give others wide latitude to leave unhappy living arrangements. Cue them in one direction, and you get one picture; cue them in another, and you get a different picture. Both pictures, contradictory as they may be, are part of the way that Americans live their family lives. Together they spin the American merry-go-round of intimate partnerships.

Support from Religion and Law

The cultural model of marriage is alive and well in southern European countries such as Italy and Spain. The individualism model is prominent in the Scandinavian countries and the Low Countries. But only in the United States do people have two strong models of family and personal life—two different sets of tools—from which they can draw. Such a distinctive cultural climate must have strong social support, because otherwise it would not persist. Models of marriage and individualism don't simply hang in the air like moisture on a damp day, and they don't just reflect lessons learned in childhood. Rather, they need to be continually communicated and reinforced. Two powerful sources of support in the United States are religion and law, which provide principles that heavily influence how people construct their family lives. Religion provides moral principles about how family life should be lived, such as the belief that adults should marry before having children. The law provides principles about what is permissible and about what rights and obligations family members have. Sometimes the religious and legal principles are consistent, as is the case with bigamy, which is both sacrilegious and outlawed in the contemporary United States. Sometimes they are inconsistent, as in the contradiction between the religious belief that husbands and wives should stay together in sickness and in health for as long as they live and the law that a divorce must be granted even if only one partner wants it. The continual stream of messages we get from sources such as church services, religious television programs, debates over issues such as legalizing same-sex marriage, and court decisions about paternity and child support affect the way we live our family lives.

From an international perspective, the strength of American religion is striking. In no other Western country is religious practice so vital and so influential in shaping people's beliefs. The percentage of Americans who say they attend religious services at least once a month is greater than in the other English-speaking countries and far greater than in most of Western Europe. Moreover, in no other country do so many people turn to religion for guidance on family matters. For instance, Americans are more likely to agree that "churches in your country are giving adequate answers to the problems of family life." The continuing intensity of religious life in the United States has surprised scholars who expect that as countries modernize they will become more secular. That has happened in many other countries, but not in the United States.

American religious faiths continue to hold marriage in high regard, as they have since the colonial era. Nevertheless, an overlooked aspect of American religion is its strong and growing individualistic element. Although many people think of American religion as promoting "traditional values," it has, in fact, embraced the cultural model of individualism. This is evident at the many "seeker churches" filled with spiritual shoppers searching for religious identities. It can be seen in sermons on topics such as how to have a more successful career. And it is visible in the religious self-help sections at bookstores that include manuals for personal improvement, such as the *Christian Family Guide to Losing Weight.*

American law also supports both marriage and individualism. When I write about American law, I have in mind two components. The first includes statutes and court decisions about family matters such as marriage and divorce. During the latter half of the twentieth century, the legal status of marriage eroded substantially. What matters for child support, for example, is no longer whether the father is married to the mother of the child but simply his individual responsibility to provide for his children, whether or not they were born into marriage. In other words, being a parent rather than being a spouse is increasingly what matters to the courts. Yet marriage still conveys legal advantages, from the right to jointly file income tax returns to the right to visit an ill partner in the hospital. As elsewhere in American culture, the cultural models of marriage and individualism sometimes clash— for instance, in determining how much a man who has chosen to start a new family owes in child support to his previous family.

The second component consists of government policies that attempt to influence how Americans live their family lives. This component is sometimes called "family policy." More than in any other Western nation, government policies make families rely on the labor market rather than social programs for support. Welfare payments, for example, now have time limits and require work. An income supplement for low-income families, the Earned Income Tax Credit, is available only to parents who work outside the home. This emphasis on work reflects the continued strength of old-style utilitarian individualism in the United States—the self-reliant, early-to-bed-early-to-rise kind. Family policy also includes the marriage promotion program passed by Congress and the constitutional amendments passed in more than half of the states by 2006 that restricted marriage to a union of a man and a woman.

To fully understand the interdependence of marriage, individualism, religion, and law, it helps to know their history. From the colonial days onward, the leaders of the nation viewed marriage as an important component of the republic. In the nineteenth century, a series of legal and social issues such as polygamy among Mormons strengthened sentiment for (monogamous) marriage. Yet American religion and law made room for divorce from the start, although in a much more restrictive way than today. Moreover, American religion placed the individual at the center of the religious experience in a way that the hierarchical churches of Anglican and Catholic Europe did not. It nurtured the individual's direct relationship with God, and it developed and spread an emotionally expressive style of worship. So as the twentieth century began, American family life was set in a historical framework that influenced the coming century of social change. It is to this history that we will now turn.

The Historical Origins
of the American Pattern, 1650–1900

In 1857, a New England woman, Abby Sage, married Daniel McFarland, a well-educated Irish immigrant, in New York. According to Abby's account, McFarland told her he had a flourishing law practice but a few weeks after the marriage admitted that he had given up the law for a career in land speculation. The marriage was an unhappy one: Abby claimed that McFarland was frequently intoxicated, had a fierce temper, and was unspeakably cruel. She spent periods of time living separately from him at her father's home. When in New York, she achieved some success as an actress, and she socialized with a group of radical literary figures associated with the *New York Tribune*. One of them was Lucy Calhoun, a journalist who supported Abby's career aspirations and urged her to leave her marriage. Another was a nationally known journalist and writer at the *Tribune,* Albert Richardson.

In 1867 Abby and McFarland moved into a boardinghouse, and a few weeks later Richardson moved into the same house. One evening, McFarland returned home to find Abby standing at Richardson's door. He tormented and abused her all night and into the next day. Abby then told him she was leaving the marriage:

> I told him decidedly that I should leave him forever; that I had borne with patience for many years great outrages from him; that he had made my life miserable, and had often put me in great dread of my life; that I could not endure it any longer; that by his outrageous conduct for the two days past, and by the language he had used when he found me at Mr. Richardson's door, he had added the last drop to my cup of endurance, and I should go away from him at once.

According to Abby, Richardson soon confessed his romantic interest in her and said he wished to marry her if she were ever free to do so. He also wrote her a passionate love letter, but McFarland intercepted it. Outraged, he followed Abby and Richardson as they walked home from the theater and shot Richardson in the thigh, inflicting a slight wound. McFarland then sued Richardson for alienation of affection.

In 1868 Abby moved to Indiana, one of the few states that allowed divorce on the grounds of marriage breakdown, whatever the reason. Having established residency in Indiana and having received her divorce decree, she returned to New York in 1869. A month later, after Richardson published a notice stating that he intended to marry her, McFarland, now the ex-husband according to Indiana law, walked into the offices of the *Tribune* and shot Richardson again. This time Richardson died, but not before surviving long enough to hold a bed-side wedding conducted by the famous pastor Henry Ward Beecher.

The McFarland-Richardson case was one of three highly publicized cases between 1859 and 1870—the O. J. Simpson trials of their times—in which current or former husbands were charged with murdering their wives' paramours. By the 1850s, judges and juries followed an unwritten law that if a husband discovered his wife in the act of adultery, he was allowed, "in the heat of passion," to kill on the spot the man involved. No other man—not the woman's father, brother, or son—could kill and get away with it, nor could the wife kill her husband's lover. If, however, the husband waited until after the act and planned the killing, he could be convicted for premeditated murder.

When the case came to trial, Daniel McFarland's attorneys depicted their client as defending not just his honor but also the sanctity of the institution of marriage. The *Tribune* circle, one of the attorneys said, conducted a "free lover conspiracy" that drew Abby away from her marriage and made her think she was independent. The actions of these "fourierites [Charles Fourier was a utopian socialist who advocated sexual freedom], agrarians, Mormons, spiritualists, [and] free lovers" had deprived McFarland of his marital rights to his wife, driving him mad. He was in a state of temporary insanity, his attorneys explained, when he killed Richardson. In his closing argument, attor-

ney John Graham read biblical passages justifying revenge and patriar-
chal authority, and he spoke to the jury about what he called "the law
of the bible":

> That man was made for God, and woman for man; and that the woman
> was the weaker vessel, is meant to be under the protection of the
> stronger vessel, man. The forfeiture of that supremacy is as much an
> infraction of the husband's right as though it was the infliction of vio-
> lence upon her or him.

The all-male jury voted for acquittal, as did the juries in the other two
murder trials.

McFarland's attorneys had succeeded in tying the *Tribune* circle to
larger forces that were threatening traditional Christian marriage.
They had convinced the jury that by acquitting their client, it could
defend marriage against the onslaught of these un-Christian free-
thinkers. That the case was controversial tells us that challenges to
"traditional" marriage were beginning to surface in the mid-nineteenth
century, providing a hint of what was to come in the twentieth. That
acquittals were obtained in all cases suggests that the principle of
husband-headed marriage was still deeply ingrained in Americans'
moral beliefs—so deeply that juries would exonerate a husband who
walked into a rival's workplace and shot him. That appeals to the Bible
were successful suggests that the principles of marriage were rooted in
a Christian interpretation of how it should be lived.

Yet if Daniel McFarland had sought a divorce on the grounds of his
wife's adultery, he would have been granted one in any state, and subsequently he could have entered into a religious as well as a civil remarriage. In contrast, at the time of the trial, divorce had been legal for just
thirteen years in Britain, and it was prohibited in France and elsewhere
in Catholic Europe. To be sure, most Americans in that era viewed
divorce as scandalous if undertaken for reasons of incompatibility or,
worse yet, a new romantic interest. Nevertheless, the principle had
been established that, under limited circumstances, a person could
end a marriage voluntarily. By the time of the McFarland-Richardson
case, a few states, such as Indiana, were even willing to expand those

circumstances to include, as an 1849 Connecticut "omnibus clause" stated, "any such misconduct as permanently destroys the happiness of the petitioner and defeats the purpose of the marriage relation." Women's rights advocates protested the composition of all-male juries and disputed the claim that women were still the property of their husbands. Avant-garde thinkers began to see sex as separate from marriage. The beginnings of a debate about the expansion of the grounds for divorce into the realm of emotional satisfaction could be discerned.

In fact, the cultural models of both marriage and individualism were embedded in American society by the end of the nineteenth century. Granted, the models were different from what they are today. The nineteenth-century marriage model gave much greater authority to the husband—as shown by McFarland's acquittal—and involved a more formal, less friendly style of relations between the spouses. Still, by the end of the nineteenth century, the legal authority of husbands had begun to erode. In many states, married women gained property rights. Several states broadened the grounds for divorce, which made it easier for a woman to obtain one. And judges increasingly awarded custody of children to their mothers, rather than their fathers, after a divorce.

The nineteenth-century model of individualism mainly supported the utilitarian, rather than the expressive, version—Horace Greeley told young men to go west to find their fortunes, but no one told them to look inward to find their true selves. And the individualists, as Greeley's exhortation shows, were thought to be men, not women. Nevertheless, the erosion of husbands' authority foreshadowed a more companionate, partnerlike relationship between husbands and wives in the twentieth century. In addition, the growing preference for maternal custody reflected an emerging view of children as individuals needing nurturance and love. This concern about children's development presaged a twentieth-century concern about adults' personal development. Meanwhile, religious worship took on an increasingly individualistic style, as revival meetings spread and sects that would grow greatly in the twentieth century gained a foothold in the religious world.

Even a quick examination of history, then, shows that the story of the contemporary American family began long ago. If you look closely, you can see the origins of the current patterns of marriage and divorce in the way that Americans lived their lives, in their laws, and in their religious beliefs. You can also detect anxiety over the family's future, so characteristic of our times, in the past. "The family, in its old sense, is disappearing from our land," wrote an essayist in the *Boston Quarterly Review* in 1859, "and not only our free institutions are threatened, but the very existence of our society is endangered." The *Continental Monthly* asked in 1864, "Do any of you who may be our readers know half a dozen happy families in your circle of friends?" These expressions of concern were written at a time when one out of twenty marriages ended in divorce, a laughably low level compared to nearly one out of two today. Yet enough change was occurring to make people worried about it, and the family was evolving in a direction that would eventually lead to what we see today.

Marriage and Divorce from the Colonial Era to 1800

In fact, the roots of the American pattern of family life go all the way back to the colonial era. Marriage with the husband as the head was a central part of the lives of the New England colonists, so central that its existence was often taken for granted rather than remarked upon. The marriage-based family of husband, wife, and children was not just the backbone of New England colonial society; in large part, it *was* society. For instance, parents in Plymouth Colony were required by law to teach reading to their children and young servants so that they would "be able to duely read the scriptures." Why didn't the schools do this? Because there were no schools. Rather, the family was school. Through apprenticeship and service with other families, children learned the skills they needed for adult life. Justices sometimes ordered people convicted of crimes to live in the homes of upstanding families. Children whose parents had died—a far more common occurrence than today—were taken in not by orphanages but by other families. In the famous phrase of historian John Demos, the Plymouth family was "a little commonwealth."

So essential was marriage-based family life that the New England colonies passed laws forbidding people to live alone. The Connecticut law of 1636 read that "no man that is neither married, nor hath any servant, nor is a publick Officer shall keep house of himself without consent of the Town where he lives." The selectmen of a Massachusetts town in the 1670s met "to setel the younge persons in such families in the Town as is most sutable for thier good." In part, these laws reflected the reality that living alone was nearly impossible in an environment where people needed family members to help them obtain the food, clothing, and shelter they needed to survive. Yet these laws (which were not enforced strictly) also reflected a moral view that the marriage-based family, with the husband at the helm, was the foundation of a virtuous community.

As every schoolchild learns, the Puritans settled in America so that they could practice their religion, a dissenting version of Protestantism at odds with the prevailing Anglican faith of the Church of England. Consequently, to say that religion was important to the New England colonists is an understatement: it was the raison d'être for their migration to the New World. All families were expected not only to attend church but to supplement it by engaging in "family worship," praying and meditating daily. As you might expect, church attendance was high in the early New England colonies—up to 70 to 80 percent of families belonged to a church. This level of worship was in striking contrast to England and most of the rest of Europe, where far fewer attended. An observer in Hertfordshire, England, wrote in 1572 that on Sunday, "a man may find the churches empty, saving the minister and two or four lame, and old folke: for the rest are gone to follow the Devil's daunce."

The Puritans were Calvinists, followers of the fathers of the Protestant Reformation, Martin Luther and John Calvin. The writings that these men penned nearly five hundred years ago have had a striking influence on American values that still can be seen today. First, they gave an important but subtle boost to individualism. Luther rejected the Catholic doctrine that salvation could be attained only through participation in the rituals of the Church, with its sacraments, prayers, and hierarchical connection from God to pope to priests to parishioners. Rather, the Protestant sects claimed that salvation could be achieved through personal faith alone. Salvation was not granted by others; rather, it was granted directly by God. It did not depend on one's relationship to the clergy. What an individual felt—whether he or she trusted in God—was paramount. Over the course of American history, this emphasis on emotional experience and personal faith grew. It led, for instance, in the early nineteenth century to the more expressive style of worship of the evangelical sects, and in the late twentieth century to a style of religion in which the quest for personal spiritual fulfillment was central. Neither Luther nor Calvin used the term "individualism," which wasn't invented until after the French Revolution and even then was used in a negative sense to mean something akin to anarchy or mob rule. They certainly would not have recognized the twenty-first-century version of individualism, with its emphasis on self-development. But their revolutionary reinterpretation of a person's relationship to God formed the basis for individualism's later growth.

Second, the Reformation elevated the position of marriage. Among Catholics celibacy was the preferred status spiritually, the way of living one's life that left a person closest to God. The Bible tells us that Paul said, "It is good for a man not to touch a woman," and, "I wish that all men were [celibate] even as I myself am." But those who could not devote their lives fully to God should marry, he said, for it was better to marry than to commit the sin of fornication outside of marriage. Luther rejected this position; for him, marriage was the most spiritually edifying form of personal life. Indeed, some of the leaders of the Reformation were former priests and brothers who had left their orders and subsequently married. Marriage was not merely the second-best choice for those who lacked the self-discipline to remain celibate; it was rather the highest form of personal life. Moreover, to the Protestants marriage was primarily a civil status, albeit ordained by God, rather than a holy status. It was part of what Luther called the "earthly kingdom" rather than the "heavenly kingdom"; it was, in his words, "a secular and outward thing." Marriage was, in fact, the foundation of civil society. This idea of creating a secular society from marriage-based families became an important tenet of American life, a standard that wouldn't be challenged until the late twentieth century.

But the greater emphasis on both marriage and individualism left a problem: how to reconcile the contradiction between them. For if marriage was the union of two people who could act as individuals, how could it be a functioning unit that society could rely on? Wouldn't the interests of husbands and wives clash? Wouldn't it split apart easily? To solve this problem, the colonists drew upon English common law, which stated that the husband was the head of the family. Under the doctrine of "coverture," husband and wife became one legal person upon marriage, and that person was the husband. A wife could not sue or sign legal documents without her husband's approval. Her assets and earnings became his property. As historian Nancy Cott writes, the husband "became the one *full* citizen of the household," responsible for, and having authority over, his wife and children. Under English common law, husbands were allowed to "chastise," or correct, their wives by hitting them, as long as the stick they used was no thicker than the average thumb—hence the origin of the phrase "rule of thumb." The New England colonists, however, believed that violence was immoral. The minister Cotton Mather told his congregation that for "a man to Beat his Wife was as bad as any Sacriledge" and that "any such a Rascal were better buried alive, than show his Head among his Neighbours any more." In 1641, the Massachusetts Bay Colony enacted the first law against wife beating in the Western world. But it's not clear how strictly this law was enforced; there were few prosecutions. And in later eras, government officials seemed even more reluctant to intervene. In any case, as long as there was only one true individual per marriage, there was no conflict between individualism and marriage. It was when the dominance of the husband (in law and culture) began to fade that the conflict emerged. That didn't begin to happen until the mid-nineteenth century and gathered steam only in the twentieth.

Within the family, then, there was little individualism. The husband and wife were engaged in a joint enterprise, struggling to subsist in the New England climate. While husbands plowed and harvested, wives tended to animals and a vegetable garden, sewed clothes, cooked, canned, and did the washing. The contributions of both spouses were essential; the idea of a "housewife" who produced little of value had not yet been invented. The typical Puritan house also discouraged individual pursuits. Often only one room, the "hall," contained enough furniture for activities other than sleeping. In this room fathers, mothers, children (Plymouth families had an average of seven or eight children), servants or apprentices, and perhaps a grandparent ate, cooked, talked, prayed, sewed clothing, relaxed, and received visitors. Individuals simply could not find a place to get away from other household members. Personal privacy, one of the taken-for-granted aspects of modern individualism, was in short supply. Even family privacy was precarious: Puritan laws required that married couples maintain harmonious relationships and raise their children properly and imposed fines on those who did not. Friends and neighbors commonly called at one another's houses without advance notice. Given all the ways in which privacy was prevented, the idea of a private, marriage-based family with its own separate space—and of individual privacy within the family—may not have been in the mind-set of most people.

Beginning in about 1650, church membership in New England began to decline. Immigrants arrived who were motivated less by a desire for religious freedom than by the promise of economic opportunity. And perhaps the second generation of settlers lacked some of the religious fervor of their parents. Moreover, church membership was never as high in most of the other colonies as in New England. For example, the founder of Maryland, Lord Baltimore, envisioned his colony as a refuge for English Catholics but was never able to attract enough of them. The largely Protestant, unskilled laborers who formed the core of the Maryland immigrant population had little in the way of organized religious worship at all. Neither North Carolina nor South Carolina had many church buildings prior to 1700. In Virginia the Anglican Church, the official religion of the colony (and the American wing of the Church of England), failed to expand the number of parishes as the colony grew.

By 1700, levels of church membership and worship in the American colonies were far lower than in the early 1600s. But religious activity began to increase in the 1700s. Immigrants brought religious traditions that would later expand into major denominations: German Lutherans, Scottish Presbyterians, English Methodists, and English and Welsh Baptists. The number of church buildings increased. A wave of revival meetings—gatherings filled with intense preaching, often lasting days—occurred in the 1730s and 1740s. Still, by 1776 only 17 percent of Americans belonged to a church. There was plenty of room for growth.

Not only was church attendance lower outside of New England, but also marriage was more disorderly. Europeans had a long tradition of informal marriage, sometimes called "self-marriage." (By "informal" I mean not casual but rather begun without legal ceremonies.) Until the Council of Trent in the mid-1500s, the Catholic Church accepted as a marriage any public statement by a couple that they considered themselves married to each other, as long as neither partner coerced the other and their marriage did not violate church laws about who could marry whom. Until 1753 the Church of England, which had broken with the Catholic Church during the reign of Henry VIII, recognized self-marriages. Such a marriage occurred in a sixteenth-century alehouse, where Robert Piercy assembled a dozen friends to proclaim his solemn pledge of marriage, his "trothplight," to Agnes Davidson. A witness at the event wrote, "Said Robert dranke to the said Agnes, and cauld hir his wyf, and she lyke manner dranke to the said Robert Piercy, and cauld him husband." They kissed, and Robert gave Agnes a ring and a piece of gold. It is unlikely that they held any other ceremony. A British historian claimed that before 1753, there were large numbers of people in England who were unsure whether they were married or not.

Even as late as 1850, informal marriage was common in England among the poorer classes. People used the phrase "living tally" to describe couples living as married but who had never wed in the church. A woman described to a British folklorist the ritual of the "besom" (i.e., broom) wedding in the mid-1800s, in which a couple jumped over a broomstick in the presence of families and friends and were considered married. Conveniently, if a couple wanted to end the marriage within the first year, they could gather witnesses and jump backward over the besom. Up to one-fifth of the rural population of Britain between 1750 and 1850 lived tally at some point in their lives.

In the American colonies and during the early years of the nation, informal marriage also occurred, especially in frontier areas, where social control was looser, and in the middle and southern colonies, where the Anglican Church did not provide enough clergy. An Anglican minister in eighteenth-century Maryland said, "If the rule was established here that no marriage should be deemed valid that had not been registered in the Parish Book, it would I am persuaded bastardize nine tenths of the People in the Country." In addition, slaves were not allowed to marry formally. As the population of the colonies outside of New England, both free and slave, grew, the practice of marriage remained quite variable. Not until the mid- to late 1800s did formal marriage become the only acceptable way of forming a union. How the courts responded to informal marriage is unclear, but it seems likely that at least some jurisdictions recognized the rights and responsibilities of informally married partners, creating something of a dual marriage system in practice. A form of bigamy was also common: a man who left his wife and migrated to a faraway state or territory was unlikely to be followed, so he could marry anew without much fear of prosecution.

Informal marriage was the only option for slaves. Owners could, and did, disregard bonds of kinship by selling slaves or by having sex with female slaves without regard to their family ties. Nevertheless, slaves celebrated marriages through informal ceremonies. For example, several reports tell of slave couples who married by jumping over a broom; perhaps they adopted this particular ritual of self-marriage from whites who brought it from Europe. In addition, slaves organized themselves into families and recognized not only parents and children but also aunts, uncles, and cousins. Slaves who were separated from their families sent letters such as one that field hand Cash sent to relatives on a Georgia plantation after he, his wife, Phoebe, and some of their children were sold away:

Clairissa your affectionate Mother and Father sends a heap of love to you and your Husband and my Grand Children, Mag. & Cloe. John.

Judy. My aunt sienna . . . Give our love to Cashes brother Porter and his Wife Patience. Victoria sends her Love to her Cousin Beck and Miley.

Slave kinship patterns may also have reflected the survivals of African cultural patterns. Traditionally, African society was organized by lineages, large groups of kin who traced their ancestry through the father's or mother's line; the members of a lineage cooperated and shared resources with each other. Adults carefully controlled and monitored courtship and marriage. What mattered most was not the happiness of the young married couple but rather the birth of children who could be retained by the lineage. Getting married was more of a process, a series of steps that occurred over a long period of time, than a single event. Childbearing could occur before the ceremony, in which case the couple were expected to marry. But on the other hand, if the couple produced no children in the early stage, the elders might cancel the marriage. It was the lineage—the larger kinship network—that mattered more than the marriage itself.

In other words, both the slavery system and cultural survivals could have influenced the development of the African American slave family. Slavery did not allow formal marriage; while African culture allowed it, the married couple was subordinated to the lineage. Slavery forced African Americans to have children outside of marriage, and African culture was tolerant of this practice because having children was so important to the lineage. Slavery forced slaves to depend on other kin because slave owners could separate parents and children, and African culture emphasized links to a network of kin in one's lineage. Whatever the mix of influences, African American families were set on a track in which marriage mattered but childbearing outside of marriage was tolerated, and ties to one's parents or siblings were relatively more important than among whites.

Despite the existence of informal marriage practices, the Protestant ideal of Christian marriage remained strong. In fact, it became a fundamental building block of the new nation. Perhaps this reflected the strong influence of the Puritans and their descendants on American culture. Under the political philosophy that emerged toward the end of the colonial era, wives (and implicitly children) consented to the rule of law by the family head just as the (white) family head himself consented to the rule of law in the American republic. To be sure, the husband ruled more like an enlightened despot than an elected official. But to most people, it seemed natural that the husband should be the head of the family. He became the crucial intermediary between the state and the other members of the family.

Despite the importance of marriage, divorce appears to have been increasing in the United States since the colonial era—slowly at first, and then faster and faster through the nineteenth and twentieth centuries. It is likely that the chance of a marriage ending in divorce has always been higher in the United States than in most of Europe. That has certainly been the widespread impression. For instance, Hendrik Hartog wrote in his history of family law in America, "For two centuries commentators have singled out America as the home of divorce, as the place where marital exits lived. America was always a comparative divorce haven." In any case, there is no doubt that the chance of divorce has always been higher in America than in Britain. Unlike in the New England colonies, where divorce was possible, even if on a very limited basis, divorce was not allowed in Britain except by an act of Parliament until 1857. Even as recently as the early 1900s, fewer than a thousand divorces per year were granted in Britain. In the United States, by contrast, there were about a hundred thousand per year. So while the population of the United States in that era was about twice the population of Britain, a hundred times as many divorces occurred in the United States.

Britain's low level of divorce stems from the circumstances of its break with the Catholic Church during the reign of Henry VIII. Under the doctrine of the Catholic Church in medieval Europe, marriage was not dissoluble. The union of a man and a woman could be ended only if it could be proven that a valid marriage never existed. That could occur if the marriage had violated Church law because, for example, the couple were too closely related, or if the marriage had never been consummated. In case of such a violation, a marriage could be annulled, that is, considered null and void. But it could not end in divorce. When Pope Clement refused the request of Henry VIII to annul his marriage to Catherine of Aragon, Henry broke with the Catholic Church and formed the Church of England, with himself as the head. But Henry did not divorce Catherine; rather, he obtained an annulment from the Church of England; and he subsequently obtained annulments for his marriages to Anne Boleyn and Anne of Cleves. Indeed, he never divorced anyone. Unlike all other Protestant churches, the Church of England, following Henry's practice, retained the Catholic doctrine of the indissolubility of marriage.

Most of the New England colonies, on the other hand, allowed divorce on the bases of adultery and desertion, following the teachings of Luther and Calvin. Luther believed that divorce was to be deplored but also allowed in limited circumstances. Most notably, he argued that if one spouse was guilty of adultery, the other spouse could obtain a divorce and remarry. In his later writings, he also allowed for divorce in the case of desertion. The willful deserter, he wrote, "shows his contempt for matrimony . . . he does not consider his wife his wedded wife." In words about the need for divorce that one could imagine Dear Abby giving as advice to Unhappily Married in Minnesota, he wrote, "Frequently something must be tolerated even though it is not a good thing to do, to prevent something even worse from happening." Calvin basically accepted this position. He also acted as counsel to his brother Antoine, who requested a divorce on the grounds that his wife—who resided with Antoine in Calvin's house—had committed adultery. Although Antoine's wife denied the charge, even after being imprisoned and tortured twice, the Calvin brothers persisted, and the divorce was granted.

It's true that divorce was difficult to obtain, seen as shameful, and never granted merely because the spouses wanted to end their marriage. Nevertheless, the seed of divorce was planted in the soil of the northern colonies. Connecticut had the most liberal laws of any colony or state in the 1700s, and divorce petitions appeared to increase in the aftermath of the Revolution. Even though the numbers were tiny by modern standards—perhaps fifteen to twenty divorces per year in the second half of the eighteenth century—the rise caused concern among prominent clergy and academics. The middle colonies were more restrictive, while the southern colonies that followed Anglican law did not allow divorce until after the Revolution.

No colony or state, however, went as far as the French National Assembly in 1792, three years after the start of the French Revolution. It passed a law, influenced by the individualistic spirit of the revolution, allowing divorce by mutual consent or at the request of only one spouse on the general grounds of incompatibility of temperament and on specific grounds including cruelty or ill treatment and desertion for at least two years. This breathtaking statute introduced principles that would not be seen again in Western divorce law for nearly two hundred years. It set off a wave of divorce and a round of opposition from conservatives, especially to the ground of incompatibility. After Napoleon seized power, the law was significantly restricted and the ground of incompatibility was dropped. (Napoleon retained other grounds and divorced Josephine in 1809.) In 1816, after the fall of Napoleon, King Louis XVIII abolished divorce altogether, returning France to the Catholic position. Over the next half century, several attempts to legalize divorce were unsuccessful. Opponents had merely to refer to the excesses of the revolutionary period to beat back divorce legislation. Only in 1884 did France finally legalize divorce.

Looking back, we can see that several of the key characteristics of the twentieth-century American family were in place by 1800: the status of marriage as the preferred family form, the central role of the marriage-based family in civic life, and the availability of divorce. In hindsight, it may seem as though the shape of the modern family flowed naturally and inevitably from the pre-1800 past. But that's too simplistic a view of history. As the nation entered the nineteenth century, other outcomes were without doubt still possible. Informal marriage, for instance, was widespread outside of New England in the pre-1800 period; given a different nineteenth century, it could have remained strong and chipped away at the privileged status of formal, legal marriage. Divorce was stigmatized and rare early on. Given a different nineteenth century, it could have remained legal but uncommon.

What a nation's early history does is give it a set of leanings and tendencies—an initial position of sorts. The initial position of the American family was different from that of the British family and the French family of the same period. That's most clear in the case of divorce, which was not allowed in Britain (without an act of Parliament) and

France (except for a brief period during the revolution) prior to 1800. Even though all three nations developed similarly in subsequent centuries, we might expect the initial position to translate into a higher level of divorce in the United States today than in Britain or France, and that is what current statistics show.

This persistent difference is an example of what social scientists sometimes call "path dependence," the principle that societies that are different in important ways early on are likely to remain different later, even if their recent experiences are similar. Think of ships that begin their journeys at different ports but try to sail on parallel courses across the sea. They are unlikely ever to cross paths. But ships do sometimes shift direction, and storms sometimes blow them off course. At the ends of their journeys they may be closer together (or farther apart) than when they started. Similarly, the leanings and tendencies of early history can be reinforced or counteracted by later events. In the case of divorce, both Britain and France eventually legalized it, and by historical standards all three countries now have divorce rates high enough to make their ancestors gasp. Early history sets the course but cannot tell us precisely where the ships will land; that depends too much on the conditions they encounter along the way. That's why we also need to look at American history in the nineteenth and twentieth centuries in order to fully understand the American family today.

Marriage and Divorce in the 1800s

Should polygamy be outlawed? Is birth control information obscene? Should newly freed blacks be encouraged to marry? Is a man who kills his wife's lover guilty of murder? Issues such as these filled the pages of newspapers during the second half of the nineteenth century, as longstanding disputes came to a head and high-profile cases came to trial. Nearly all of these matters were resolved in ways that emphasized the primacy of monogamous, lifelong marriage, with the husband as its head. In fact, so often was marriage the winner, so many knockout punches did its advocates throw, that by the end of the century the nation had developed what Cott calls an "atmosphere of moral belligerence" about marriage. Any challenge to it was met by a spirited, almost militant defense. In 1888, for instance, Supreme Court justice Stephen Field wrote that marriage, as "creating the most important relation in life, as having more to do with the morals and civilization of a people than any other institution, has always been subject to the control of the legislature." (The idea that marriage is central to both personal and civic life would have sounded familiar to the Puritans.)

The longest-running morality play was the effort by the federal government to end the practice of polygamy among the Mormons—the Church of Jesus Christ of Latter-Day Saints—the majority of whom lived in the Utah territory. To the Mormons, the issue was one of religious freedom. They believed that God had revealed to their founder that marriage should follow the Old Testament model, in which a man could take more than one wife. In the 1850s, after their epic trek across the country, they began to do so. Yet to most easterners, polygamy was an affront to Christian marriage. Congress passed a law in 1862 that made polygamy a crime in the territories, but because Utah did not record marriages, and because juries were reluctant to convict, the law proved to be unenforceable. Congress then passed additional laws, and in 1879 a case, *Reynolds v. U.S.,* reached the Supreme Court. The Court ruled that Congress did have the power to prohibit polygamy in the territories. Chief Justice Morrison Waite wrote that monogamous marriage was one of the principles on which American democracy rested. In the 1880s Congress enacted even more restrictive legislation, denying the vote to any man who refused to swear that he was not a polygamist. The Supreme Court continued to reject Mormon appeals: an 1884 ruling stated that monogamy was "wholesome and necessary" to a "free self-governing commonwealth." Another justice wrote that polygamy was "a blot on our civilization . . . contrary to the spirit of Christianity and of the civilization which Christianity has produced in the Western world." Finally, in 1890, the Mormons capitulated and suspended the practice of polygamy, which allowed the Utah territory to become a state in 1896. The lesson for Americans who followed this decades-long dispute was that Christian marriage was a fundamental aspect of American society and that Congress and the courts would act forcefully to defend it when necessary.

Anthony Comstock, a reformer from New York, was one man who worried about threats to Christian morality, even within marriage. To Comstock, sexual intercourse undertaken for purposes other than to conceive children, whether by a married couple or not, was a depraved act. It undermined morality by separating sex from childbearing. It endangered the primacy of marriage by encouraging people to have sex outside of marriage. (In fact, that's precisely what happened almost a century later, when the birth control pill was introduced.) Therefore, argued Comstock, any sexual aids that reduced the risk of pregnancy were obscene. He successfully lobbied Congress to pass the eponymous Comstock Act in 1873, outlawing the use of the U.S. mail to send "obscene, lewd, or lascivious" information—a category that included any information about birth control—and had himself named as a special post office agent to enforce the act. Many states followed with laws forbidding the distribution of birth control devices. These prohibitions reinforced the principles that marriage is the proper place for sexual relations; that men, as the traditional heads of households, should control women's sexual relations; and that the purpose of sex is to have children rather than to experience intimacy or pleasure.

The public also was eager to impose marriage on members of minority groups who had been unable or unwilling to marry in the past. After the Civil War ended, the newly formed Freedman's Bureau, which oversaw the relief efforts for emancipated slaves, issued marriage rules. The bureau told African Americans, who could not marry under slavery, that now they must marry: "No parties . . . will be allowed to live together as husband and wife until their marriage has been legally solemnized," read an 1865 rule. Several southern states passed laws making living together without legal marriage a misdemeanor punishable with a fine. Similarly, in the late 1800s the Bureau of Indian Affairs encouraged Western-style marriage and destroyed the communal landownership of many Indian tribes by offering land and citizenship only to "household heads."

In the 1870s and 1880s, informal marriage came under direct attack from reformers concerned about the rising divorce rate and a perceived decline in traditional marriages. In a high-profile Kansas case in 1886, Lillian Harman, the daughter of the editor of a leading free-love periodical, and Edwin C. Walker conducted a "free marriage" ceremony without clergy or a marriage license. Their union directly challenged the authority of the state to control marriage and the authority of husbands over their wives. Walker told Harman she would "be free to repulse any and all advances of mine . . . She remains sovereign of herself." Harman said she was retaining her maiden name and "the right to act, always, as my conscience and best judgment shall dictate." However, the day after the ceremony, Harman and her partner were arrested for marrying without a license from the state or the participation of a minister. They were tried and convicted, with Harman sentenced to forty-five days and Walker to seventy-five days. The couple actually prolonged their incarceration by not paying court costs while national interest grew and their case worked its way to the appeals court. Four months later, the Kansas Supreme Court reaffirmed that a marriage must comply with state marriage statutes, although they did rule that a wife could keep her maiden name.

Earlier in the nineteenth century, in contrast, influential legal figures such as Chief Justice James Kent of the New York Supreme Court had argued in favor of recognizing informal, "common-law" marriages begun without legal ceremonies. "No peculiar ceremonies are requisite by common law to the valid celebration of marriage," Kent wrote in 1826. "The consent of the parties is all that is required." Through the middle of the century, most state courts accepted the common-law view that marriage could be inferred from public statements by the couple that they considered themselves to be married and from the fact of living together. But the reformers of the 1870s and 1880s charged that this position encouraged hasty, unwise marriages that were more likely to end in divorce. They argued for state regulation of marriage as a step toward reducing what they saw as social disintegration. By the end of the century, almost all states had revised their laws to require that couples obtain licenses in order to marry; although common-law marriage endured at lower rates, formal marriage was ascendant.

What explains this sudden burst of attention to heat-of-passion murder trials, polygamy, free love, and birth control? The second half of the nineteenth century was a time of social turbulence. There was, of course, the disruption of the Civil War. But there were subtler forces, too. The nation was beginning to urbanize. Fifteen percent of Americans lived in urban areas in 1850; by 1900 the figure was 40 percent. Urbanization put people closer together in settings where their behavior was often unsupervised by family and neighbors. Albert Richardson, the murdered journalist, could not have moved into the same boardinghouse as Abby Sage McFarland if they had been living in rural villages. Moreover, as industrialization began, wage work drew husbands out of their homes and into factories, a development that undermined the older husband-wife partnership that had sustained farm families.

In addition, the technology of the telegraph allowed Americans, for the first time, to follow stories from around the country. Beginning in the 1850s, newspapers began receiving telegraphic feeds from their own reporters and from the newly formed New York Associated Press. The mass-circulation newspapers of the penny press, so named because of the low cost of their issues, found that their readers wanted stories about crime, romance, conflict, and intrigue—in short, the very topics that drive the mass media today. They covered the McFarland-Richardson murder trial and the dispute over polygamy because their readers clamored for the latest news. The penny press was CNN and *USA Today* for the nineteenth century, the first approximation of today's twenty-four-hour print and video news cycle. Had Harman and Walker lived a half century earlier, they would not have prolonged their stay in jail in order to build national interest, because the media infrastructure for quickly building interest didn't yet exist. Through the penny press, message after message about marriage was passed to the masses.

The moral belligerence about marriage was not as visible in Europe—at least not in Britain and France. To be sure, formal marriage strengthened in British society, too. Historian John Gillis called the period from 1850 to 1960 in Britain the "era of mandatory marriage." The single greatest cause of this era, Gillis writes, was the rise of factory work. In England, as in the United States, a male-breadwinner ideal developed, in which husbands were to do wage work while wives cared for home and children. But British society did not have the same antipathy toward alternatives to husband-headed marriage—the same intensity of campaigns against nonconformists or the same kinds of interventionist statements by the courts. Consider Margaret Sanger, the American birth control activist. When Sanger was indicted in 1914 under the Comstock Act for publishing a radical feminist magazine, the *Woman Rebel,* that argued for women's right to practice birth control, she fled to Britain. Contraception was legal there, and no Comstock-like campaign was to be seen. Rather, as the British birth rate declined in the 1890s, advertisements for birth control devices and manuals appeared in magazines, catalogs, and pamphlets. Entrepreneurs started firms to produce and distribute contraceptive devices (sponges, cervical caps, condoms) and abortifacients. It was a safe haven for Sanger, who remained there for a year before returning to the United States to face trial.

Birth control devices were available in France, too, although soon to be banned. A 1920 law outlawing contraception and abortion reflected the long-standing concern about population growth. The French birth rate had begun to fall in the early 1800s, before any other country experienced a decline. After the French defeat in the Franco-Prussian War of 1870–71, the size of the French population, especially in relation to the German military threat, became a major issue. Rather than focusing on marriage, national leaders called for efforts to improve maternal and infant health. In 1896, when the National Alliance for the Growth of the French Population was formed, no less a social critic than Émile Zola became a founding member. In 1899, he published a novel, *Fécondité,* usually translated as "fruitfulness" but also meaning "fertility," serialized in the popular press, that glorified a couple who had fifteen children while decadent Frenchmen and -women all around them rejected the idea of large families, to their ultimate ruin. If any observers were concerned about marriage, their voices were lost in the chorus of cries for the French to have more children.

Other continental countries shared the concern about low birth rates. Pronatalist logic was even carried to the extreme of arguing for more liberal divorce laws. In 1783, Frederick the Great of Prussia wrote to his cabinet:

[Divorce] must not be made too difficult, lest the population be hindered. For when two spouses are so angry and irritated with each other that no further connection between them is to be hoped for . . . then also will they produce no children with each other, and that is detrimental to the population. On the other hand, if such a pair is divorced, and the wife then marries another fellow, then surely children are likely to come along.

In short, if two spouses hate each other, they will stop having sex and will not produce any more children. It is in the state's interest to allow them to divorce and remarry so that they'll start having sex again. Some French writers offered similar arguments. There is no record of anyone making a similar argument in the United States.

Despite the strength of husband-headed marriage as an ideal, the authority and privileges of American husbands were gradually reduced by changes in family law during the 1800s. By the end of the Civil War, a majority of states had modified their laws to allow women to own their own property and to take some legal actions. The best-known and most influential statute was the Married Women's Property Act, enacted in 1848 by the State of New York. The act was passed in response to protests from early feminists and others who saw the old principle as discriminatory. The passage of these laws may also reflect the first stirrings of a more companionate style of marriage, in which husband and wife would be partners. This kind of relationship became more common in the late 1800s and even more so in the 1900s.

Moreover, a sea change occurred in judges' rulings on who gets custody of the children after divorce. In 1800, judges gave custody to fathers in most cases; by 1900 they gave custody to mothers in most cases. This reversal reflected the emergence of a new view of children. Early in the century they were seen legally as property—a cut above farm animals, but property no less. The father owned the rights to their labor just as he owned all the other property in the family. As the century progressed, however, adults began to view children as growing beings with their own interests and needs. As such, they were seen as requiring nurturance and moral guidance—and therefore best cared for by mothers. Consequently, under the new doctrine of the "best interests of the child," judges increasingly assigned custody of them to their mothers. Children were becoming little individuals, and the family was becoming a place that nurtured individual development, a trend that accelerated in the twentieth century.

The nineteenth-century changes in the law, however, were more evolutionary than revolutionary. Despite the new marital property laws, conservative judges still found reasons to rule in favor of husbands' ownership of assets. When the first casebooks on domestic relations law appeared in the 1890s, they chronicled cases that sought to modernize and amend coverture, rather than to end it. Even as late as the 1950s, casebooks presented rulings that preserved the husband's right to manage resources and make decisions for the family. Not until the second half of the twentieth century did the law finally extinguish the embers of coverture. Moreover, not until the second half of the twentieth century did the legal system seriously confront the problem of domestic violence. In the nineteenth and early twentieth centuries, few statutes and little case law protected women against abuse; by and large, husbands retained the right to hit them.

As the ideal of marriage strengthened, so did religion. And while religious beliefs supported the husband-headed family, they increasingly left room for individual spiritual pursuits. Between 1776 and 1850, the percentage of Americans who belonged to a church doubled, from 17 percent to 34 percent. It was during this interval, not during the colonial era, that the first great expansion of religion occurred. The growth of new churches between 1780 and 1860 was substantial, even considering that the American population increased tenfold, from about three million to about thirty million during this sixty-year period. Baptist congregations grew from about 400 to 12,150, a thirtyfold increase. Methodist congregations grew from about 50 to 20,000, and Roman Catholic congregations from about 50 to 2,500. Moreover, after 1800, independent black churches began to emerge. According to one estimate, the number of black Baptists grew from 25,000 in 1800 to 150,000 by 1850. After the Civil War, black churches expanded at a rapid pace, with the number of black Baptists increasing to nearly

500,000 by 1870. The total number of Christian congregations grew from about 2,500 in 1780 to 52,000 in 1860—a twentyfold increase. What's more, religious publications mushroomed: religious newspapers increased from fourteen in 1790 to six hundred by 1830. A million Bibles and about six million books and tracts were published in 1830.

The new churches that expanded rapidly, such as the Methodists and Baptists, emphasized introspection, individual responsibility to God, emotional expressiveness, and a transformative, "born-again" experience. The themes of introspection and expressiveness foreshadowed twentieth-century modes of thought about personal life. Methodist "circuit rider" preachers tirelessly spread their message on horseback across the nation. They had little more education than the people to whom they preached, and they emphasized personal faith rather than theology. Large crowds attended camp meetings—outdoor revival meetings that combined preaching, prayer, song, and body movement in an atmosphere designed to create converts to Christ. The organizers of these meetings left behind notes, lectures, and drawings worthy of the modern impresarios of rock-and-roll festivals. At the heart of their success was an intense emotional experience. For instance, Charles Grandison Finney, one of the leading evangelists of his time, wrote in 1835: "Men are so spiritually sluggish, there are so many things to lead their minds off from religion, and to oppose the influence of the gospel, that it is necessary to raise an excitement among them, till the tide rises so high as to sweep away the opposing obstacles."

Illustrations of camp meetings portray women and men standing near the stage, gesturing, shouting, and swooning. This participatory, expressive, personal style was what attracted the crowds. By 1850, the Methodists were the largest denomination in the United States, accounting for one-third of all American church members. The Baptists comprised another 20 percent. In contrast, only 4 percent of church members were Congregationalists (the descendants of the Puritans) and only another 4 percent were Episcopalians (the descendants of the Anglicans).

Meanwhile, divorce continued its climb during the nineteenth century, foreshadowing even greater increases in the twentieth century. The passage of Connecticut's "omnibus clause" in 1849 was a shocking development to many traditionalists, and after decades of protests the clause was repealed in 1878. Indiana had added an omnibus clause in 1824, and its laws allowed migrants to establish temporary Indiana residence easily. By the 1850s it had become the first state to which people migrated in significant numbers in order to obtain a divorce—the first "divorce mill." That's why Abby Sage McFarland temporarily moved to Indiana to obtain her divorce. Although the number of migratory divorces in the United States was small, probably never exceeding 5 percent of all divorces, the cultural impact was larger. During the McFarland-Richardson trial, the *New York Times* editorialized, "An Indiana divorce is not only a farce, but a disgusting farce." Many Indianans also were unhappy with the state's reputation. In 1873, the legislature passed a new, much stricter divorce law and the state's career as a divorce haven ended.

After Indiana tightened its laws, those seeking migratory divorces generally moved westward to the Dakotas and south to Arkansas. In fact, the history of migratory divorce is of states passing liberal laws, attracting migrants seeking divorces, engendering opposition to the practice among their own citizens, and then passing more-restrictive legislation—until, that is, migratory divorce reached Nevada, which embraced it as a revenue-producing mechanism. When other states tried to reduce their residency requirements to compete with Nevada, the Nevada state legislature decreased theirs to three months and then again, in 1931, to six weeks. Nevada had become the last divorce mill. Its place was secure until the 1970s, when most states passed liberal divorce laws, reducing the need for unhappy individuals to obtain a Nevada divorce.

By the 1890s, divorce had become a national issue. Between 1865, the first year for which good statistics exist, and 1890, the proportion of marriages ending in divorce had doubled, from about one in twenty to about one in ten. Progressive reformers urged passage of new, more restrictive divorce laws. Between 1889 and 1906, state legislatures enacted more than a hundred restrictive divorce regulations. For example, fifteen states forbade remarriage until one or two years after a final divorce decree, and six eliminated some grounds for divorce. In 1905, after ordering a study of divorce, President Theodore Roosevelt wrote in a message to Congress: "There is widespread conviction that the divorce laws are dangerously lax and indifferently administered in some of the states, resulting in a diminished regard for the sanctity of the marriage relation." Roosevelt called for states to voluntarily adopt uniform, restrictive divorce legislation to counter the overly liberal laws in some of them.

Yet despite this call to action, despite the passage of restrictive legislation in some states, and despite vociferous opponents of liberalized divorce, few states passed the uniform divorce legislation drawn up at national conferences. The movement to restrict divorce failed. Some states, such as Nevada, wanted to protect their divorce-related business. Others, such as New York, wished to protect their even more restrictive laws. In addition, voices began to be heard suggesting that divorce was a personal matter, even an individual right, in which the state should not intervene.

In 1910, the monthly magazine *Current Literature* ran a long article entitled "The Most Difficult Problem of Modern Civilization." Among the experts quoted was former Supreme Court justice Henry Billings Brown: "It is not perceived why the partnership created by marriage should so far differ from a commercial partnership that one may be dissolved at pleasure while the other is indissoluble." Such a view would have been repugnant to nineteenth-century thinkers such as Justice Field, who regarded government regulations of marriage and divorce as proper and necessary. Throughout the nineteenth century divorce was more like a reprimand than a grant of freedom. "Divorce was not a right," Hartog notes, "only a remedy for a wrong." But it was an allowable and increasingly tolerated remedy.

By 1900, the ideal of marriage and the reality of divorce were firmly embedded in American society and culture in a way not seen in Britain or France or, most likely, other Western nations as well. American culture promoted and defended marriage—or at least a particular kind of marriage in which the husband was the head—more strongly than did British or French culture. American Protestantism disapproved of divorce but, unlike the Anglican and Catholic churches, tolerated it.

American law, unlike British or French law, allowed it from the start. This history predisposed the United States to have both a high level of marriage and a high level of divorce in the twentieth century.

In retrospect, we may wonder why marriage won all of its battles in the second half of the nineteenth century—why it was able to knock out polygamy, informal marriage, and the like. Without doubt, the influence of Protestant religion, which had strengthened earlier in the nineteenth century, was critical. In addition, as the wage labor economy grew, the American family was able to evolve in a way that preserved the husband-headed marriage as its core: in the new male-breadwinner family, the husband was to be the wage earner while the wife cared for home and children. This clever adjustment to the changing economy helped husband-headed marriage remain the heavyweight champion of family life throughout the first two-thirds of the twentieth century, after which, like an aging fighter, it lost its crown. Let us now examine the remaining decades of its reign, after which we will conduct a requiem for the heavyweight.

The Rise of the Companionate Marriage, 1900–1960

By the middle of the twentieth century, most people took the connection between romantic love and marriage for granted. They would readily have agreed that you should be romantically attracted to the person you choose to marry. That meant not only loving the person but also being *in love*—feeling an intense emotional pull. People knew that there were other qualities you should look for in a spouse, such as dependability and a pleasing disposition, but if you weren't in love with a person, you shouldn't get married. The prevailing view, as synopsized by Sinatra, was that love and marriage go together like a horse and carriage.

Prior to the twentieth century, however, many people would have questioned this link between romantic love and marriage. Romantic love was seen as a risky basis for marriage. When it faded—and people thought it would fade quickly—you might be left with a partner who couldn't manage a farm, earn a living, or run a household. And if you were stuck with such a person, you were in trouble, because there were no welfare programs, no Social Security benefits, and no farm subsidies. Rural men and women needed competent, hardworking partners to make a go of farming. City dwellers needed marriages in which the husband was a steady wage earner and the wife raised children, sewed clothes, and perhaps earned some money by taking in boarders and lodgers. Without enough help from your spouse, you could become destitute. People hoped and expected to love their partners in a spiritual way, but they believed that following the lure of romance and sex would lead to poor choices they couldn't afford to make.

The diary of Isabella Maud Rittenhouse, of the famous Philadelphia family for whom a square is named in that city, illustrates this distrust of romantic love. Between 1882 and 1884, Maud was courted by several suitors. She was romantically attracted to one of them, Robert Witherspoon, a dashing, handsome, cultured man. Yet she worried that his character was flawed. He had, she wrote "beauty of feature and charm of tongue with little regard for truth and high moral worth." Another suitor was a plain-looking, socially awkward man named Elmer Comings, who nevertheless had an "inward nobility in him." Maud chose Elmer over Robert even though she knew what she was giving up: "If I do marry [Elmer] it will be with a respectful affection and not with a passionate *lover* love." To give in to romantic feelings and choose Robert was too big a risk. Elmer was dependable, steady, and morally upright; he was the safe choice—until, that is, some shady business dealings caused Maud to reject him, too.

Maud wrote these words near the start of what historians call the Progressive Era, which lasted from 1880 to 1920. As she was making her decisions, the meaning of marriage was beginning to change. Historian Elaine Tyler May writes of an "overlapping of cultural values" among married couples during this period. On the one hand, they still expected to have husband-headed marriages. The Married Women's Property Acts that many states had enacted in the 1800s gave women some control over assets they brought to a marriage or would inherit, but the courts tended to interpret these provisions in ways that preserved husbands' authority. The Illinois Supreme Court ruled in 1867 that a wife could not freely dispose of real estate she owned separately without her husband's approval, even though a state statute clearly said that she could. "It is simply impossible," wrote the court in this leading case, which law students were still studying in 1900, "that a woman married should be able to control and enjoy her property as if she were sole, without leaving her at liberty, practically, to annul the marriage tie at her pleasure." In other words, if wives controlled their own assets, they could leave their marriages if they were unhappy, and no state legislator in his right mind, the court thought, could possibly have meant to allow that.

Judges spoke euphemistically of preserving "domestic harmony" or "marital privacy" rather than of husband and wife as being one legal person, but their decisions still, for the most part, favored husbands.

For example, in *Thompson v. Thompson,* a case that reached the Supreme Court in 1910, a wife attempted to sue her husband for $70,000 in damages because he had assaulted her many times—she listed seven instances in her complaint. The Thompsons lived in the District of Columbia, where Congress had passed a law allowing wives to sue "as fully and as freely as if they were unmarried" for harm they incurred. But the Supreme Court ruled that this law did not include the right of married women to sue their husbands. Allowing such suits would be unwise, wrote Justice William R. Day for the majority, because it

> would, at the same time, open the doors of the courts to accusations of all sorts of one spouse against the other, and bring into public notice complaints for assault, slander, and libel, and alleged injuries to property of the one or the other, by husband against wife, or wife against husband. Whether the exercise of such jurisdiction would be promotive of the public welfare and domestic harmony is at least a debatable question.

Upholding domestic harmony, that is to say, was more important than allowing wives legal remedies against abusive husbands. After all, Justice Day wrote, abused women could always get a divorce if their marriages became intolerable. So the Supreme Court left the domestic harmony of the Thompson household, in which Mr. Thompson repeatedly beat his wife, undisturbed.

In fact, through the mid-twentieth century the entire legal system treated wife battering as a private matter that called for counseling rather than legal action. Reformers pushed for family courts in which problems such as these could be treated separately from crimes or lawsuits. Couples were urged to reconcile, and wives were encouraged to consider how their own actions might have contributed to their husbands' assaults. The police hesitated to intervene in private matters between husbands and wives such as physical abuse unless grave injury or death occurred. A training bulletin from the International Association of Police Chiefs in the 1960s offered this advice on how to handle domestic violence:

For the most part these disputes are personal matters requiring no direct police action. However, an inquiry into the facts must be made to satisfy the originating complaint. . . . Once inside the home, the officer's sole purpose is to preserve the peace. . . . In dealing with family disputes the power of arrest should be exercised as a last resort. The officer should never create a police problem when there is only a family problem existing.

These mere family problems remained invisible to the public. Except for severe cases, men were rarely prosecuted for beating their wives. The concept of "marital rape" was unknown, because the law assumed that when a woman married a man she gave him consent to have sexual relations with her at any time. Social scientists saw no need to study family violence: between 1939 and 1969, the leading academic journal on marriage and family life did not publish a single article on the subject. Within broad limits, what went on between husbands and wives was seen as beyond the reach of the law. A man's home was still his castle.

The other overlapping cultural value of the Progressive Era was the emerging concept of "marital happiness," as yet not clearly defined but having to do with emotional satisfaction. Maud may have been struggling with that concept when she wrote about improving Elmer's knowledge and interests to the point where she could have a satisfying personal relationship with him: "All the time I am planning to bring him up to a standard where I *can* love him." This newer view of marriage spread as the nation industrialized and more people worked for wages while fewer farmed the land. The exodus from the countryside that had begun in the second half of the nineteenth century continued during the first half of the twentieth. In 1900, 40 percent of Americans lived in urban areas; by 1950, 64 percent did. In cities, young adults were more independent of their parents. They frequently lived as boarders or lodgers in other people's homes before they married. Because men took factory or office jobs that paid wages, they did not need to inherit the family farm. This greater independence encouraged them to choose partners based more on emotional attraction than in the past.

Men were seen as the ones who should work for wages outside the home while wives cared for home and children. It was always easier for prosperous families to reach this ideal status, because poor families could not live on the husband's wages alone. Even so, very few married women worked outside the home in 1900—just 6 percent according to Census Bureau estimates. Women depended heavily on the steady earnings of their husbands. Husbands, in turn, depended on their wives to handle demanding chores such as washing clothes by hand, buying food almost every day (home refrigerators were unknown in 1900), and caring for an average of three or four children per family. All but the most prosperous men also depended on their wives to earn some supplementary income by taking in work. Many young adults would have shared some of the reservations Maud had about romance. Nevertheless, little by little the role of romantic love increased.

The shift from farm to city also changed the costs and benefits of raising children. Farm families had functioned as labor cooperatives headed by the husband, and children had contributed valuable labor from an early age. But as industrialization proceeded in the twentieth century, the need for child labor declined. Parents began to realize that children required a longer period of schooling so that they could obtain better jobs as adults. These material changes led married couples to have fewer children. Moreover, infant and child deaths declined sharply, which meant that parents were less likely to lose a child. In turn, the decline in births, along with lengthening adult lives, meant that wives and husbands could choose to spend several years together before having children and could expect many more after they were finished raising them. Marriage in Western nations, perhaps for the first time in human history, included long periods without small children at home. Suddenly, more space opened for companionship and personal growth.

Companionate Marriage
and the Male-Breadwinner Ideal

As a result, what observers called the "companionate marriage" arose during the late nineteenth and early twentieth centuries. It was based on the importance of emotional ties between wife and husband—their companionship, friendship, romantic love, and sex life. Eventually the factors that Maud hesitated to rely upon became the center of married life. In her day, experts on marriage thought that sexual intercourse should be limited to once or twice a month. The purpose of sex was to have children rather than to satisfy one's desires, and it was thought unseemly to have sex more often. But by the 1920s and 1930s, marriage manuals offered explicit advice on how to achieve sexual pleasure and assured skittish readers that by achieving mutual satisfaction they would strengthen their marriages. Theodor van de Velde, in his popular 1930 book, *Ideal Marriage: Its Physiology and Technique,* told his readers that "a vigorous and harmonious sex life" was one of the "four cornerstones of the temple of love and happiness in marriage." (The others were a good choice of partner, a good psychological attitude, and an agreement on how and whether to limit the number of children.) He also argued that sex without mutual satisfaction and variety would become so boring, particularly to the wife, that the couple would reduce the frequency of intercourse and drift away from each other. He then proceeded to discuss lovemaking in great detail and encyclopedic breadth. A helpful table summarized the pluses ("when the summit of voluptuous pleasure is desired by both") and minuses ("avoid this in the first acts of intercourse") of the ten basic positions he described.

By the 1920s, according to historian Stephanie Coontz, "love and marriage had become vital to most people's sense of personal identity, with attachments to parents, siblings, and friends paling by comparison." But it was a kind of marriage in which the husband was still the family head and the breadwinner. In fact, an underlying tension existed between the husband-headed marriage and the love-based, companionate marriage. In the former, wives are supposed to defer to their husbands' wishes, while in the latter wives and husbands are supposed to act as friends and as partners. The first is an unequal relationship, but the second is a relationship of equals. The first also implies separate roles for the husband and wife, but the second implies togetherness—joint activities and joint experiences. In the first husbands and wives are to be as one in facing the outside world; in the second they are to be two individuals in relating to each other. These opposing tendencies coexisted in marriage for the first two-thirds of the twentieth century. So entrenched were both that few people saw any contradiction between them. Instead, this historically novel combination was hailed as the highest form of family life.

The male-breadwinner ideal was strong enough when the Great Depression struck for observers to criticize wives who worked outside the home for taking scarce jobs that should be reserved for husbands. Following this sentiment, Congress passed a law in 1932 that prohibited two people in the same family from holding federal jobs at the same time. The law resulted in about fifteen hundred women (but almost no men) losing their government jobs in its first year. The male-breadwinner ideal received a further boost from one of the first major pieces of social welfare legislation in American history, the Social Security Act of 1935. The law assumed that almost all working-age adults would be married and that husbands' earnings would support their wives and children. Working-age men received no government assistance until retirement except for temporary unemployment benefits to tide them over while they looked for work. Women also received no support except if their husbands died, in which case they and their children received benefits through the Aid to Dependent Children program. (The act ignored divorced or never-married mothers, whose numbers later expanded greatly.) Here, then, was family life according to the designers of the act: Men and women were supposed to get married before having children and stay married. Men were supposed to work for wages and support their wives and children, and when they retired they were to receive a government pension. Women were supposed to remain at home, raise the children, and rely on their husbands for support. Should their husbands die before their children were grown up, they were to receive a modest amount of cash assistance. Should they be widowed later in life, they would receive a portion of their husband's Social Security benefits.

The dominance of the male-breadwinner ideal was further enhanced by the 1944 GI Bill of Rights, which provided government benefits to veterans, such as low-interest mortgage loans. The only way for women to obtain these benefits was to marry veterans, which millions, of course, did. In the 1950s, new homes mushroomed in the suburban rings around nearly every city, and married couples bought most of them. The government also provided veterans with subsidies for higher education and job training, gave them preference in hiring for civil service jobs, and provided them a longer period of unemployment compensation. American tax law also encouraged the male-breadwinner marriage: as of 1948, a man could reduce his tax burden if he married a woman who earned little outside the home. All of these benefits encouraged young men and women to form families based on the husband's work outside the home and the wife's work inside the home.

Other nations had made different policy choices during the first half of the century. Maternity leave benefits that provided at least partial wage replacement for women workers were introduced by Germany in 1883, and by 1940, eighteen Western countries offered them. In France, encouraging births was always the highest priority. A 1939 law even required that population issues be taught in schools. From an American perspective, one might expect that the goal of increasing births would have led French policy makers to reinforce the "traditional" male-breadwinner marriage. However, the French were so focused on subsidizing motherhood that they paid less attention to whether wives worked outside the home. As a result, France developed a generous support package that helped mothers whether or not they were employed. In contrast, British policies (like American policies) continued to support the male-breadwinner model and to provide substantially less public support to families than France's.

In the 1950s, the overlapping ideals of the love-based companionate marriage and the husband-headed, breadwinner-homemaker marriage reached their peaks. About 95 percent of adults who came of age in the 1950s got married. There was no other acceptable way to raise children. Having what was called an "illegitimate" child—one born outside of marriage—was shameful and, among the middle class, often resulted in a pregnant girl being sent to a home for unwed mothers to give birth. I remember the location of such a home, mentioned in hushed tones, in the town where I grew up in the 1960s; by the 1980s it had become a home for the elderly. Living together outside of marriage was unacceptable except among the poor and the bohemian. The only path to respectable adulthood was marriage, and people walked down that path quickly: about half of all women were married by age twenty. One expert, writing in the *New York Times Magazine* in 1953, warned, "A girl who hasn't a man in sight by the time she is 20 is not altogether wrong in fearing that she may never get married." In addition, couples tended to have their first child sooner after marrying than did their parents' generation. All told, Americans married at younger ages and had children at a faster pace than in any other twentieth-century decade.

Moreover, a man's rights over his children, and his responsibilities toward them, depended almost entirely on whether he was married. For instance, if a married woman bore a child, her husband was treated as the legal father even if everyone in the community knew he wasn't. The original purpose of this archaic but still-on-the-books law was to protect a father's rights to the labor of his children. His control could be threatened if another man claimed to be the child's father, especially since no good way existed until recently to determine who the father really was. But what should happen if an *unmarried* woman gave birth? Her child would pose a threat to the system of assigning children to fathers through marriage. So the law prohibited any legal relationship between the father and the child—they were said to be "legal strangers" toward each other. The birth was called illegitimate because only a birth within marriage was legitimate. An illegitimate child could not inherit any wealth from the father. In turn, the father had no responsibility to support the child. And even if the mother died, the father could not be awarded custody. Unmarried mothers also were stigmatized and their children penalized in order to enforce the dominance of marriage. The stigma had its effect: in the 1950s, the "shotgun marriage," with its evocation of a young pregnant woman's angry father forcing the couple to marry at gunpoint, was common. Well over half of all unmarried women who became pregnant married before the birth of their children. Only about 5 percent of the children of mothers in their teens and early twenties were born outside of marriage.

The tension between companionate relationships and the husband's authority remained latent in the 1950s, hidden behind a surge of child-bearing. In the early 1900s, the birth rate had continued its slow, long-term fall, and then had fallen precipitously during the Great De-pression. Couples in the 1930s simply could not afford to have as many children as their parents had. The birth rate was so low that academic experts worried about a long-term decline in the American population. World War II further disrupted marriage and childbearing. But after the war was over, birth rates rose to levels not seen since 1900. They stayed high throughout the 1950s baby boom—the only sustained rise in childbearing in the twentieth century—before declining in the early 1960s.

A quieter baby boom occurred in Britain and France. Like the United States, the British and French had emerged victorious from World War II. Young adults may have shared what one demographer has called a renewed trust in public institutions: a greater sense of con-fidence that postwar government would continue to provide stability and that the labor market would continue to provide opportunities. In the 1950s and early 1960s, the proportion of young adults who married increased to well over 90 percent in Britain and France. Births also increased, although not as much as in the United States. Women who married at the peak of the American boom in the 1950s had 3.2 chil-dren on average. The comparable figure was 2.8 for French married women in the 1950s and 2.5 for British married women when the boom peaked there in the early 1960s. Moreover, the American divorce rate, although stable, remained far higher. In the 1950s, the number of divorces for every thousand people was three times as high in the United States as in France or Britain. But, as we know, the birth rate and the divorce rate had long been higher in the United States; the gaps were nothing new.

A Spirituality of Dwelling

One key cultural difference between the United States and Western Europe, however, had grown by the 1950s—and it was a difference that mattered for family life: religious vitality. By the 1950s church membership had been increasing in the United States for more than one hundred years. In 1850, 34 percent of Americans were affiliated with a church. By 1906 the figure had reached half, and by 1950 it stood at 59 percent. In much of Europe just the opposite had occurred: church records in Britain, for instance, show a sharp and almost continuous decline in attendance at religious services from 1850 to the present. So by the baby boom era, religious participation was far higher in the United States than in Britain. According to a 1950 survey, just 23 percent of the British said they attended church at least monthly, whereas in the United States the comparable figure was probably twice as large or even larger.

What happened in Britain is an example of secularization: the decline of religious ideas and practices in social and personal life. It's what you might expect to occur when a country modernizes. The size of the government grows and provides an alternative source of authority to religious doctrine. The rise of modern science with its rejection of the supernatural leads to nonreligious explanations for how the world works, such as the Darwinian theory of evolution. The growth of industrialism and wage labor frees people from economic dependence on their families, which weakens the effects of the religious traditions that families may hold. As individuals come to see that religion has less power and authority, they are more likely to choose not to participate in it. Secularization, many experts think, is an inevitable part of modernization.

This theory seems to work well for most Western nations, but it doesn't work for the United States. Why has religious vigor increased as the United States has modernized? The leading explanation is, at first glance, surprising and counterintuitive: competition. In most of Europe, including Britain and France, the state supports one official church through taxes and other revenues. In France it is the Catholic Church; in England it is the Anglican Church. The vast majority of the population at least nominally follows what is called the "established" religion—the official church—but attendance is generally low. In the United States, however, the First Amendment to the Constitution says, "Congress shall make no law respecting an establishment of religion, or prohibiting the free exercise thereof."

It might seem logical that the lack of an established church should have depressed religious activity in the United States. After all, established churches have the authority of the state behind them and are supported by a stream of state revenue. They have an infrastructure of clergy and buildings. They have a tradition of being the official religion. But the proponents of the competition explanation argue that the separation of church and state in the United States set off a contest that was, and is, the source of American religious vitality. Think of a "religious economy," analogous to a market economy, in which churches are like competing firms producing a product (in this case, spirituality) and individuals are the potential consumers. The winners in the spiritual marketplace are the religious firms with the most innovative and attractive goods. The older churches tend to be the losers in this market because they aren't used to competition, may find it distasteful, and may not wish to redesign their product. Competition, then, has allowed American religion to evolve. It has been able to redesign its message, its rituals, and the services it offers to fit with social change. Consistent with this theory, old-line denominations have lost members over time, while newer ones have gained.

Whether because of the religious economy or other factors, large numbers of Americans attended religious services in the 1950s. The style of worship they experienced reflected what sociologist Robert Wuthnow has called a "spirituality of dwelling." People wanted a religious experience that made them feel at home. Inhabiting the sacred space of a church or synagogue gave them a sense of membership in a community. The distinctive architecture (the spire towering over the town green, the stained-glass windows, the vaulted ceilings) signified that they were in what was commonly called a house of worship. The familiar text and music, repeated every week—including the wish to dwell in the house of the Lord forever—were comforting. In this way, most 1950s congregations provided a secure spiritual home.

In a similar way, so did most 1950s families. The spirituality of dwelling fit with a family- and home-centered decade in which marriage and children were a central part of almost every adult's life. "Homes and congregations," Wuthnow writes, "acquired special spiritual significance because they were the places where children were being raised." Much of the growth in religious involvement occurred in the suburbs, as married couples bought homes, had children, and sought churches to join. The suburban churches offered a standard package of family-related programs: Sunday schools, teen groups, Scouting, women's and men's groups, and so forth. Following the male-breadwinner ideal, these activities often presumed a two-parent family with a mother who did not work outside the home. Women's groups, for example, often met during the day so that homemakers could attend and still have their evenings free for their families. The 1950s family and the 1950s church supported each other.

Still, liberal Protestant and Jewish religious leaders began to endorse the use of birth control devices, such as the diaphragm and the condom, by married couples. Most often their approval came in the context of endorsing "family planning": spacing and limiting the number of births a couple had. That meant accepting the idea that married couples were having sex for pleasure, not just to have children—a big shift from the attitudes that were prevalent at the beginning of the century. An Episcopal leader said that using contraception was a "positive duty" for married couples who did not want a child at the time. By 1961 the National Council of Churches had approved the use of birth control devices. The devices available in the 1950s were not completely reliable—the birth control pill was not introduced until the 1960s—so couples still had to worry about unintended pregnancies. Moreover, the Catholic Church maintained its prohibition of artificial contraception, and Catholic couples had more children, on average, than did non-Catholics. But except for Catholic teachings, the idea that religiously observant married couples should have pleasurable sex lives even when they didn't want to have more children was well established by the end of the 1950s.

The connection between religion and family life was necessarily weaker in Britain, France, and many other Western European nations because levels of religious activity were much lower. Nevertheless, the affinity between religion and the baby boom can be seen even in Britain. During the 1950s, a short-term rise in religious involvement occurred for one of the only times in the long history of British religious decline. Membership in the major Protestant churches in Great

Britain, which had been dropping since a temporary peak after the end of World War I, increased in the 1950s. Other records show that the number of people taking communion in the Church of England rose between 1955 and 1965. By the end of the baby boom, however, rates of attendance and communion had resumed their downward drift.

In the United States, the 1950s values of security and stability could also be seen in the stable divorce rate. During the first few decades of the twentieth century, the divorce rate had continued its long-term rise. It dropped briefly during the depths of the Depression, not because wives and husbands were getting along better but rather because it was too difficult economically to live in separate households. Just after World War II a temporary spike in divorce rates occurred as hasty post-war marriages failed. Then, during the 1950s, the divorce rate was stable—the first sustained period since the mid-1800s in which divorce did not increase. Perhaps one in three marriages ended in divorce, a total that would have shocked nineteenth-century Americans but now seems modest compared to the approximately one-in-two level today.

Popular religion encouraged married couples to take pride in playing the roles of husbands and wives, breadwinners and homemakers, and fathers and mothers. In 1952, Norman Vincent Peale, a Methodist-ordained minister in New York City, published a self-help guide, *The Power of Positive Thinking*. Peale drew upon both religion and psychology. He advised that if you think of yourself in positive terms and have faith in God, you will succeed in life. *The Power of Positive Thinking* shot to the top of the best-seller lists and stayed there for two years. It sold two million copies in the 1950s and many more after that. Peale became a national celebrity, appearing regularly on the young medium of television and writing frequently for magazines and newspapers.

The book consists largely of anecdotes about individuals who achieved success through prayer and positive thoughts. Although most stories focus on the "businessman," several relate to family life. Read today, they seem steeped in 1950s values. Peale tells a story he heard from a minister about a woman who wanted to save her marriage despite the loss of "old-time companionship" and her discovery that her husband was interested in other women. When she discussed the problem with the minister, he whimsically repeated the maxim that "God runs a beauty parlor," meaning that women can become beautiful as they age if they have an inner spiritual life reflected on their faces. He then suggested that she picture herself as capable and attractive and hold on to a mental image of the good times earlier in her marriage. When her husband asked for a divorce, she requested a ninety-day delay before a final decision. Night after night, as her husband went out, she sat at home, praying and painting a mental image of the better days of their relationship. Toward the end of the period, he began to remain home, and when the ninety days were up, he told her, "I couldn't possibly get along without you. Where did you ever get the idea that I was going to leave you?"

As for men, Peale tells the story of a prominent citizen who was involved in an affair with a married woman. He had tried to break it off, but she threatened to tell her husband if he did, which would have led to the prominent citizen's disgrace. Peale urged him "to do the right thing," which was to break off the affair, seek God's forgiveness, and leave the outcome to God. He did, the woman did not tell her husband about the affair, and he was not disgraced. Another man, Bill, was passed over for the presidency of his company. His wife was angry and wanted him to quit his job, but he was unsure. Peale met the couple, led a few minutes of quiet prayer with them, and then asked God's blessing for the new president. "I also prayed," he writes, "that Bill would be able to fit in with the new administration and give more effective service than before." Bill decided to stick with the company and was rewarded two years later when the president quit the firm and Bill was given the position.

Peale presents these stories as great successes. The wife who stayed home alone night after night was able to save her marriage through her faith in the positive images she was picturing. The prominent citizen was able to end his affair without a scandal. Bill eventually became president of his company by loyally keeping his job. Beyond the message about method—think positively, have faith—was a message about the rewards that were valued in the 1950s, such as saving your marriage and sticking with your job. Think positively and you, too, can get married, stay married, have children, keep your job, play your role, stay the course—those were the 1950s values that Peale was conveying.

The Distinctiveness of the 1950s

The 1950s family was idealized in television situation comedies that you can still stumble upon while channel-surfing: *Father Knows Best, Ozzie and Harriet,* and *Leave It to Beaver.* These shows have become so iconic that their very names now conjure up an image of the era. They connote a cheerful and contented family in which the dad works for pay and the mom stays home to raise the kids and do the housework. Their biggest problems are on the order of the dad's clumsiness in the kitchen or a child's difficulty in finding a date for the junior prom. In reality, of course, family life was not that idyllic. But was there something about the 1950s family that made it more stable and less susceptible to divorce than the historical trend of continually rising divorce rates would have predicted?

At the time, experts pointed to the sharp division of labor between husband and wife as the source of stability. The leading sociological theorist Talcott Parsons argued that small groups such as families do better if their members specialize in the activities they perform, with one person becoming the task leader (the husband, as he marches off to earn money) and another becoming the social-emotional leader (the wife, as she cares for the children and comforts her husband on his return home). The husband does the market work, the wife does the emotion work, and the family functions better. Gary Becker, an economist whose theories of the family were to later win him a Nobel Prize, drew an analogy between two nations with different strengths: a developed nation that is more efficient in factory work and a less developed nation that is relatively more efficient at growing crops. According to economic theory, said Becker, the two countries gain if each specializes in what it does best—industrial production for the former, farm production for the latter—and then trades goods with the other. So just as two countries might trade tractors for grain, the efficient family maximizes its gains when the husband, whose higher wages are taken to mean that he is better at earning money, trades his earnings for the domestic services his wife performs.

There are problems with this happy framework, however. It takes as a fact of nature that men are substantially better at earning money and women at nurturing children. Even if there are some differences in men's and women's capabilities and preferences, the gap between them was greatly exaggerated by the male-breadwinner ideal that was so popular at the time. Not just sitcoms but also books and magazines portrayed women's roles in ways one can't imagine seeing today. For instance, Peale tells the story of a woman who came to see him because she wanted to get married but couldn't find a man she liked who would marry her. When he appeared five minutes late for the appointment, "it was obvious that she was displeased for her lips were pressed firmly together." She chided him for his tardiness, then told him her problem and asked him to tell her why she couldn't get married. Peale studied her and, speaking frankly, said the problem was her attitude. He writes:

> Then I said, "You have a very firm way of pressing your lips together which indicates a domineering attitude. The average male, I might as well tell you, does not like to be dominated, at least so that he knows it." Then I added, "I think you would be a very attractive person if you got those too-firm lines out of your face. You must have a little softness, a little tenderness, and those lines are too firm to be soft."

For good measure, he added that she might get her hair done better, use a little perfume, and get a dress that hangs better. "Well," she remarked, "I never expected to get this combination of advice in a minister's office." Peale then told her the "God runs a beauty parlor" saying. Many years later, after finishing a speech, Peale was approached by "a lovely looking lady with a fine-looking man and a little boy about ten years of age." It was—guess who?—the woman with the pursed lips, now happily married and a mother. She thanked Peale for his valuable advice and said that putting into practice the principles he suggested had worked. This is the type of lesson about family life that Americans learned in the 1950s. It helps to explain why theorists assumed that women were naturally better at the stay-at-home role.

But reading Peale takes us only so far in understanding the mysteries of the 1950s—where the era came from, why it happened, whether it will return. Why, we might ask, were so many people receptive to Peale's message? Why did so many of them buy his books and watch his television appearances? Why did so many of them start breadwinner-homemaker families? I think the answer can be found in the remarkable lives of the generation of Americans who were born during the Great Depression. None of the observers who were writing in the 1950s seemed to appreciate how their unique life histories could be influencing their era in ways that would change once the era had passed. My parents were among those who grew up during the Depression. My father, who was born in 1909, had to drop out of high school to help support his mother and four brothers after his father died. He continued to live at home and work during the Depression. My mother, born in 1916, was one of ten children in a family that survived the Depression because of the contributions the older children made. She was told she could attend nursing school or what was then called a "normal school" if she wanted to be a teacher, but she could not attend a liberal-arts college. My grandparents, struggling to get by, wouldn't spend money to provide a daughter with a broad college education. Then, in 1941, the start of World War II forced young adults such as my parents to further delay marriage. Three of my father's brothers went off to war, making his support for his mother even more important. My mother met few eligible men because most were overseas.

In 1946, with the end of the war, their luck improved. The postwar prosperity finally allowed the members of my parents' generation to marry and start their own families. Deprived of this opportunity for so long, the Depression generation seized it. My parents married in 1947. Nearly all of their friends married between 1946 and 1950, and most of them soon had children; I was born in 1948. Moreover, job opportunities were plentiful for my father and his male friends (none of their wives worked outside the home at the time). When the economy expanded in the postwar years, the demand for workers outstripped the supply of now-grown-up Depression children, and wages rose. Depression, war, prosperity: no other generation in the twentieth century, we now know, had a life course filled with this many calamities and opportunities. By the time the ups and downs ended, they had embraced marriage and childbearing as no other twentieth-century generation had done or subsequently would.

I think that we are unlikely to see a reversal of family life of this magnitude—a large-scale return to marriage, home, and child rearing—unless a future generation faces a similarly cataclysmic series of events. Only then would the exhaustion and the desire for an inward, nurturing family life that we saw in the Depression generation resurface. That series of events, of course, could happen. With nuclear proliferation, international terrorism, climate change, and environmental degradation all posing potential threats, I could imagine a generation—perhaps even one that is alive today—having a life as difficult. I hope not. But in any case, that's the scale of events it would take, I think, before a similarly exhausted future generation would turn as eagerly to home and children as did the women and men of the Depression generation. The return of the 1950s, in sum, is very unlikely but cannot be ruled out.

When I was in elementary school, my mother went back to work part-time as a secretary. (She had, to her everlasting regret, declined the opportunity to go to normal school.) Most of her friends also returned to the workforce part-time when their children were all in school. In this way, the women of the Depression generation slowly but steadily began to undercut the male-breadwinner ideal. Someone who married in her early twenties and had three children in six or seven years (a not-uncommon pattern) would only be in her early thirties when her youngest child entered kindergarten. If she looked at the help-wanted ads in the newspaper, she would find an increasing demand for jobs that had become typed as "women's work": secretaries, telephone operators, nurses, teachers. These positions were in the growing service sector of the economy. By 1960 about 40 percent of married women whose children were all in school were working for pay.

The experts also ignored the dissatisfactions of some stay-at-home mothers: the "problem that had no name," according to Betty Friedan's famous 1963 book, *The Feminine Mystique*. The housewife role, which seemed natural to Americans at midcentury, was actually new. Until then, wives had always been important to the family economy in ways that went beyond child rearing. Farm wives tended a garden, canned fruits and vegetables, and sewed clothes, among other things. Even in the urban families of the early 1900s, wives still performed some of these tasks. But with a rising standard of living that allowed couples to purchase goods such as store-bought clothes, processed foods, and washing machines, wives became consumers rather than producers. With refrigerator-freezers in the home, they no longer needed to shop every day for meat or dairy products. There were no gardens to tend, no fruit to can. In short, they produced less, and what they still produced, such as clean clothes, they could accomplish more quickly.

In part, they compensated by ratcheting up standards of home-making, so rugs were cleaned and clothes were washed more often. Departments of home economics emerged at state universities with the goal of improving homemaking through scientific methods. "Home ec" became a popular major for the growing number of "coeds," as female students were called. While these programs did provide a better understanding of nutrition, hygiene, and child development, they could not hide the fact that homemaking was not a lifelong, full-time job. Yet when they returned to the paid labor force, married women found it difficult to develop satisfying careers. Most returning mothers held a series of jobs that offered few opportunities for promotions. Even today, when far more married women work for pay, a woman who takes time out of her career to raise children pays a "marriage penalty" of about 7 percent of her wages per child. The reduction in wages occurs because of a combination of lack of experience, part-time rather than full-time work, and employer discrimination.

Although the primary messages in the media provided Peale-like paeans to the stay-at-home wife, some support for wives who were working for wages could be seen. A few articles in monthly magazines celebrated women's achievements outside the home, supported wage work for women, and expressed ambivalence about domestic life. A 1954 article in *Reader's Digest,* "That Amazing Secretarial Shortage," argued in before-its-time terms:

For the young mother with small children, going back to an office is likely to be a losing proposition—the cost of baby-sitters demolishes her earnings. "Thousands of mothers," said a business school principal, "would be willing to return to full-time jobs if the Government allowed them to deduct on their income-tax returns the cost of domestic help."

Eventually, Congress would enact legislation to do just that. The pioneers of this movement of women into the labor force were the baby boom mothers who dropped out to have and raise children and then returned.

The Family at Midcentury

In hindsight, we can see that the 1950s formed an unusual interlude in the history of American family life. But to many observers at the time, the companionate marriage, with the husband as breadwinner and the wife as homemaker, seemed more like the end of family history— a crowning achievement that was likely to remain the dominant family form as long as industrial society survived. Observers assumed that near-universal, early marriage was here to stay, and they celebrated the rise in births. They ignored the distinctive history of the generation who grew up during the Depression, fought World War II, and then built their families during the prosperous Pax Americana of the late 1940s and the 1950s—the great period of peace and prosperity in the United States following the Allied victory in World War II. They paid little attention to the growth of the service sector of the American economy and its increasing need for the kinds of jobs that were seen as women's work. They ascribed little significance to the many mothers in their thirties and forties who took these jobs. In retrospect, the 1950s-style homemaker role looks less like a timeless tradition than a temporary detour on the road to smaller families and greater involvement in paid work.

The 1950s marriage was held together not just by its division of labor but also by the emotional satisfaction that husbands and wives obtained from each other and from their children. Spouses took pleasure in being good husbands, wives, fathers, and mothers. But beyond playing their roles well, husbands and wives were supposed to be companions, friends, and lovers, in a fashion that was new to family life on a large scale. According to historian Jessica Weiss, *McCall's* magazine coined the term "togetherness" in 1954 to describe what an article described as "this new and warmer way of life, not as women *alone* or men *alone,* isolated from one another, but as a *family* sharing a common experience." This new way of relating implied equality and sharing in marriage. It undermined the idea that husbands were the authorities in families and that their wives should defer to their decisions. While the ideal of husband-headed marriage held during the 1950s, it would decline later in the century.

Moreover, no one seemed to consider the possibility that once emotional satisfaction became a central focus, it might be difficult to limit it to marriage. No one foresaw that Americans might seek love and companionship with live-in partners and sexual pleasure with casual acquaintances, or that large numbers would think it justifiable, if they were unhappy with their intimate lives, to obtain a divorce and find a better relationship. Instead, experts seemed to think that increasing the emotional rewards of marriage would prevent people from wanting any other kind of relationship. Van de Velde's sex manual, reprinted many times through midcentury, was addressed entirely to married couples, as if there were no reason why an unmarried person would need to read it. Even Margaret Sanger, the birth control crusader, restricted her focus to married couples. She argued that traditional birth control methods such as coitus interruptus (withdrawal prior to ejaculation) left women sexually frustrated, which reduced their satisfaction with their partners and weakened their marriages. If wives and husbands were both sexually fulfilled, she reasoned, their marriages would be stronger. Artificial contraceptive methods such as the diaphragm and the condom, Sanger said, could provide both partners with sexual fulfillment without the fear of unwanted pregnancy. "Marriages built upon the shifting sands of [sexual] fear, shame, and ignorance can never lead to happiness," she wrote. In a similar vein, the author of a widely used college textbook on marriage and family life wrote in 1955, "It is unlikely that anyone who was happy and contented with his or her sex life would be interested in experimenting outside of marriage." Later decades would show, however, that the emphasis on emotional satisfaction encouraged people to critically examine their marriage and sometimes to seek alternatives to it.

The 1950s family was supported by laws and legal precedents that had changed little since 1850. The law still reinforced the position of husband as head of the household. He had fewer prerogatives than in the past, but his authority was still substantial. Courts hesitated to establish individual rights within marriage for fear of reducing domestic harmony, a reluctance that left the husband as the lead singer. As long as he inflicted no serious injury, a husband could be reasonably certain that he would not be punished for abusing his wife. Moreover, marriage made all the difference: children born outside of marriage had no rights and established no parental responsibilities. To obtain a divorce, a person still needed to prove that his or her spouse had committed a serious breach of marital behavior, such as having an affair or abandoning the family. This long-standing legal framework also seemed timeless, yet beginning in the mid-1960s it would be swept away.

In addition, the 1950s family was supported by the religious vitality of the nation. Church attendance had grown to an all-time high, in contrast to the diminishing numbers of parishioners who populated the pews of Western Europe. Most churches and synagogues offered a style of worship and a package of services that attracted married couples with children. The style emphasized being together in a holy place, much as family life emphasized being together at home. It was not a style that encouraged introspection or questioning of one's personal life. All that being religious appeared to require was sitting at weekly services, repeating familiar prayers and hymns and listening to sermons. The standard package of family-oriented activities assumed a breadwinner-homemaker marriage. In these ways, religion reinforced the 1950s family. Yet American religion, too, would change greatly in subsequent decades. It would emphasize a quest for spiritual growth that required a look at one's own needs and preferences. This new style of religion, like the broader culture around it, would encourage a more individualistic perspective on personal life. Those who took the new tack tended to make more changes in their personal lives, which could include ending their intimate partnerships and starting new ones. As law, religion, and the larger culture changed, marriage and family life would soon look very different from its 1950s form.

4

The Individualized Marriage
and the Expressive Divorce, 1960-2000

McCall's magazine may have popularized the term "togetherness" in the 1950s, but in the 1970s and 1980s its editors began to print stories about separateness. Suddenly wives were encouraged to think about their own needs and to create a personal space within their marriages. The author of "Love vs. Privacy" wrote in 1977:

> Marriage in America is unique in its emphasis on the premise that husband and wife should function as a "couple." In most other cultures, marital partners are freer to have separate identities, individual friendships, personal interests. This is not considered any reflection on their relationship. But in this country husband and wife are all too often viewed as a unit.

He cautioned, "The person who insists on sharing everything runs the risk of alienating a partner, rather than drawing him or her closer."

A 1980 article asked the question "Time for Yourself: Must It Hurt Your Marriage?" and answered that, on the contrary, it helps by allowing "the attainment of a private space in which individual growth can continue within the intimacy of a marriage." One man told the author:

> When Sharon [his wife] and I were in our twenties, we were overwhelmingly concerned with how to be a husband and wife. Now we're concerned about how to be our private selves within that marriage, and we nearly split up before we were willing to face it.

By 1990, the focus on privacy within marriage was so strong that an article asserted, "What Every Woman Needs: A Place to Call Her

Own." Women, according to the article, need private space to develop their own identities rather than merely being the persons their husbands wish them to be.

Articles such as these show that a new style of marriage was emerging in which both the wife and the husband were expected to develop a separate sense of self, to communicate more openly about their needs, and to have more flexible roles rather than the rigid breadwinner and homemaker roles of the 1950s marriage. Women and men could still get some satisfaction from playing the old-style roles, but that kind of satisfaction was no longer enough. Each spouse also wanted her or his individual life to be fulfilling in a personal sense. Marriage was not just a partnership in which two functioned as one but also a relationship in which two people maintained their individual selves. When wives and husbands evaluated how satisfied they were with their marriages, they began to think more in terms of self-development, as opposed to the satisfaction they gained through pleasing their spouse and raising their children. They asked themselves questions such as: *Am I getting the personal satisfaction I want from my marriage?* and *Am I growing as a person?* The result was a transition from the companionate marriage to what we might call the individualized marriage.

The transition began in the 1960s and accelerated in the 1970s. Like a paleontologist carbon-dating a skull, Francesca Cancian pinpointed it by examining 128 articles in mass-circulation magazines such as *McCall's* and *Ladies' Home Journal* that offered marital advice aimed at women between the early 1900s and the 1970s. She noted whether the advice in each article fit one of three themes that characterize the individualized marriage. The first theme is self-development: each person should develop a fulfilling, independent self instead of merely sacrificing oneself to one's partner. The second is that roles within marriage should be flexible and negotiable. The third is that communication and openness in confronting problems are essential. She then tallied the percentage of articles in each decade that contained one or more of these three themes. About one-third of the articles in the first decade of the twentieth century, and again at midcentury, displayed these themes, but the proportion began to rise in the 1960s, and by the

1970s two-thirds displayed these themes. The author characterized this transition as a shift in emphasis "from role to self."

Before probing the significance of this shift, however, we need to briefly consider the larger context: the breathtaking scope of social and political change that occurred in the 1960s and 1970s. From the perspective of a nation that had just glided through the quiet 1950s, it was extraordinary. To be sure, the early years of the civil rights movement had given 1950s Americans a hint of what was to come. But no one save Betty Friedan expected the feminist movement to appear, no one anticipated the sexual revolution, and no one foresaw the disruption of the urban riots and the anti–Vietnam War protests. A half century later, the questions still remain: Where did this upheaval come from? Why the 1960s instead of, say, the 1930s or the 1990s? The full answer is probably unknowable. But let me suggest an explanation: it happened in the 1960s because of the prosperity and progress of the 1950s. The latter decade nurtured a generation in which most young adults, unlike any earlier generation in American history, did not have to worry about their material standard of living. They were confident—perhaps too confident—that they would lead comfortable lives. As a result, their minds were freed to contemplate what some theorists have called higher-order needs, such as personal freedom and self-fulfillment. For African Americans, modest but real improvements in the standard of living helped produce a revolution of rising expectations that found its voice in the civil rights movement. A similar rise in expectations led to the feminist movement. A more inward turn led to sharp increases in premarital sex and cohabitation.

The young adults of the era also sought greater knowledge. The proportion of them with college degrees doubled between 1950 and 1970. What college teaches you above all, I tell my students, is critical thinking—the ability to examine one's environment and make judgments about it. Critical thinkers are more apt to question the values and institutions they find around them and to imagine how things might be better. This facility makes them more likely to protest and to challenge the existing order. It's understandable, then, that college campuses played an important role in the antiwar protests, the feminist movement, and the changing morality of sex and love. In this way, the progress made in expanding higher education also played a role in the upheavals of the 1960s and 1970s. It was not the prior poverty and deprivation of the Depression that caused such a period of change, nor has the recent loss of jobs due to globalization and automation triggered such change. Rather, the Pax Americana brought it about in a stunning display of the law of unintended consequences.

The 1960s and 1970s

In any case, the shift from role to self was part of a broader increase in expressive individualism in American culture—the kind of individualism that involves growing and changing as a person, paying attention to your feelings, and expressing your needs. Expressive individualism encourages people to look inward to see how they are doing, and it encourages them to want personal growth throughout adulthood. It is not incompatible with lifelong marriage, but it requires a new kind of marriage in which the spouses are free to grow and change and in which each feels personally fulfilled. Such marriages are harder to keep together, because what matters is not merely the things they jointly produce—well-adjusted children, nice homes—but also each person's own happiness. Since people can find happiness in other relationships, they have less reason to stay together if they are unhappy. Moreover, if relationships are primarily about the feelings of the two partners, rather than raising children together, there's less reason why relationships need to be formalized as marriages. Consequently, expressive individualism allows, and perhaps even encourages, people to find personal satisfaction in intimate relationships outside of marriage. More effective contraceptives such as the birth control pill, which Margaret Sanger and others had thought would strengthen marriage, instead allowed people to lead active sex lives outside of marriage without fear of pregnancy.

Given this more individualistic view of intimate relationships and the availability of the pill, it's no coincidence that in the 1970s the number of couples who lived together before marrying began to increase. There have always been some living-together relationships among the poor, but the phenomenon of middle-income couples living together was new, as my parents learned to their dismay from me. Just 8 percent of couples who married in the late 1960s had lived together beforehand; but by the mid-1980s the proportion who had lived together was 49 percent. Throughout this era, people without college educations were more likely to cohabit, but the numbers increased sharply among the better-educated, too.

As I noted, the feminist movement strengthened in the 1960s, and its leaders challenged the dominance of men, including husbands in male-breadwinner marriages. They urged husbands to do more housework and child care and to share decision-making authority with their wives. They encouraged wives to take paying jobs, and they pushed for greater government support for the care of children whose mothers worked outside of the home. Meanwhile, married women continued to join the paid workforce in large numbers. In the 1950s, mothers with school-age children had led the way, but during the 1960s and 1970s, mothers with preschool-age children also took paying jobs in large numbers. By 1970, 49 percent of women with school-age children were in the paid workforce, as were 30 percent of women who had at least one preschool-age child.

Gradually, the government began to respond to the needs of working mothers. It backed into assisting them in 1975, when Congress enacted a cash assistance program for low-income families, the Earned Income Tax Credit. The EITC provided what's called a refundable tax credit to low-income working families with children. "Refundable" means that even if you don't pay income taxes because your wages are low, you can still qualify to receive a "refund" check from the Internal Revenue Service. Instead of taking your money, the IRS gives you some. Conservatives thought that the EITC would strengthen the male-breadwinner family because only one parent had to be employed in order for the family to qualify. But liberals realized that it would also aid other kinds of families for two reasons. First, lone parents could receive EITC benefits if they were employed because a worker did not need to be married to qualify. Second, two-earner families could receive benefits because there was no requirement that one parent stay home. In fact, few of the working-poor families who received EITC benefits fit the breadwinner-homemaker mold because most low-income families felt they couldn't afford to keep a parent at home. After several increases during subsequent decades, the EITC currently provides a maximum benefit of more than $4,000 to a family with two children and an income of about $10,000 to $15,000. Although little known outside the world of government agencies and low-income families, the EITC now provides benefits that cost the United States Treasury twice as much per year as the program people call "welfare."

In 1976, twenty-two years after an article in *Reader's Digest* suggested giving employed parents tax breaks for child care expenses, Congress enacted the Dependent Care Tax Credit. It allowed parents to deduct from their taxable income part of the money they paid for the care of their children while they worked outside the home. Its benefits went almost entirely to lone mothers and to two-earner, two-parent families. Meanwhile, the beneficiaries of Aid to Families with Dependent Children, as welfare was then known, shifted from the widows it was designed to protect in the 1930s to separated, divorced, and never-married mothers. Improvements in health care had reduced the number of widows, while divorce and nonmarital childbearing had increased the latter groups. The level of assistance AFDC provided was modest, but it did help mothers assemble a support package that could allow them to live separately from the fathers of their children. AFDC recipients typically combined their government benefits (which could also include food stamps, health insurance through Medicaid, and housing subsidies) with other sources of assistance, such as help from kin, support from absent fathers, and off-the-books work.

Working outside the home gave married mothers more authority within the home. Because they contributed to the family's income, they had more of a claim in deciding how to spend it. Working for pay also made them more independent of their husbands. They could more credibly threaten to leave a marriage if they were unhappy. Few made that threat in everyday family life, of course, and women's low wages made it difficult for them to support themselves and their children. But leaving was a greater possibility than when most wives stayed home. This source of independence seems to make a difference: many studies have found that women who work outside the home have more power within the home. They tend to spend less time doing housework and their husbands tend to spend more time doing it.

The movement of married women into the workforce was a momentous development for American family life. Yet the contrast with the breadwinner-homemaker families of the 1950s made it seem like a greater change than, in historical perspective, it really was. Wives had always done productive work in addition to raising children. In hunter-gatherer societies, they gathered the fruits, vegetables, and grain that provided much of the food for their band. In agricultural societies, they were full partners with their husbands in managing the farm. Even in the early twentieth century, when few wives worked for wages, they took in boarders and lodgers, did other people's laundry, or did piecework at home. It was only in the mid-twentieth century, at the height of the male-breadwinner family, that women withdrew from productive work apart from child rearing. The 1950s was the more unusual time. Starting in the 1960s, married women returned to the productive role they had always had, but they did it this time by bringing home a paycheck.

Another domain in which swift and important change occurred was family law. After changing little since the mid-nineteenth century, family law was transformed in the last third of the twentieth in ways that lessened the legal significance of marriage, reduced the authority of husbands, and strengthened individual rights. In 1965 and 1972, a century after the Comstock law was enacted, the Supreme Court issued two decisions that finally put it to an end. In *Griswold v. Connecticut,* the Court in 1965 invalidated a vestigial Connecticut law that prohibited the counseling or medical treatment of married couples for the purposes of birth control. Justice William O. Douglas, writing for the majority, asserted a right to privacy within marriage that the state must respect. The Court soon extended that right to privacy in a 1972 decision, *Eisenstadt v. Baird.* Unmarried persons, the Court ruled, also could not be denied access to birth control services. Justice William J. Brennan conceded that *Griswold* had established a right to privacy only within marriage, but he reasoned: "Yet the marital couple is not an independent entity with a mind and heart of its own, but an association of two individuals each with a separate intellectual and emotional makeup." One hundred years earlier, or perhaps even fifty years earlier, the marital couple *had* been viewed legally as an independent entity with a mind of its own, and that mind was the husband's. Brennan's position represented a major shift. It came at a time when a more individualistic view of family and personal life was already gaining ground, and it helped to accelerate that trend.

The same view was reinforced by court decisions that virtually abolished the legal significance of whether a child was born to married parents or not. One important case involved Peter and Joan Stanley, who lived together intermittently in Illinois for eighteen years in the 1950s and 1960s and had three children but never married. Theirs was not an ideal home: their oldest child was declared a ward of the state in a neglect proceeding. Then Joan Stanley died. According to the law at the time, Peter was a "legal stranger" to his children: he had neither rights to them nor responsibilities for them. But he claimed that he loved and supported them, and after Joan's death, he arranged for the two younger children to live with a couple he knew. When a state agency learned of the arrangement, however, it invoked an Illinois law stating that the children of deceased unwed mothers are wards of the state and tried to take the children. Peter appealed this decision and asked for a hearing on his fitness as a parent. The agency denied his request because he had not married the children's mother, and the Illinois Supreme Court agreed with this denial. Peter then took his case to the U.S. Supreme Court, which overruled the lower courts in 1972 and stated that he was, indeed, entitled to a hearing despite being an unmarried father. "The private interest here," wrote Justice Byron R. White for the majority, "that of a man in the children he has sired and raised, undeniably warrants deference and, absent a powerful countervailing interest, protection." But until that point, judges had considered not the private interest of an unmarried man but rather the public interest of assigning children to fathers through marriage. Now, implied Justice White, it is the individual relationship of a father to his children that counts, and marriage is no longer a powerful enough principle to countervail that interest. In other words, when it comes to children, parenthood matters more than marriage.

This more limited view of the legal importance of marriage would be affirmed and expanded in a series of legal decisions that strengthened individual rights. Just three weeks after deciding the Stanley case, the Supreme Court rejected the practice of excluding illegitimate children from receiving benefits through their relationship to their fathers—such as receiving death benefits if their father died in a work accident. Justice Lewis F. Powell Jr. wrote for the majority that "visiting this condemnation on the head of an infant is illogical and unjust." Through decisions such as these, the courts established that if an unmarried woman gives birth, the biological father and the child have rights and responsibilities toward each other that are very similar to what the law prescribes for a former husband and his child after a divorce. The father—who can now be identified with near certainty through genetic testing—can ask the court for visitation privileges or for custody, and he can be required to provide financial support for the child. The child can inherit the father's property and collect damages in wrongful-death or unemployment compensation cases.

The trend toward abolishing the category of illegitimacy also has occurred in most other Western nations. In Germany, for example, the Civil Code of 1896 stated, "An illegitimate child and its father are not deemed to be related," but a 1969 revision of the Civil Code effectively overturned this rule. In all countries, the legal recognition of nonmarital childbearing was spurred by two other legal trends. The first was a greater focus on the rights of children, rather than parents, in families formed by births outside of marriage or by divorce. Courts became more interested in ensuring that children in these situations received adequate support and care and had the same rights as children born in marriages. The second was a decline in the use of the law to punish sexual activity outside marriage. Doing so seemed untenable in an era where sex outside of marriage was becoming common and where sexual acts between consenting adults were considered for the most part as private matters.

In 1969 California further advanced individual rights within the family by becoming the first jurisdiction to allow people to obtain divorce decrees merely by stating that their marriages had irretrievably broken down, whether or not their spouses agreed. Prior to the passage of California's law, a person who wanted a divorce had to show that his or her partner had committed a specific act—desertion, infidelity, abuse, mental cruelty—that state law recognized as grounds for granting a divorce. But now the State of California would grant you a divorce if you felt that you and your spouse had grown apart, were unable to communicate adequately, or did not sufficiently love each other. You could obtain a divorce if you felt your marriage was adequate but limited, perhaps because it did not allow you to grow and develop as an individual. These kinds of reasons are consistent with the expressive individualism that was becoming so prominent in American culture—the kinds of reasons that led Barbara Whitehead to write of the rise of "expressive divorce."

In the decades leading up to the new divorce laws, couples who agreed to divorce had increasingly colluded to satisfy the fault-based provisions of state laws. For instance, they would pretend that the husband had been mentally cruel to his wife. In fact, a legal historian claims that a majority of divorces had been collusive for a century. By the 1960s the artifice was so common that a young Woody Allen incorporated it into his stand-up comedy routine. Allen described how he and his wife wanted a divorce but discovered that in New York adultery was the only ground: "And that is weird because the Ten Commandments say 'Thou shalt not commit adultery.' But New York State says you have to." The growing sense that fraud and manipulation were commonplace in divorce suits was an important reason for the new laws. Still, the Western world had not seen divorce laws like these since the short-lived divorce reform of the French Revolution.

By coincidence, American automobile insurers were changing the way they handled claims about the time the California law was introduced. Previously, a driver whose car had been damaged in an accident had to get in touch with the other driver's insurance company and prove that the other driver had been at fault. Under the new rules, dubbed "no-fault" by the media, each driver received benefits from his or her own company regardless of who was at fault. Fresh from reporting this change, the media labeled California's new status "no-fault divorce," a name that stuck, even though the bill's sponsors had not meant to suggest that no one was at fault in a divorce. By the 1980s most states had followed California's lead by enacting some form of no-fault divorce.

The divorce rate, which had stabilized in the 1950s, began to rise again in the early 1960s and shot up to an all-time high by 1980. A marriage begun around 1980 had a nearly 50 percent chance of ending in divorce. It's not clear how much of this change was produced by the no-fault divorce laws. A short-term spike in divorce typically occurred after a state introduced no-fault criteria. But social scientists are still debating whether the laws caused much long-term change. The new laws probably both reflected attitudes that were already changing and also furthered those changes.

The no-fault divorce revolution swept over most Western nations during the 1970s and 1980s but with an important difference: most laws were more restrictive than in the typical American state. In England, France, and Germany, for example, a person who requested a no-fault divorce without the consent of his or her spouse had to wait five, six, and three years, respectively, before it was granted. Even then, judges had the authority to reject the divorce if they thought it created exceptional hardship for the unwilling spouse or the children. In twenty-two American states, in contrast, the waiting period for a no-fault divorce was one year or less, and the courts had no authority to deny it. Except in Sweden, American-style no-fault divorce, automatically granted after a short waiting period, was seen as too liberal, too potentially harmful to children, to fully adopt.

Throughout the 1970s, changes in family law continued to reduce the power of husbands over their wives. In 1973, the famous *Roe v. Wade* decision affirmed the right of women to choose, in consultation with their doctors, whether to obtain abortions in the first trimester of pregnancy. And after the feminist movement made wife beating a social issue in the late 1960s, battered women's shelters were opened, police became more aggressive in responding to calls, and laws were passed creating stronger civil protection orders for victims of violence. All of these changes reduced the ability of husbands to impose their will on their wives, and all reinforced the notion of marriage as a partnership of individuals.

The 1980s and 1990s

By the 1980s the cultural upheavals of the 1960s and 1970s had diminished, and so had the pace of change in American family life. The divorce rate sat at a high plateau through the 1990s. After reaching a low point in the mid-1970s, the birth rate stabilized and then increased slightly, so in 1999 the average woman was projected to have 2.0 children. The percentage of births to unmarried women continued to increase, but that increase was deceptive. First, the increase was caused as much by married women having fewer children as by unmarried women having more. More important, nearly all the increase in births to "unmarried" women since the early 1980s has reflected a rise in the number of births to cohabiting couples, not to lone mothers (government statistics don't differentiate between unmarried women who are living without a partner and unmarried women who are cohabiting). What's happened is that the percentage of babies that are born to women who are cohabiting has been increasing.

In fact, the continued rise in cohabiting relationships was the major source of change in living arrangements in the 1980s and 1990s. By the early 1990s cohabiting relationships, which had stunned middle-class parents such as mine twenty years earlier, were an entrenched part of the American family system. More than half of first marriages began as cohabiting relationships. A large majority of remarriages began as cohabiting relationships. Although the percentage of young adults who were married dropped sharply, the percentage who were in a partnership of some kind—cohabiting or marital—dropped much less. Said otherwise, young adults weren't marrying as much as they used to, but they were living in intimate partnerships almost as much. Cohabiting had become a complex phenomenon: it included childless young adults who were not thinking about marriage, others who were testing a relationship to see if it was worthy of marriage, others who had had a child together but were not actively considering marriage, and lone parents who were bringing a potential stepparent into the household.

Ask anyone to picture a cohabiting couple in their minds, and chances are they will envision two young, well-educated, childless people. But in that list, only "young" is accurate, and even that attribute is changing. Are they well educated? Although many people think of cohabitors as college-graduate trendsetters, cohabiting relationships in the United States have continued to be more common among the *less* well-educated. In 1995, for example, 59 percent of women of childbearing age without high school degrees had cohabited, compared to 37 percent of comparably aged college graduates. A difficult job market is one reason why the less-educated cohabit more. Young men are still expected to have good, steady jobs in order to marry, and less-educated men have had a harder time finding them, especially as the globalization of production moved factory jobs to other countries in the 1980s and 1990s. A cohabiting relationship may be all a young man with a low-paying or temporary job can aspire to, or all that he can find a partner to agree to. Are they childless? Cohabiting couples raise children more commonly than is thought: 39 percent of opposite-sex cohabiting couples had the children of one or both partners present in 2000.

Moreover, the connection between cohabiting and marrying varies greatly. Many cohabiting couples have given little thought to marrying when they first move in together. A 2002 study of young adults in the Toledo, Ohio, area, a majority of them high school graduates without college degrees, found many of them drifting into cohabiting relationships without a deliberate decision to live together. A computer consultant described the start of his cohabiting relationship this way:

> It began by attrition of this thing at her parents' house. In other words, she stayed at my house more and more from spending the night once to not going home to her parents' house for a week at a time and then you know further, um, so there was no official starting date. I did take note when the frilly fufu soaps showed up in my bathroom that she'd probably moved in at that point.

Other relationships started on the first date or involved individuals who alternated between two households. These relationships, if they last, eventually lead the partners to contemplate their future, but at first there may not be much discussion about it. Some of them merely seem like the twenty-first-century equivalent of what was called steady dating, or "going steady," in the mid-twentieth.

Nevertheless, most cohabiting relationships of any type end relatively quickly in a marriage or a breakup. It's still rare in the United States to see a long-term cohabiting relationship, particularly with children present. In fact, it's rare enough that in the 1990s the average length of a cohabiting relationship in the United States was less than in any other Western country. In some European nations, such as Sweden and Denmark, long-term cohabiting relationships are becoming acceptable as alternatives to marriage, and most cohabiting families with children consist of two biological parents. In the United States, on the other hand, cohabiting by and large remains a short-term arrangement: more than half of cohabiting relationships end within two years, and the percentage that end in a breakup rather than a marriage has been rising. For American children born to cohabiting couples, the result is a high likelihood that one parent will move out of the home. About 60 percent of American children who are born to cohabiting parents see their parents split up by ages nine to ten. That's a higher risk of family breakup than children born to married parents face. The rise of cohabitation has increased the number of children who experience the breakup of their parents' partnerships.

Overall, children living in cohabiting families with a parent and a nonparent seem to have more problems than children living with married biological parents or even than children living with a married parent and a stepparent. They are more likely to be expelled from school, to steal something, or to get into fights. It is hard to figure out, however, whether cohabiting relationships are the cause of these problems; people who cohabit might have characteristics that would make them less effective parents whatever their living arrangements. For instance, cohabiting parents spend more money on alcohol and tobacco than do married parents. It's doubtful that moving in with a partner causes teetotalers to turn to drink; rather, the kinds of people who cohabit rather than marry may also be the kinds who drink and smoke more. Their children might have as many problems even if they were to marry.

Children's experiences in two-biological-parent cohabiting families may not differ much from those of children living with married biological parents. But two-thirds of American children in cohabiting families are living with one biological parent, usually their mother, and another adult, usually a man, whose relationship to the child is highly variable. At one end of the continuum are men who should be considered stepparents because they are deeply involved in the children's lives and likely to marry the mothers after a period of living together. At the other end are mothers' short-term romantic liaisons who may have little to do with the children and may be around only for a few months. In between is a gray area of men in the household who are not taking on a parental role but who do spend some time with the children and may be present for a year or two. The presence of these short-termers could be problematic for children. Overall, cohabitation is still a work in progress, evolving and diversifying as it becomes increasingly common. We will need to watch carefully to see how well it is meeting the needs of the children who are involved with it.

Within marriage, the dominance of husbands was reduced further in the 1980s and 1990s by changes in the law. Until the 1980s, a husband had the right to have sex with his wife anytime he wanted to, whether she was willing or not. Women, legal doctrine said, gave their husbands unrestricted sexual access by virtue of marrying them. The term "marital rape" was therefore an oxymoron. Gradually, though, the courts became concerned about violence and sexual abuse within marriage. In 1984, the New York Court of Appeals affirmed the conviction of a man for raping his wife. Mario Liberta was under a court order to stay away from his family home because he had been beating his wife, Denise. One day she allowed him to take her and their son to the motel room where he was living, after he assured her that a friend would be there at all times. Once they were in the room, however, the friend left, and Mario threatened to kill Denise and forced her to have sexual intercourse with him. Denise swore out a legal complaint the next day, and Mario was arrested and convicted of rape. He appealed his conviction, arguing that because he was married to Denise he was exempt from rape statutes. The appeals court ruled that just as a husband cannot use the privacy of marriage to justify beating his wife, neither can he justify actions that constitute rape.

Yet given the fascination of Americans with the lifestyles of the rich and famous, perhaps it shouldn't be surprising that the issue of family violence didn't get the attention it deserved until a celebrity was involved. Within two weeks of O. J. Simpson's arrest in 1994 on the charge of murdering his ex-wife, both *Newsweek* and *Time* had cover stories on domestic violence. Within days of Simpson's arrest, the New York state legislature passed a bill that required the police to arrest suspected perpetrators of domestic violence whether or not the victim was willing to press charges. Los Angeles County immediately allocated millions of dollars of additional aid for shelters for battered women. Within two months, the House of Representatives had approved nearly all the provisions of the Violence Against Women Act, which had first been introduced, without success, six years earlier. The act included funds for a national hotline for victims of abuse; for the training of police officers, prosecutors, and judges about gender-linked crimes; and for encouraging states to require that police always arrest people who are accused of abuse by their spouses or partners. These developments clearly reduced men's power over their wives and partners. Mexican immigrant men told an anthropologist that men cannot control women in the United States the way they can in Mexico because American women can call the police, who are much more responsive to claims of violence than are the Mexican police.

Legal scholar Sanford Katz, looking back over the previous fifty years, wrote in 2000 that the most important change in family law had been "the recognition and protection of individual rights." The spread of individual rights into the household is a major advance. Few would argue for stripping children born to unmarried mothers of their right to be supported by their fathers. Virtually everyone applauds the progress that has been made against domestic violence. Few miss the legal charade that "fault" divorce had become. No one would argue that husbands ought to be able to sell their wives' property without their permission. Yet the advance of individual rights, as laudable as it may be, has made marriage less necessary and, when it occurs, less stable. People simply have more options—living with a partner or raising a child as a lone parent. Within marriage, it's easier for an unhappy partner to leave. As Stephanie Coontz argues in her history of marriage:

> Over the past century, marriage has steadily become more fair, more fulfilling, and more effective in fostering the well-being of both adults and children than ever before in history. It has also become more optional and more fragile. The historical record suggests that these two seemingly contradictory changes are inextricably intertwined.

The growth of individual rights in family law, for better or worse, probably increased family instability.

From Dwelling to Seeking

Throughout the late twentieth century and into the twenty-first, the gap in religious vitality between the United States and most other Western countries remained vast. The percentage of the American population that belonged to a church or other religious body peaked at nearly two-thirds in the 1970s and 1980s and has fallen only modestly since then. Meanwhile, the long-term decline continued in many Western European countries. According to the 1999 to 2002 World Values Surveys, 60 percent of Americans claimed that they attended religious services at least once a month; even if there was some wishful thinking in that response, it dwarfed the levels reported in most other Western countries. For instance, among Western Europeans, 25 percent of the Germans, 19 percent of the British, and 12 percent of the French said that they attended church at least once a month. The responses were slightly higher in non-European Western countries: 36 percent of Canadians, 25 percent of Australians, and 22 percent of New Zealanders said they attend church that often. But the only Western country with higher attendance than the United States was Ireland (67 percent). Even in Italy, home to the Vatican, only 54 percent said they attended church that often. Clearly, religious attendance in the United States is very high by Western standards. Compared to Britain and France, in particular, a far larger percentage of Americans attend services every month.

The difference extends beyond church attendance. When Americans were asked, "Independently of whether you go to church or not, would you say that you are a religious person?" far more (83 percent) said yes than did people in most other nations. In addition, Americans were more likely to believe in both heaven and hell than were people in any other Western country: 88 percent of Americans said they believed in heaven and 75 percent in hell. The British and French were much more skeptical: 56 percent of the British and just 31 percent of the French believed in heaven, and 35 percent of the British and merely 20 percent of the French believed in hell. I could go on, but several other questions in the surveys showed more of the same: the United States is one of the most religious countries in the Western world, and only Ireland and Italy approach its level of religious vitality. I was recently at a conference in Europe where a French sociologist referred to her country as a "postreligion" society. No one would describe American society that way.

Religious activity, in fact, remains the greatest cultural difference between the United States and most other wealthy nations. In our search for reasons for the distinctiveness of American family patterns, there is still no more obvious suspect to round up. And enough evidence exists to make an arrest. For instance, Americans say they apply the lessons learned in church to their family lives. When asked, "Generally speaking, do you think that the churches in your country are giving adequate answers to the problems of family life?" 61 percent of Americans said yes—the highest percentage of any Western country. Yet if we look closely, we will see that the message churches were giving to Americans at the end of the century was different from the message they gave at midcentury. The new message, moreover, was more consistent with the new style of family life.

Without doubt, the landscape of American religion has changed over the past half century. In the mid-twentieth century, American Protestantism was still dominated by the older so-called mainline denominations, such as the Episcopalians, Congregationalists, Presbyterians,

Lutherans, and Methodists (who had left their revival-meeting origins to become more urban and middle class). Mainline Protestants tended to be more liberal both theologically and politically. They did not interpret the Bible's words literally, they accepted the theory of evolution, and they embraced the social gospel of assisting the less fortunate elements of society. They accounted for about 25 percent of all church adherents in 1940, although their percentage was declining and would continue to decline throughout the century. So-called conservative Protestants were still a minority, accounting for about 10 percent of church adherents in 1940. By and large, they interpreted the Bible as the inerrant word of God, they accepted the creation story of Genesis and rejected the theory of evolution, and, until the last few decades of the century, they kept their distance from social and political action. Many would also accept the label "evangelical," which signifies an emphasis on saving souls for Christ and a "born-again" conversionlike experience.

At midcentury, Catholics comprised about 20 percent of all church adherents. Discrimination against Catholics had declined but still existed as the children and grandchildren of European immigrants moved up the social ladder. When John F. Kennedy ran for president in 1960, his Catholicism was an issue. No less a public figure than Norman Vincent Peale associated with a group opposed to Kennedy's election on religious grounds before a public uproar forced him to withdraw from it. Similarly, discrimination against Jews—a much smaller group but visible in many urban areas since their large-scale immigration from Eastern Europe—was declining but still present.

As American society and culture changed after the 1950s, so did American religion. Numerically, the major religious trend was the continued growth of conservative Protestantism and decline of the mainline denominations. By the 1990s, nearly as many Americans identified themselves as belonging to conservative Protestant bodies (26 percent) as to mainline Protestant denominations (29 percent). Another 25 percent identified as Catholic, while smaller numbers identified as Jewish (2.5 percent), as members of other non-Christian faiths (2 percent), or as having no faith (16 percent).

Across all of these denominations, American religion had moved from the spirituality of dwelling that characterized the 1950s to what Robert Wuthnow calls a "spirituality of seeking." Rather than relying on a religious home that provides security, stability, and familiar beliefs and rituals, individuals sought information on a variety of faiths. "Spirituality," writes Wuthnow, "has become a vastly complex quest in which each person seeks in his or her own way." A spirituality of seeking is less secure than a spirituality of dwelling but also less constraining. You are free to decide which rewards are most important to you and then to choose the faith that best provides them. Congregations become less a source of stability and more a source of information and services. Take the example of Sam, a thirty-seven-year-old computer programmer who was interviewed by Wade Clark Roof for his book *Spiritual Marketplace.* Sam was a committed evangelical Christian who belonged to large congregation in California, which he describes as an evangelical "seeker church." He told an interviewer:

> This church has a class where you can ask about Christianity. Most of the people there don't know what to believe. A lot of us don't know about all the teachings. But it's okay that you don't know, or maybe even don't always agree with some things as long as you believe in Jesus Christ, and learn and grow in your faith.

At Sam's church, the style of music and preaching was contemporary. Nowhere in his account did he mention whether his church belongs to a denomination. The seeker-style churches also deemphasize architecture, iconography, and theology and encourage everyone to come as they are. In many of the megachurches founded in the 1980s and 1990s—usually defined as congregations with two thousand or more congregants—almost all signs that the building is a house of worship were absent. There were no crosses, no stained-glass windows. No one wore a tie, and jeans were common. Christian rock music, with lyrics projected on large screens, replaced choirs and hymns. Lee McFarland, the pastor of Radiant Church in a Phoenix exurb, preached in a Hawaiian shirt to five thousand parishioners per week. "We want the church to look like a mall," he told a writer for the

New York Times Magazine. "We want you to come in here and say, 'Dude, where's the cinema?' "

It was also not a coincidence that Sam's church was evangelical. It was the conservative churches, rather than mainline churches, that were the innovators in catering to seekers. They built market share while the mainline churches continued to decline. Radiant Church offered free coffee and Krispy Kreme doughnuts, had video games to occupy the kids, and advertised its "rockin' worship music" on its Web site. What it did not advertise was its denomination. Only after a couple of mouse clicks could a Web surfer find an indirect statement of Radiant's affiliation with the conservative Assemblies of God. The purpose of this strategy is clear: "I'm just trying to get people in the door," Pastor McFarland said. "For people who haven't been to church, or went once and got burned, the anxiety level is really high. 'Is it going to be freaky? Is it going to be like what I see on Christian TV?' So we've tried to bring down those visual cues that scare people off."

American Catholics altered their beliefs in a similar way in the 1980s and 1990s. They placed less emphasis on the Church as an institution and more on individual responsibility for one's own faith, they shifted toward viewing God as loving and forgiving rather than as punitive and judgmental, and they placed greater importance on personal exploration and discovery. When presented in a survey with six elements of being a Catholic and asked how important each was to them, 76 percent of American Catholics chose "spiritual and personal growth" as very important, compared to 70 percent who chose "the Catholic Church's teachings about Mary as the mother of God" as very important, and 45 percent who chose "the teaching authority claimed by the Vatican." In fact, the percentage choosing spiritual and personal growth was second only to the 80 percent who chose "the sacraments, such as the Eucharist and marriage." Personal growth, exploration, and discovery: the spirituality of seeking was apparent by the 1990s in a faith noted more for its hierarchy and top-down spirituality than for self-development.

Across Protestant and Catholic religious life, the spirituality of seeking was not about laws or doctrines but about finding a style of spirituality that made you feel good, that seemed to fit your personality. Just so, the individualized marriage was not about rules and traditions but rather about finding a style of family life that gave you the greatest personal rewards. Religion became a site for self-development—a place where you could continually "learn and grow," as Sam said—and so did marriage. Rather than inheriting your faith from your forefathers, you were free to choose your own through a process that might involve exploring several churches. Similarly, you were free to choose your spouse through a process that might involve living with more than one partner in order to make that choice. And should you become personally dissatisfied with your church, you could leave in search of another, more fulfilling one. So, too, could you leave your marriage if you became dissatisfied with it. Both the spirituality of seeking and the individualized marriage became part of the larger project of developing your self-identity, a quest that became the focus of personal life for more and more Americans during the last several decades of the twentieth century.

As the divorce rate rose in the 1960s and 1970s and remained high in the 1980s and 1990s, an increasing number of divorced congregants turned to their churches for solace, support, and assurances that they had not done anything morally wrong. In response, most religious groups—even conservative Protestant and Catholic churches—modified the way they responded to divorce. The traditional Protestant view of divorce was that only adultery and desertion were valid reasons for ending a marriage. In a modern world in which most people's whereabouts can be determined, few divorce actions are brought to the courts for desertion, leaving adultery as, in practice, the only biblically acceptable ground for divorce. Moreover, only the nonadulterous partner is allowed to remarry. The traditional Catholic view is that even adultery does not justify divorce. Couples may separate following one spouse's unfaithful behavior, but a divorce is not possible. An annulment (a ruling that a marriage is invalid) can be obtained only if the marriage itself was never properly begun according to Church law. Without an annulment, remarriage is not allowed. Judaism has long allowed divorce, although in such a way as to give the husband more freedom to obtain a divorce than the wife.

During the 1950s, however, mainline Protestant denominations, such as the Episcopalians, Lutherans, and Presbyterians, accommodated the long-term rise in divorce by allowing remarriage after virtually any type of divorce. Since then, mainline churches have been more likely than conservative Protestant churches to adopt a rhetoric of tolerance toward people who are divorced or who live in other types of families that do not fit the two-parent ideal. In a 1998 survey, all of the pastors in four upstate New York communities were asked whether they agreed with this statement: "There have been all kinds of families throughout history, and God approves of many different kinds of families." Eighty-eight percent of the mainline Protestant pastors agreed. In contrast, none of the conservative Protestant pastors agreed. The Catholic priests, despite their church's formal opposition to divorce and remarriage, were much closer to the mainline pastors than to the conservatives: 83 percent agreed with the statement.

Responses such as these might lead you to think that conservative Protestants take a hard line against divorce and do not welcome divorced people into their congregations. You would be wrong on both counts. Instead they show what one observer called "a surprising range of opinions on the subject." Some conservative pastors do not attempt to limit divorce and remarriage to biblical grounds, arguing that compassion and forgiveness should govern responses to divorce. Others follow the biblical restrictions but interpret them so broadly as to allow most divorced people to remarry. For instance, in 2007 a biblical scholar offered a new reading of the restrictions in light of the writings of rabbis from Jesus' time. In an article in *Christianity Today,* a conservative Protestant magazine, he concluded that divorce is allowable not only for adultery and desertion but also for abuse and for emotional and physical neglect.

As for welcoming divorced people, it seems that conservative Protestant congregations have more lone parents attending their services than do mainline ones. This could be a social class difference: mainline Protestants are better educated, and people with more education are less likely to divorce. But in addition, conservative Protestant churches (along with Catholic churches) appear more likely to minister to divorced people. Pilgrim Baptist, for instance, an evangelical church in upstate New York, teaches that the two-parent, male-breadwinner family is the best kind, and its leadership views lone parents and their children as "broken families." Nevertheless, Pilgrim Baptist has programs for divorced congregants and does informal family counseling with its own staff. It has also changed the times of some of its activities to accommodate the schedules of children who alternate between the homes of their divorced parents.

Some divorced individuals may react more positively to conservative Protestant churches' frank rhetoric that divorce is sinful and creates broken families than to the acceptance of divorce in many mainline churches. Conservative Protestant pastors combine their antidivorce rhetoric with a desire to help divorced people heal and recover from the experience. Joseph Tamney tells of the experience of Iris, who went to the minister in her mainline church to talk about the possibility of getting a divorce. The minister told her that "if she wanted to do it, she needed to do it." Iris found this statement unsettling rather than reassuring, and went to a conservative church, where the pastor preached against divorce but explained to her that there were some biblically acceptable reasons to divorce, and hers was one of them. She felt better after that. Some divorced people, it seems, do not want to be told that divorce is acceptable, quite possibly because they do not agree. Rather, they want to be told that divorce is not okay but that they can recover with the church's help. In addition, mainline churches, despite their more inclusive rhetoric, often reflect their midcentury organization around two-parent households, and they continue to attract young couples with children who attended mainline churches as children themselves and want to give their children a religious education. The result is that a separated or divorced adult may feel less welcome and comfortable in a mainline Church than in a conservative church.

Catholics who have remarried without having their previous marriages annulled are prohibited from receiving communion. But American Catholics and their clergy have backed away from complete opposition to divorce. In 1999, 64 percent of American Catholics agreed that a person could be a good Catholic without following the Church hierarchy's teaching on divorce and remarriage. (In contrast, only 23 percent thought one could be a good Catholic without believing that Jesus rose physically from the dead.) And the percentage of Catholics who thought that individuals, rather than church leaders, should have the final say about whether a divorced Catholic could remarry without getting an annulment rose during the 1990s.

The Catholic clergy, meanwhile, has adapted to the rising rate of divorce and the changing sentiments of Catholics by approving an avalanche of annulments. Prior to the Second Vatican Council, held from 1962 to 1965 and known as Vatican II, the American Catholic Church granted approximately four hundred annulments per year. At Vatican II, the official description of marriage was modified in a way that made approval of annulments easier in the case of problems in the couple's initial exchange of consent. These include problems that rendered one spouse incapable of giving full and free consent to be married. Many dioceses interpret this "defective consent" ground broadly to include psychological difficulties such as neuroses, personality disorders, and, to quote one prominent interpreter, "even the situation where neither partner to the marriage suffers from a true disorder but they still remain incapable of establishing a marital relationship with each other." The number of annulments grew enormously in the 1970s and by the 1980s exceeded fifty thousand per year. Annulment has become de facto religious divorce for American Catholics.

Still, Catholics, conservative Protestants, and mainline Protestants have different formal positions on divorce: prohibited, adultery only, and broad grounds, respectively. If these positions matter, you might predict sizeable differences in the divorce rates of these three groups. If strict religious doctrine encourages "traditional" behavior, Catholics should have a low divorce rate, conservative Protestants should have a moderately low rate, and mainline Protestants should have a substantially higher rate. In fact, the differences in divorce rates among these three groups are minimal. Only Mormon couples have a markedly lower risk of divorce. How restrictive a religious denomination is toward divorce seems to make little difference in how frequently its adherents divorce. Catholics and conservative Protestants must be ignoring formal church teachings on divorce in large numbers.

What does make a difference is having any religious affiliation at all. During the first fifteen years after marrying, an estimated 41 percent of women who have any religious affiliation would separate or divorce, compared to 56 percent of those who have no religious affiliation. The latter group may have other factors in their backgrounds that predispose them both to reject religion and to have unstable marriages. For example, they may have grown up in families where the parents divorced and the children received little religious training. Nevertheless, having a religion—any religion—is associated with a lower risk of divorce. Another survey question, "Currently, how important is religion in your daily life?" gives similar estimates. Thirty-nine percent of those who say "very important" would separate or divorce within fifteen years, compared to 54 percent of those who say "not at all."

From an international perspective, however, even Americans who say religion is "very important" have a high divorce rate. Compare the United States with Sweden, for example, which is often considered the country where marriage is weakest and where only 9 percent attend church at least once a month. The rate of separation or divorce in Sweden is the highest in Western Europe. Yet the percentage of Swedes who will separate or divorce within the first fifteen years of marriage is estimated to be only 28 percent. That's considerably lower than the 39 percent figure for Americans who say religion is very important. In other words, religious Americans are more likely to divorce than secular Swedes. It's true that secular Americans are even *more* likely to divorce; nevertheless, religious Americans have raised the floor of the American divorce rate above the ceiling in most other countries. In that sense, both secular and religious Americans have contributed to keeping the American rate higher than in other countries.

It may seem odd to suggest that, by international standards, religious Americans have high divorce rates. After all, isn't American religion "traditional"? Don't some conservative Protestants, in particular, tout "traditional" profamily values? Although one does hear this rhetoric, there's not much evidence that Americans are more traditional than Europeans. In the World Values Surveys, Americans responded in ways that might seem traditional on two topics close to their religious values: abortion and homosexuality. Thirty-two percent of Americans agreed that homosexuality is never justified, a higher figure than in most other countries. Thirty percent of Americans agreed that abortion is never justified, which was similar to the responses in Canada and Italy but more than in many other countries. Yet these views are more accurately labeled as conservative rather than traditional. Abortion, for instance, was legal in the United States until the last third of the nineteenth century, and its criminalization was less the result of religious objections than of opposition by the American Medical Association and nativists who wanted more white, native births to combat the rising tide of immigrants. Rather than being a traditional concern, then, opposition to abortion is a modern one: it became a cause célèbre for religious conservatives only after its legalization in the early 1970s.

On several other questions in the World Values Survey, moreover, the differences are small or are in the opposite direction from what a view of the United States as a traditional society would predict. Take divorce, for example. A society with traditional family values should frown upon divorce. Yet only 8 percent of Americans said that divorce is never justifiable. What about male dominance in economic life? Shouldn't a traditional society think that men should work for wages and women should stay home? The survey asked people whether they agreed with the statement "When jobs are scarce, men should have more right to a job than women." Only 10 percent of Americans agreed, a low figure compared to most other countries. Authoritarianism? Given a list of five aims for their country for the next ten years, fewer Americans chose "maintaining order" than did the French, Germans, or Swedes.

In short, the World Values Surveys do not show that the United States is more traditional than other countries. They show that it is more religious. The distinction is important, because thinking of American religion as "traditional" can blind us to the significance of the great, recent changes in spirituality in the United States. Without doubt, no cultural difference between the United States and the rest of the Western world was as stark at the end of the twentieth century as the difference in religious vitality. But it was not the same type of religion as in the 1950s. Rather than staid worship in the house of the Lord, it was, in some ways, a throwback to the expressive, individualistic religious practices of the nineteenth-century camp meetings—

"raise an excitement among them," Finney had advised. Drawing from that strand of worship, Americans in the late twentieth century applied a questing, personal style to their religious lives—and to their family lives.

Still, it's hard to determine the extent to which the spread of a spirituality of seeking *caused* the changes in family life or was the *result* of the changes in family life. I think both religion and the family were swept up in the larger, more fundamental cultural change, the rise of expressive individualism. It encouraged the pursuit of personal growth, whether through church or family, and the search for self-identity, whether through spirituality or intimacy. What happened, I would suggest, is that the changes in religion and family reinforced each other. If you were focused on your self-development, an individualized marriage and a church that helped you to grow as a person might both be appealing. Or if you were searching for a partner, you might be drawn toward a parallel search for a church.

One could, of course, find the rise of expressive individualism in the decisions other Westerners were making about their intimate lives. Cohabiting relationships became even more common, and support for marriage weaker, in some other countries than in the United States. Only in the United States, however, could you find so much expressive individualism in the context of a thriving religious life. The American version of the rise of expressive individualism produced not a secular society but rather a questing one in which individuals searched, sometimes again and again, for the kind of spirituality and family ties that fit their needs.

By the turn of the twenty-first century, then, both family law and religion were more individualistic in nature than they had been a half century earlier. Nevertheless, the law reserved many privileges to married couples, such as jointly filing a federal income tax return or receiving a spouse's Social Security benefits upon his or her death, and religion retained a preference for marriage. Religion and law, in other words, supported both of the cultural models—individualism and marriage—that could be found in the American family at the end of the century. To some observers, though, marriage seemed to be fading away. It had become an optional lifestyle, one that could be avoided more easily than during past times when cohabiting relationships and lone parenthood were not socially acceptable. It was a fragile lifestyle, because divorce rates had increased so much. It no longer commanded as many legal advantages. Marriage would not, however, disappear in the early twenty-first century. Indeed, it would remain the most highly valued way of living one's family life, even though people spent less time actually being married than in the past. It would enjoy a resurgence of support as both the defenders of "traditional" marriage and the advocates of same-sex marriage battled over how to define it. Marriage would be greatly changed in nature but still identifiable as a central part of American family life. And it would continue to have a more prominent role in the United States than in many other Western countries.

The American Way of Marriage

In the early 2000s, with the male-breadwinner family in deep decline and more than one-third of all births occurring outside of marriage, two groups campaigned in support of conventional marriage. One group opposed attempts by gay and lesbian activists to legalize same-sex marriage. Another partially overlapping group extolled the benefits of heterosexual marriage and encouraged young adults to take advantage of them. No effort on this scale occurred in any other country in the Western world—make that the *entire* world. No other government provided funds for programs to promote heterosexual marriage. Nowhere else was the debate over same-sex marriage so intense. Nowhere else did the stakes seem so high. And yet the individualistic view of family life that strengthened in the last third of the twentieth century continued to flourish. People still sought personal rewards and self-development. Cohabiting relationships, many begun with little thought of marriage, became even more common. Exploring this strange terrain, in which marriage seemed to increase in value even as people spent fewer years being married, can help us make sense of American family life today.

Who Owns Marriage?

In a sense, the marriage wars began in the early 1980s with the spread of AIDS, which was then largely an illness of gay men. As the epidemic grew and gay men tried to care for seriously ill partners, they found that they were denied visiting privileges that hospitals routinely granted to spouses, that they could not authorize or withhold treatment as spouses could, that they had a limited role in making funeral arrangements, and that they could be evicted from a deceased partner's apartment. Nor could a gay or lesbian person who had health insurance through an employer obtain coverage for his or her partner. These restrictions were widely seen as unfair. In response, municipalities began to create registered partnerships that provided gay and lesbian partners with limited but important benefits such as hospital visitation rights. One of the first such registries was established by the city of West Hollywood, California, which has a large gay population, in 1985. Registered partnership laws spread in the late 1980s and the 1990s, mainly in gay-friendly cities such as San Francisco (in 1989) and New York (in 1998). Some large firms decided on their own to offer health benefits to the same-sex partners of employees. These local reforms and employer-based benefits, founded upon empathy for people who were ill with AIDS and their caregivers, caused little controversy.

However, the issue became more prominent when gay and lesbian activists began to demand that states grant them an officially recognized status or, more radically, the right to marry. In 1990, three same-sex couples walked into the State of Hawaii marriage license bureau in Honolulu and requested licenses. The bureau refused. This did not come as a surprise to the two lesbian couples and the gay male couple; indeed, they had intentionally entered as a group in order to create the grounds for a lawsuit. Following the denial of their requests, they sued the State of Hawaii, charging that it was an unconstitutional violation of their rights to restrict marriage to heterosexual couples.

A lower-court judge ruled against the couples and in favor of the state's interpretation of the marriage laws. But in 1993, after the couples appealed, the Hawaii Supreme Court disagreed with the lower-court ruling. It sent the case back to the lower court with orders to retry it and to grant the marriage licenses unless the state could show that it "furthers a compelling state interest" to exclude same-sex couples. On September 10, 1996, testimony in the case, *Baehr v. Miike,* began before Judge Kevin S. C. Chang. News of the impending case had attracted great interest around the country. Opponents of same-sex marriage had persuaded the U.S. Congress to pass the Defense of Marriage Act in 1996, which decreed that other states need not recognize a marriage license granted to a same-sex couple in Hawaii or elsewhere. Many state legislatures also enacted measures stating that they would not recognize out-of-state same-sex marriages.

Attorneys for the two sides—the couples and the State of Hawaii—presented a total of eight witnesses. Two were sociologists who studied the family, one for each side: David Eggebeen of Pennsylvania State University testified in opposition to allowing same-sex marriages, and Pepper Schwartz of the University of Washington testified in favor of allowing them. That social scientists rather than, say, religious leaders were key witnesses showed how debates about the family had moved from the moral discourse of the nineteenth century to a more pragmatic weighing of costs and benefits. Still, Eggebeen spoke of the importance of marriage in terms that a nineteenth-century court would have understood:

> *Eggebeen:* Well, to me it's the . . . the conclusion is clear that marriage represents a gateway to becoming a parent. When people get married, by an extraordinary margin they intend to become parents.
> *Attorney for the State:* So in the minds of people marriage would be synonymous with having children?
> *Eggebeen:* When 98 percent of the married individuals intend to become parents, I would say that's a very valid conclusion.

Eggebeen then argued that same-sex marriages may not provide optimal settings for raising children. He claimed that gay couples with children are like stepfamilies because often the children were conceived in heterosexual marriages that the gay parent later left (although this is becoming less and less true as gay male couples adopt children and lesbian couples use donor insemination). Therefore, he said, same-sex marriages should be discouraged because research shows that stepfamilies are not as good for children as two-biological-parent families. Eggebeen admitted that there wasn't much research on whether or not same-sex couples are fit parents, but he drew the conservative conclusion that in the absence of data, society should not take what he saw as a risk to children's development.

In contrast, Pepper Schwartz, testifying on behalf of the couples, spoke of the meaning of marriage in ways that would have puzzled many nineteenth-century jurists but which fell easily on the ears of late-twentieth-century Americans:

> *Attorney for the Couples:* Well, on the topic of what marriage means to people, Dr. Schwartz, why do people get married?
> *Schwartz:* . . . What people think of when they want marriage is they want companionship, they want love, they want trust, they want someone who will be with them through thick and thin. Now, I wouldn't say this is what marriage means in all cultures but in our own it's an aspiration for—for intimacy and security. And that is the definition of marriage as people first and primarily think of it.

Children are an important part of marriage, she suggested, but they aren't as central as Eggebeen claimed:

> *Schwartz:* Yes, having children is a deep desire of the majority of young Americans . . . most of whom want kids when they get married. But it isn't, I think the reason that everyone gets married. They get married to have this partnership. It [having children] is a reason among many that people want to be married.

Schwartz was suggesting that the most important part of marriage is the emotional reward that couples get from their relationship. But Schwartz and the attorneys for the couples realized that in order to win a favorable ruling from the judge, they had to address the question of whether allowing same-sex marriage is in the best interests of children. So, under friendly questioning from the couples' attorneys, Schwartz argued that, according to social scientific research, gay parents could be as good as heterosexual parents. (My reading of the literature is that children raised by gay and lesbian parents don't seem to differ much from children raised by heterosexual parents.)

Judge Chang ruled on December 3, 1996, that the State of Hawaii had failed to prove that prohibiting same-sex marriage furthered a compelling interest. He was not persuaded that enough negative evidence existed to plainly show that being raised by same-sex partners harms children, and he concluded that children being raised in same-sex partnerships would be helped if the partners were allowed to marry. He therefore declared the law unconstitutional and prohibited the State of Hawaii from denying a marriage license solely because the applicants are of the same sex. Public opposition to the decision was so negative, however, that in 1998 Hawaii voters approved an amendment to the state constitution that authorized the legislature to restrict marriage to a man and a woman, which it did.

Same-sex couples had greater success in two other states. In Vermont, three couples sued the state in 1997 after they were denied marriage licenses. The Vermont Supreme Court ruled that they were entitled to the benefits that the state granted to married couples and ordered the Vermont general assembly to either make same-sex marriage legal or create an alternative status that would provide its benefits. The assembly took the latter option, and in 2000 Vermont became the first state to have a legal marriagelike status for same-sex partners, which it called a civil union. In 2003 the Massachusetts Supreme Court, responding to a similar suit, struck down the statute limiting marriage to opposite-sex couples and instructed the state legislature to change the law.

What's notable about the Massachusetts court's decision is how strongly it was based on the relationship-centered meaning Schwartz emphasized rather than the child-centered meaning Eggebeen emphasized. "Civil marriage," the majority wrote, "is at once a deeply personal commitment to another human being and a highly public celebration of the ideals of mutuality, companionship, intimacy, fidelity, and family." Without the ability to marry, they added, "one is excluded from the full range of human experience." The court's view of marriage became clearer when the Massachusetts state legislature, hoping to avoid same-sex marriage, crafted a plan to enact civil unions for same-sex couples using the Vermont model. The legislature then asked the court whether their plan was sufficient; after all, if the issue is benefits, then a civil union that provides all the benefits should be good enough. But the court rejected the plan, arguing that allowing civil unions but not marriage would create a "stigma of exclusion," because it would deny to same-sex couples "a status that is specially recognized in society and has significant social and other advantages." Providing all the legal benefits of marriage was not sufficient for the judges, because marriage to them was more than just a collection of benefits. It was a special status, and to deny same-sex couples access to it would be to stigmatize them. The Massachusetts constitution, the judges wrote, "forbids the creation of second-class citizens." The court's view suggested that marriage is an important status symbol for Americans, a marker of a first-class personal life.

Same-sex marriage became legal in Massachusetts in May 2004. By that time it was also legal in several Canadian provinces. Along with weddings that the City of San Francisco conducted illegally for a few months and impending legalization at the national level in Canada, the events in Massachusetts elicited strong opposition from social conservatives. With the 2004 election approaching, the debate quickly became politicized. President Bush announced that he would support a federal constitutional amendment to protect the "sanctity of marriage" by restricting it to heterosexuals. He and his supporters invoked the moral language about marriage that had been so prominent a century ago but had faded from public view. At the announcement, he said:

The union of a man and woman is the most enduring human institution, honoring—honored and encouraged in all cultures and by every religious faith. Ages of experience have taught humanity that the commitment of a husband and wife to love and to serve one another promotes the welfare of children and the stability of society.

After the amendment failed in Congress, opponents of same-sex marriage took their campaigns to the states, and by 2007 more than half had amended their own constitutions to ban same-sex marriage. In at least eight of these states, the amendments also banned or restricted same-sex partnerships. Opponents argued that registered partnerships are just same-sex marriages by another name and should not be allowed, or they made the more nuanced argument that legalizing registered partnerships would undercut the social status of marriage, thereby further weakening it.

In 2008 Massachusetts was joined by Connecticut (and briefly by California before a ballot proposition prohibited it) as the only states in which same-sex marriage was legal, although Rhode Island and New York will recognize same-sex marriages begun elsewhere. Three states (New Hampshire, New Jersey, and Vermont) had enacted civil unions; and four more states (Hawaii, Maine, Oregon, and Washington) and the District of Columbia had enacted less sweeping domestic partnership laws. So as some states were outlawing same-sex marriage and registered partnerships, others were starting them. These contradictory developments created a patchwork quilt in which some states had allowed same-sex marriages or registered partnerships, some states had banned them, and others had taken no action. (Because marriage and divorce law is enacted at the state level, no national legislation will occur.) In this respect, the United States stands in contrast to most Western countries. At this writing, same-sex marriage is legal in Belgium, Canada, the Netherlands, and Spain, and national registered partnership laws exist in Britain, Denmark, France, Germany, New Zealand, Norway, Switzerland, and Sweden. These laws vary in how they view partnerships and in what benefits they provide, but all of them give at least limited legal standing to same-sex couples (and in some cases to unmarried opposite-sex couples as well). In most other countries, then, the principle of providing some sort of registered partnership has been accepted.

Moreover, to many Europeans, marriage is not as special a status as it was to the Massachusetts Supreme Court, and civil unions are not seen as second-class citizenship. For instance, no effective movement for same-sex marriage has emerged in Great Britain or France, in part because British and French gay activists are more ambivalent than American gay activists about the value of having access to marriage. Many feel that marriage, with its implied social roles of breadwinner and caregiver, is too restrictive. One British gay man said, "Marriage in heterosexual terms is such an oppressive institution, and I wouldn't like to see lesbians or gay men simply reflecting that." Only in the United States has a major battle over same-sex marriage occurred, because only in the United States is marriage so important to people's sense of who they are, regardless of sexual orientation. In 2004 Britain legalized "civil partnerships" ("with hardly a murmur of protest," according to John Eekelaar) that are similar to civil unions in the

American states that have them. France enacted a somewhat different form of registered partnership, the *pacte civil de solidarité,* or PACS, in 1999 for both same-sex and opposite-sex partnerships.

Nevertheless, in some Western countries registered partnership legislation has been controversial, but not for the reasons found in the United States. The more contentious issue in Western Europe is not whether same-sex couples should be granted the legal privileges of marriage but how much assistance they should receive in becoming parents. The French debate about the PACS, consistent with the nation's parent-and-child-oriented social policies, focused on the kinship rights and relationships of the children of domestic partners rather than on marriage. Opponents of a broad registered partnership law argued that same-sex couples should have civil rights but that children should have the continuity of being raised by their biological mothers and fathers and of having the ability to trace their family lines. This "symbolic order" of family life, it was said, should not be disrupted. When the PACS law was finally approved, it prohibited registered partners from using assisted-reproduction services such as insemination with the sperm of a donor. Nor did it allow them to adopt children. And France is not alone in its anxiety over who should have children: in Norway women in same-sex partnerships do not have access to assisted reproduction, and in Switzerland domestic partners may neither access assisted reproduction nor adopt children. In fact, hesitancy exists in much of Europe toward providing lesbians, single or partnered, with access to assisted reproduction.

Even in Britain the opposition to registered partnerships centered more on childbearing than on marriage. The Fertilization and Embryology Act of 1990 states, concerning assisted reproduction, "A woman shall not be provided with treatment services unless account has been taken of the welfare of any child who may be born as a result of the treatment (including the need of that child for a father)." The parenthetical phrase in this provision discourages clinics from offering reproductive services to unmarried women and to same-sex couples. Although some private clinics accept lesbians who want to become pregnant, their access to the National Health Service has been limited. In 2006 the minister of health announced that the government wished to revise the act to allow greater access to services, probably by replacing the phrase "need for a father" with something like "need for a family." But in the face of a perceived shortage of donated sperm and a long list of heterosexual couples waiting for insemination, the extension of reproductive services to lesbians remained controversial. For example, a 2006 investigation by the newspaper *Scotland on Sunday* found that the public health service was funding treatment for lesbian patients "despite a nationwide shortage of sperm donors." The newspaper reported, "The revelation has been welcomed by gay rights campaigners but has angered infertility support groups, who fear healthy gay couples are harming the chances of parenthood for heterosexual couples with fertility problems."

Americans, in contrast to their greater concern about who can marry, tend to be liberal about adoption and tolerant of high-tech reproductive assistance. They therefore are indifferent toward gay and lesbian parenthood in a way that would seem odd to many Europeans. Access to assisted reproduction in the United States is largely unregulated and open to anyone a clinic cares to serve. The Sperm Bank of California, founded in 1982, claims it was the first to serve lesbians and single women. Social scientists began writing of the "lesbian baby boom" due to assisted reproduction in the 1990s. They are now beginning to write about gay male partners who choose to become fathers by adopting children whom agencies find difficult to place or about other gay men who enter into agreements with surrogate mothers to carry their babies. In most states, adoption laws do not cover same-sex parents, so judges have flexibility in determining whether a placement is in the best interests of the child. In addition, more than twenty states allow "second-parent adoptions." These usually occur after a lesbian gives birth following donor insemination or a gay man adopts a child. The parent's partner then adopts the child in order to become the second legal parent. All this is relatively uncontroversial in the United States. But let these adoptive or donor-assisted same-sex couples ask to marry, and Americans become deeply divided by politics, religious belief, and region.

Opposition to same-sex marriage was one of the two tracks on which the engine of marriage promotion rode in the 2000s. The other track involved efforts to encourage heterosexual young adults to marry. The major concession that marriage promoters made to the times was to accept that both spouses in a contemporary marriage are likely to be employed. By 2005, 75 percent of married women with school-age children and 60 percent of married women whose youngest child was preschool-age were working outside the home. The American public approved of this transformation overwhelmingly. A large majority saw women's employment as a necessity: 85 percent agreed with the statement "Most women have to work these days to support their families." But most Americans approved of married women's employment even if it is not a necessity. When asked, "Do you approve or disapprove of a married woman earning money in business or industry if she has a husband capable of supporting her?" 81 percent said that they approved. While some conservatives still regard the male-breadwinner family as preferable for raising children, many have made their peace with women's employment.

The marriage promotion movement in the early 2000s consisted of a loose group of conservative and centrist activists, religious leaders, academics, and intellectuals who wanted to strengthen the institution of marriage. Some of them believed that the marriage-based family is morally superior to other kinds of families based on biblical or philosophical grounds. Others were more pragmatic conservatives who believed that the growth of lone-parent families was the fundamental cause of poverty and who saw marriage as the solution. The latter group had been influenced by a controversial report about poverty among African Americans, "The Negro Family: The Case for National Action," written by Daniel P. Moynihan for President Lyndon B. Johnson in 1965. The "Moynihan Report," as it has come to be known, identified childbearing outside of marriage and the resulting single-parent families as the most important reason for the high rates of persistent, long-term poverty among African Americans. Still others in the promarriage camp, including most of the social scientists, favored marriage on the grounds that, in their reading of the evidence, the marriage-based family maximizes children's well-being. On the other side were what we might call the "diversity defenders," liberal activists, feminists, and sympathetic social scientists who argued that lone-parent families can be just as good for children if they receive the support they need. They advocated for public policies along the European model that would provide more generous income support, child care options, and family leave arrangements for lone-parent families. Although they eschewed the language of morality, they implicitly favored a moral position in which independence and equality were highly valued.

The antipoverty conservatives had succeeded in including language about the virtues of marriage in a landmark bill in 1996 that overhauled cash assistance to the poor and is usually referred to as "welfare reform." Its first section included these "findings" of Congress:

1. Marriage is the foundation of a successful society.
2. Marriage is an essential institution of a successful society that promotes the interests of children.

When the welfare reform law needed to be reauthorized by Congress in the early 2000s, promarriage conservatives proposed that funds be included for promoting marriage. The Bush administration wished to use the funds for a "Healthy Marriage Initiative" to help low-income couples get married and stay married. When the law was finally reauthorized in 2006, it included $150 million per year for promoting marriage.

Although $150 million is relatively modest compared to the total cost of welfare, the proposal generated more controversy per dollar than any other part of the bill. Advocates of promoting marriage stressed that they wished to use the funds to support only marriages that are relatively conflict-free and that they would not support programs that coerced couples to marry or to stay married. States could use the funds to develop high school curricula on the value of marriage, or they could support public advertising campaigns like the one in Baltimore. (Most recently, I saw a bus with the broadside "Married people earn more money.") But the most discussed type of program is a relationship skills course that engaged or married couples might attend for one or two hours per week for several weeks. This course would endeavor to teach skills such as the ability to listen to a partner, speak clearly and positively, manage anger, and resolve disagreements. Similar programs for middle-class couples seem to have helped them to improve their communication skills and have increased their satisfaction with their relationships. But it is unclear whether these programs can be adapted to help the poor and near-poor. The government agency leading the Healthy Marriage Initiative therefore is sponsoring some large-scale studies to find out.

Yet despite the social scientific studies, the controversy over the marriage promotion provision of the welfare bill was, at heart, a debate over symbolism more than statistics. Should the government state symbolically that marriage is preferred over other family forms, or should it make the symbolic statement that all family forms are equally valued? Such statements are important because they may influence the way people view marriage and family life, even if they never participate in a federally funded marriage enrichment course. That's what was at stake in the legislative battle over the $150 million annual commitment to marriage promotion. That the promarriage side prevailed suggested the strength of their movement in the mid-2000s.

There were other signs that belief in the superiority of heterosexual marriage remained widespread. In 2006, more than one hundred promarriage legal and family scholars signed a statement opposing some proposed changes in family law that would further weaken the place of marriage. The proposed changes, advocated by a prestigious legal institute, would treat all unmarried couples who meet certain qualifications, such as living together for two or three years, intermingling their finances, or assuming joint responsibility for a child, as if they were married. The opponents of this proposal argued that marriage is not just a legal category to be determined through tests such as length of coresidence; rather, it is a social institution of great value to society— the best context for raising children and for promoting responsible behavior among adults. "The state," they wrote, "therefore must exercise special care not to undermine this web of meanings sustaining our increasingly fragile marriage culture." The proposed changes would send a "social signal" to Americans that being married is no longer important, they said, which would weaken the institution of marriage to the detriment of American society.

It's hard to find such strenuous efforts to promote heterosexual marriage and such passionate debates about marriage's merits in other countries. Britain probably comes closest, but British political debates have centered more on ensuring family stability, especially stable care arrangements for children. Although British government officials stated that marriage is the best foundation for stable families, they qualified that position in a way that promarriage American policy makers did not. One British government report on family life offered this opinion:

> It is not for the state to decide whether people marry or stay together. There are strong and mutually supportive families and relationships outside marriage and many unmarried couples remain together throughout their children's upbringing and raise their children every bit as successfully as married parents.

Compare the British view to this statement by Wade Horn, an American official in charge of the Healthy Marriage Initiative during the Bush administration:

> There is something fundamentally different about the commitment two people make within a marriage relationship versus a cohabiting relationship. In a cohabiting relationship, the commitment of each of the partners primarily is self-serving. By contrast, the marriage commitment is about serving one's spouse. This is a fundamental difference, and one that ought to be reflected in our social policy.

The British policy priority is that parents remain together while caring for children; the American priority is that they marry.

The public debates about law and policy that have occurred since West Hollywood created domestic partnerships in 1985—the battles over whether to extend marriage to same-sex partners, the claims of welfare reformers that the decline in marriage underlies the poverty problem, the liberal defense of family diversity, the argument over whether to spend federal funds to promote marriage—have raised the profile of marriage in the national culture. These events have signaled to the public that marriage is important, whatever side you are on. As the activists have argued about who owns marriage, the message has gone out that marriage is still worth owning. It was a different message than the French and British public received from their debates over domestic partnerships, which centered on the right to have children rather than the right to marry. That may be why far fewer Americans in the 2000 World Values Survey agreed that marriage was an outdated institution than did the British or the French.

It seems natural to many Americans to hold marriage in such high regard and to think of it as such a central concern. Yet to many Europeans it's just as natural for births to be the central concern. The sharp contrast between the United States and Western Europe illustrates how distinctive is the American emphasis on marriage. It stems from a country formed by Protestant settlers who arrived with a moralistic vision of marriage as the center of both religious life and civil society. It stems from a country that has never worried about having enough people because it was open to immigrants and because the Atlantic moat protected its castle from would-be invaders. On the other side of the ocean are smaller countries, packed against each other, fearing that a neighboring nation might grow larger and stronger—and with good reason, given the history of European warfare. Moreover, these countries don't have a tradition of welcoming immigrants and are only now dealing with the difficulties of multiculturalism, as unrest in the North African suburbs of Paris and unease about Turkish immigrants in Germany attest. In addition, European birth rates have plunged so low that these countries are already top-heavy with elderly people and concerned about having too few working-age adults to support them.

So we can see that the debates about marriage in the United States are not occurring because of its natural place in the social order, although its advocates believe it has such a place. Rather, the debates are occurring because of the history and culture of the United States. These debates reflect not just its Protestant heritage but also the very public nineteenth-century battles over polygamy and other challenges to conventional marriage. They further reflect the heritage of slavery, with its prohibition on formal marriage, and the legacy many observers believe that prohibition has had for African American families. They are influenced by our collective memory of the marriage-centered era after World War II. It's easy to get so swept up by the issues of the day— same-sex marriage, welfare reform—that you overlook this background. Simply put, marriage matters more here, and it always has.

Your Best Life Now?

Yet at the same time it's also clear that the meaning of marriage has changed. The relationship-based, self-oriented meaning that Schwartz testified to and the Massachusetts Supreme Court embraced has become the predominant sentiment, although the older child-based, breadwinner-homemaker meaning still has its passionate advocates. The ideal of self-development through marriage and family life is being conveyed to Americans in ways rarely seen in Europe. Contemplate again the peculiarly American phenomenon of the megachurch, with its shopping-mall philosophy and media-savvy ministers. Each week in Houston at least thirty thousand people attend the services of the nondenominational Lakewood Church, by some accounts the largest church in the United States. They assemble in an arena formerly used by the city's National Basketball Association team. Another seven million people watch television broadcasts of the sermons of Lakewood's senior pastor, Joel Osteen. His 2004 book, *Your Best Life Now: 7 Steps to Living at Your Full Potential,* sold more than three million copies.

Osteen proffers a positive-thinking message similar to Norman Vincent Peale's in the 1950s. "Quit dwelling on those disappointments, mourning over something you've lost," writes Osteen, "and start believing in God for a fantastic future!" But that's where the similarity ends. Whereas Peale stuck to inspiring stories about people he had met, Osteen tells many more stories about himself. Most of those stories illustrate what happens when you think positively and live "favor-minded," that is, expect favors from God. In the book he tells how his favor-minded attitude helped him find a good parking space, sink the winning shot in a pickup basketball game, and get upgraded to first class on a plane flight. And while Peale urged readers to stay married, be good parents, and behave responsibly, Osteen advises readers to try to have successful marriages but not to worry too much if they don't. It's true that he tells readers not to give up if they go through difficult times in their marriages. But he also makes it clear that God is ready to forgive those who transgress. Have you committed adultery? Then ask God's forgiveness, think positively, and move on, he suggests, citing the story of David:

> Israel's second ruler, King David, made a lot of mistakes. He committed adultery and even ordered a man to be murdered. But when he repented and sought forgiveness, God forgave him and gave him a new start. The Bible compliments David, saying, "He was a man after God's own heart." David didn't focus on his faults or on the things he had done wrong. No, he lived favor-minded.

Regarding divorce, Osteen tells a story about his own family. His father, the minister who founded Lakewood Church, married at a very young age, and unfortunately the marriage failed. In the darkest hour of his life, he made a decision to accept God's forgiveness and mercy, and God restored his spiritual strength. "God doesn't condone our sins," Osteen writes. "He doesn't wink at our wrongdoings. But God doesn't automatically condemn us either."

In its orientation toward the self rather than toward social roles, *Your Best Life Now* is very much a twenty-first-century book. It is a late-modern version of what Peale once called "applied Christianity," where the application is to leading a successful life, however the culture defines it at the time. Its market niche is sometimes labeled "prosperity theology," although the theology is limited at best: the most common word in the book is "God," appearing 1,788 times according to Amazon.com's helpful concordance, but neither "Jesus" nor "Christ" makes the list of the top one hundred words. "Joel" and "money," in contrast, do. It's easy to dismiss applied Christianity of the Peale/Osteen variety as lightweight religion. Nevertheless, religious self-help books such as Osteen's and the associated television programs and video and audio recordings are among the prime sources of religious information for millions of

Americans who do not attend services regularly and even for some who do.

Osteen's book sales, while impressive, can't match the sales of *The Purpose Driven Life,* by Rick Warren, pastor of Saddleback Church, a megachurch in Orange County, California, that claims to have an average weekly attendance of twenty thousand. *BusinessWeek* reported in 2005 that *The Purpose Driven Life* had become the fastest-selling book of all time, with more than twenty-three million copies sold. Many were sold in bulk to study groups at churches around the country and the world. Warren tells readers that God has designed a purpose for every person's life. Their task is to discover what it is. When they find it, they will be able to serve God by serving other people.

Even though Warren's book often sits on the same bookstore shelf as Osteen's, Warren takes great pains to dissociate it from the Christian self-help literature. "It's not about you" is the first sentence of Chapter 1. Later he remarks, "Sadly, a quick review of many popular Christian books reveals that many believers have abandoned living for God's great purposes and settled for personal fulfillment and emotional stability. That is narcissism, not discipleship." No one could mistake Warren's book for prosperity theology; its aim is indeed to help people serve others. He has made reducing world poverty and disease a priority for his church. Still, *The Purpose Driven Life* fits perfectly with the spirituality of seeking. It guides the reader through a personal quest: "This is more than a book; it is a guide to a *40-day spiritual journey* that will enable you to discover the answer to life's most important question: What on earth am I here for?" Warren instructs you to read one of his forty brief chapters a day. Each ends with a question for you to consider about yourself. Day 16: "Honestly, are relationships my first priority? How can I ensure that they are?" Day 25: "What problem in my life has caused the greatest growth in me?"

Consider a remarkable two-sentence excerpt that encapsulates the book's approach:

> Christianity is not a religion or a philosophy, but a relationship and a lifestyle. The core of that lifestyle is thinking of others, as Jesus did, instead of ourselves.

In the second sentence, Warren rejects self-oriented goals: it's not about you. Yet in the first sentence, he embraces a seeker-oriented spirituality. A relationship is personal, a direct connection between you and someone else or, in this case, God. A lifestyle is a way of living that you choose. At heart, then, Christianity is not a moral code, according to Warren, nor a set of God's laws, nor collective worship in a holy place. Rather, Christianity is something you must construct by establishing a personal relationship with God, by choosing how you want to live your life, and by discovering how you can best serve others. To accomplish all that, you must embark on a spiritual quest, and *The Purpose Driven Life* will help you find your way.

The problem is that once religious leaders encourage this kind of quest, people tend to generalize it. They may critically examine not just their spiritual lives but also their family lives. They may make relationships their first priority but evaluate them in more self-centered terms than Warren would recommend. They may discover that some relationships are standing in the way of their greatest growth. And they may feel empowered to make changes in their family lives that will take them on the new journey they have chosen. Warren lets the genie of self-development out of the bottle in order to get people to serve others by serving themselves. But in an individualistic culture, there is no guarantee that people will make only selfless choices.

The enormous appetite of the American public for self-oriented religious messages in print and on television (a newer book by Osteen, for which he signed a contract potentially worth $10 million, made the best-seller list in 2008) suggests both the continuing strength of religion in the United States and the extent to which it now focuses on self-development. To be sure, nearly all American religious denominations still value lifelong marriage. A high cultural value on marriage is, in fact, a necessary part of a family system in which people have multiple partners over their lifetimes. Such a system needs people to enter, and reenter, marriages. If they don't enter in large numbers, they can't exit in large numbers. American religion does not, of course, encourage divorce. Even at the liberal extreme, divorce is seen as an unfortunate occurrence that may be for the best. When married people decide to divorce, however, religious faiths that endorse an ethic of self-development have a hard time stopping them. Instead, churches focus on ministering to separated and divorced individuals, both longtime congregants and newcomers, who need help in coping with the end of their marriages. As Wuthnow writes concerning the role of religion in guiding people's behavior:

> The meaning of [divine] guidance shifted subtly away from behavioral norms and focused instead on reassurance. People talked about receiving divine guidance, but what they meant, when pressed to explain, was that they felt better about what they already were doing.

Many churches seem to take the line that people make choices about how to live their lives, and some of these choices, such as divorce, are unfortunate and even sinful, but if people ask for forgiveness and give themselves to God, they can remain (or become) good congregants and move on with their lives, much as King David did. This tolerance of ending a relationship for personal reasons and this willingness to help those who do so makes it easier for religious individuals who are unhappy to divorce. It also makes it easier for divorced people to turn to religion.

Consequently, American religion, in its focus on both marriage and self-development, tends to encourage marriage, promote an individualistic mode of thinking about personal life, tolerate divorce, and accept or even encourage remarriage. It also encourages cohabiting couples to end their relationships within a few years if they are unwilling to marry. In this way, it accommodates people who have more than one partnership. It is a powerful institution in the United States because it reaches such a large share of the population compared to other countries. Choosing one's religious beliefs and choosing one's family life have become interconnected parts of American life. With its promarriage ideal and its increasing emphasis on the personal quest, contemporary religion reinforces the cultural models of both marriage and individualism. Religious Americans, as we know, not only marry more than secular Europeans but also divorce more than secular Europeans. They get divorced not because religion tells them that divorce is good but because it tells them that self-development is good and that if they divorce, they will be forgiven and cared for.

African American churches constitute an exception to this pattern: they place less emphasis on marriage and self-development and more emphasis on perseverance and shared struggle. The roughly fifty thousand churches in the United States that have predominantly African American congregants are sufficiently distinct in their history and in their spiritual orientations that most religious scholars characterize them as a separate Protestant tradition from the conservative and mainline denominations. Although often referred to collectively as "the black church," they comprise churches with divergent religious beliefs. A sociologist who studied an African American neighborhood in Boston with twenty-nine churches found a "dizzying diversity of institutions that make up the 'Black Church.' "

These churches, be they Baptist, Methodist, or Pentecostal, remain focused on the struggles of the community. They strive to provide an uplifting spiritual message while also providing assistance to their congregants and neighborhoods. African American scholars often name the black church and the black family as the two "enduring institutions" of the African American community in the double sense of lasting through the difficult American experience and also helping African Americans cope with hardship. Cheryl Townsend Gilkes, a sociologist and a minister, writes, "Church and household at times overlapped in fulfilling the functions of the family. It is this tradition of overlap that is a critical source of strength for African-Americans, as individuals and as a group." She notes that kinship terms such as "brother" and "sister" are still commonly used and that many black congregations "are gatherings of family networks" that support each other until old age. Some black churches have an informal position of "church mother," occupied by an older woman who has been active and is highly respected.

What is missing from this type of religious practice, however, is marriage. Whereas conservative Protestant church leaders and, to a lesser extent, mainline Protestant and Catholic leaders hold the marriage-based family of husband, wife, and children as the ideal form, black church leaders and black scholars of religion speak more of parent and child, of larger kin networks, and of ties with the broader family of one's church. They may decry the conditions in which black youth are growing up, but few call for a renewal of marriage as the solution. Instead, they point to the decline of industrial jobs, racism, or the alleged failures of government policy. The nineteen-page index to a well-known book on the black church has no entry for marriage. The book about the twenty-nine Boston churches does not mention marriage. Nor was marriage mentioned in an article, "Changing Church Confronts Changing Black Family," in the African American mass-circulation magazine *Ebony.* One bishop quoted in the article was particularly concerned about the plight of the black male. Another said the black church needs to begin working with heads of households. But neither said anything about marriage. In fact, heads of households could be of either gender, according to one of the bishops: "The head of the household, male or female, must be a strong person who is conscious of the moral image they project." This deemphasis on the marriage-based family reflects the historically greater role of the larger family in the African American experience: marriage has never been as central to African American culture as it has to European American culture. It also reflects the church's focus on long-term and continuing deprivation rather than who is heading the household.

Marriage as Capstone

Although the meaning of marriage has changed, most people still get married: nearly 90 percent, according to a recent estimate. Granted, that's less than the approximately 95 percent or so who married during the 1950s, but it's still a high percentage. In fact, at a time of great public concern about the supposed decline of marriage, it's remarkably high. Keep in mind that marriage is more of an option now than it ever was in American history. Until a half century ago, little family life occurred outside of it. Today, you may live with a partner, or sequentially with several partners, without an explicit consideration of whether a marriage will occur. You may choose to have children on your own or in a cohabiting relationship. And yet most people want to marry and eventually do. A survey of high school seniors conducted annually since 1976 shows no decline in the importance they attach to marriage: the percentage of young women who respond that they expect to marry has stayed constant at roughly 80 percent (and has increased from 71 percent to 78 percent among young men), and the percentage who respond that "having a good marriage and family life" is extremely important has also remained constant, at about 80 percent for young women and 70 percent for young men. Why don't more people just want long-term cohabiting relationships such as many French or Swedish couples have? (The Socialist candidate for president of France in 2007, Ségolène Royal, had four children by her long-term partner without ever marrying.) After at least 150 years of anxiety about marriage (remember the *Boston Quarterly Review*'s lament in 1859 that the family was disappearing from our land) and after the huge pendulum swing of change since the 1950s, the real puzzle is not why there is so little marriage but why there is so much of it. In short, why does anyone bother to marry anymore?

Let's dispense quickly with one possible explanation: that it's in our genes. Although our DNA may influence the way we live our family lives, it's unlikely that humans have developed an innate preference for marriage as we know it. Evolutionary theorists think that among our hunter-gatherer ancestors, women sought stable pair bonds with men because their capacity to reproduce was limited by pregnancy and by breast-feeding (which delays the time when they are fertile again). Their best strategy was to find men who would remain with them long enough to provide assistance and protection while their children were young. The standard evolutionary view of hunter-gatherer men is that they tried to maximize the number of children they sired by impregnating many women. Rather than being natural, marriage was described in classic anthropological writing as the great social invention for keeping men around—it supposedly domesticated them and solved the problem of the sexually wandering male. No evolutionary theorist has proposed that women and men both have a genetic predisposition for lifelong, monogamous pair bonding.

Standard economic theory also isn't very helpful. You'll recall the economist Gary Becker, who argued that the gains from marriage are greatest when men specialize in working for wages and women specialize in child rearing and housework. His framework predicts that as more women work outside the home, the gains a person gets from marriage should decline. So it offers a very good explanation for why marriage rates have dropped from their peak levels in the 1950s. But it can't explain the persistence of marriage rates at relatively high levels.

One benefit that marriage still provides (although its advantage over cohabiting is lessening as time goes by) is what I call enforceable trust. Getting married requires a public commitment to a long-term, possibly lifelong, relationship. This commitment is usually expressed in front of relatives, friends, and religious congregants. At a wedding I attended, the minister said, "Will all of you witnessing these promises do all in your power to uphold these two persons in their marriage?" We all answered, "We will." Cohabiting, in contrast, requires only a private commitment, which is easier to break. As a result, marriage lowers the risk that your partner will renege on promises to act in ways that would benefit you and your children. It allows you to put time, effort, and money into family life with less fear of abandonment by your partner. For instance, it allows you to invest financially in joint, long-term purchases such as homes and automobiles. It allows you to spend more time with your children—an investment that (unlike strengthening your job skills) would not be easily portable to another intimate partnership.

Nevertheless, the difference in the amount of enforceable trust that marriage brings, compared to cohabitation, is eroding. Although relatives and friends will view a divorce with disappointment, they will accept it more readily than their counterparts would have two generations ago. Because cohabiting couples are increasingly gaining rights previously reserved to married couples, it seems likely that over time the legal differences between cohabitation and marriage will become minimal in the United States, as they already are in some European countries. Today, for example, a married couple can use divorce laws to gain an acceptable settlement if the marriage ends, but a cohabiting couple cannot. That could change in the future. If it does, the advantage of marriage in enhancing trust will then depend almost solely on the public commitments, both secular and religious, of the partners.

Why, then, is marriage still so prevalent? The answer, I suggest, is that although the practical importance of marriage has declined, its symbolic importance has increased. In the mid-twentieth century, being married was almost a requirement for being a respectable adult. Having children outside of marriage was stigmatizing, and a person who remained single through adulthood was morally suspect. Because everyone was marrying as soon as they could, being married was not a symbol of being special but rather a mark of fitting in. Your union was your union card for membership in the adult world. Later in the century, as other lifestyle options became more feasible and acceptable, the need to be married diminished. As people spent fewer years in married life, often cohabiting beforehand and afterward, being married became more distinctive. It remained the preferred alternative for most people. Now, however, getting married is a step one does not take until one's life course is farther along than in the past. Being "ready" to marry may mean that a couple has lived together to test out their compatibility, saved up for a down payment on a house, and possibly had children to judge how good they are at parenting together. Marriage's place in the life course used to come before those investments were made, but now it often comes afterward. Whereas marriage used to be the foundation of adult family life, now it is often the capstone.

For instance, young adults in their twenties say that marriage is a status you build up to: 62 percent agreed in a survey that "living together with someone before marriage is a good way to avoid an eventual divorce," and 82 percent agreed that "it is extremely important to you to be economically set before you get married." Moreover, most twenty-somethings see marriage as centered on intimacy and love rather than on practical matters such as finances and children: 94 percent of those who had never married agreed that "when you marry you want your spouse to be your soul mate, first and foremost." In contrast, only 16 percent agreed that "the main purpose of marriage these days is to have children." And over 80 percent of the women agreed that it is more important "to have a husband who can communicate about his deepest feelings than to have a husband who makes a good living." The authors of the report conclude: "While marriage is losing much of its broad public and institutional character, it is gaining popularity as a SuperRelationship, an intensely private spiritualized union, combining sexual fidelity, romantic love, emotional intimacy, and togetherness."

Said otherwise, the rewards of marriage are more individualized now. Being married is less of a social role and more of an individual achievement—a symbol of successful self-development. Marriage is not just one type of family relationship among many; rather, it remains the most prestigious form. But it is a personal choice, and individuals construct marriages through an increasingly long process that often includes cohabiting and having children beforehand. It still confers some of its traditional benefits, such as enforceable trust. Yet it is increasingly a mark of prestige, a display of distinction, a part of what has been called the "do-it-yourself biography."

Meanwhile, couples are deferring marriage until they have a firm economic base. The 2002 Toledo study included in-depth interviews with over one hundred working-class and lower-middle-class adults who were, or recently had been, cohabiting. Many of them did not want to marry until they had an economic package in place that often included homeownership, being out of debt, and having a stable, adequate family income. One twenty-five-year-old woman said that she and her partner were interested in marrying. However, a lot had to be accomplished first:

> Um, we have certain things that we want to do before we get married. We both want very good jobs, and we both want a house, we both want reliable transportation. I'm about to start taking cake decorating classes, and so I can have me some good income, and he—he's trying his best you know? He's been looking out for jobs everywhere, and we—we're trying. We just want to have—we gotta have everything we need before we say, "Let's get married."

A half century ago, most young couples first said, "Let's get married," and then looked for better jobs, bought cars, and found homes. But cohabiting relationships were not an option then. If you wanted to live with an intimate partner, you had to get married. Today, with cohabitation as an acceptable option, many young couples are postponing marriage until they have passed the milestones that used to occur in the early years of marriage.

Even the wedding has become an individual achievement. In the distant past, a wedding was an event at which two kinship groups formed an alliance. More recently, it has been an event organized and paid for by parents, at which they display their approval and support for their child's marriage. In both cases, it has been the ritual that provides legal and social approval for having children. But it is now becoming an event centered on and often controlled and paid for by the couple themselves, having less to do with family approval or having children than in the past. You might assume, then, that weddings would become smaller and that many couples would forgo a public wedding altogether. But that does not appear to have happened for most couples. According to the recollections of Detroit-area women, couples today are more likely to have a religious wedding, a wedding reception, a bridal shower or bachelor party, and a honeymoon than was the case two or three generations ago. The contemporary wedding, as Rebecca Mead puts it, "is an individualistic adventure rather than a community sacrament."

In recent decades, then, when partners decide that their relationship has finally reached the stage where they can marry, they generally want a ritual-filled wedding to celebrate it. Without doubt, the desires of brides (the desires of grooms seem to be ignored) are shaped by the wedding industry: the professional wedding planners, the exotic destinations (Disneyland, Aruba) competing for business, the bridal magazines thick with ads (Vicki Howard notes that the 1,271-page spring 2000 issue of *Bride's* made the *Guinness Book of World Records* as the largest magazine ever produced), the Web sites, the videographers, and so forth. Yet the industry is also responding to an increased demand for showy weddings. Young couples want to display to relatives and friends—and to themselves—that they have made it to the altar. Even low- and moderate-income couples who have limited funds, who may already have children, and who may be living together seem to view a substantial wedding as a requirement for marriage.

Some of the cohabiting adults interviewed in Toledo raised the wedding as an issue, even though the interviewers had not asked questions about it. Several made a distinction between a "downtown" wedding, which meant marrying at a courthouse or at a justice of the peace's office, and a "church" wedding. Simply going downtown was not acceptable to most people. A home health care aide said she was waiting for her boyfriend to change his mind about a church wedding, because "until he does, we just won't get married. I'm not going downtown. . . . I say, you don't want a big wedding, we're not going to get married." Through wedding ceremonies, individuals hoped to display their attainment of a prestigious, comfortable, stable style of life. The continuing enthusiasm for wedding celebrations suggests that people marry now as much for the symbolism it represents as for the social benefits it provides.

Marriage, in sum, has not faded away; rather, it has been redefined. It has become the ultimate merit badge—the marriage badge. It shows you have acquired the resources necessary for wedded life: a decent job, a good education, and the ability to attract a partner who is likely to treat you fairly, be loyal, and stay with you indefinitely. But to earn a merit badge, a Boy Scout must show he has gained a practical skill. It's not clear that the marriage badge reflects anything that helps you survive in the woods of adulthood. After all, nearly half of marriages end in divorce. It's almost as though obtaining the marriage badge has become an end in itself. An observer sometimes gets the sense that what matters to some young adults is not so much *being* married as *getting* married—that the exercise is more about status than survival. Some people act as though once they can display the badge, they have accomplished their goal. The focus on the wedding is so complete that they sometimes seem unprepared for how to live their married lives after the celebration is over.

There's one other explanation for the persistence of marriage that deserves a brief mention: cultural lag. William F. Ogburn, who first wrote about it in the 1920s, said that cultural lag occurs when one part of the culture (usually technology) changes faster than another (usually behavior). Ogburn noted that families were buying many of the products—clothes, soap, leather goods—that housewives used to make;

consequently, there was less reason for married women to remain at home. That they still remained at home, he said, was due to cultural lag. Well ahead of his time he predicted that the housewife role would eventually diminish. Applied to the present day, cultural lag says that people are marrying because they are still following the cultural practices of their parents and grandparents, even though there's no longer a good reason to follow those practices. They don't fully grasp that, because of technological changes such as the birth control pill and legal changes such as the extension of benefits to cohabiting partners, they can obtain most of the benefits previously reserved for married people merely by cohabiting, or even by having children as a single parent.

Ogburn said that cultural lag rarely lasts more than a generation or two. By that time people's behavior has caught up to the new realities. For example, by the 1960s, the housewife role was indeed in decline. Perhaps someone a generation or two from now, upon finding a crumbling copy of this book gathering dust on a bookshelf, will confirm with a nod that the persistence of marriage was merely cultural lag and that no one does it anymore. We cannot say for sure today. Yet let's note that although these predictions of the demise of marriage have been made for a long time, marriage has outlived them. It's not clear that it has lost its usefulness for Americans, even if that usefulness is different in nature now than it has been in the past.

6

―⊃⊂―

The M-Factor

When I meet people and tell them what I'm studying, they often offer their own explanations (I doubt this happens to physics professors). Unmindful that I have spent several years puzzling over the facts that they are just hearing about, they confidently tell me the answers to the riddles I am trying to solve. Over the past few years, when casual acquaintances have heard that I'm writing a book about why Americans have so many partners, several have told me that it's because Americans are always on the move. They tire of what they have been doing and try their luck in a new neighborhood, a different part of the country, another occupation—and, by implication, in another marriage. This is said with a knowing smile, as if it's obvious that a certain restlessness—an urge to see if opportunities are better over the horizon, a sense that life is good but could be better, an openness to new experience—is the essence of the American personality.

This is clearly a story Americans tell themselves, part of the lore of the American experience. It's supposedly the reason for the dynamism of the American economy: our love of the new and distaste for the old leads to cycles of creation, destruction, and re-creation—as when railroads replaced rivers and canals as the main way of shipping goods and were themselves replaced by trailer trucks and superhighways. It encourages inventiveness, from the telegraph to the Internet. Literary critic Philip Fisher writes, "Uniquely, in the culture of the United States there has been for the whole of the past one hundred and fifty years a clear stake in newness itself."

The many essays and books on restlessness don't focus on family life. No one is touting the high divorce rate as one of America's great contributions to the world. Rather, the story of restlessness is about the peopling of the frontier, the opportunities afforded to the working class, or the breakthroughs of the Wright brothers or Bill Gates. But could this same restlessness, this search for the new, also affect how Americans lead their family lives? Could this search for someplace better lead to a search for someone better? Could the quest for the new reinforce the quest for self-development? "America has always signaled the right to a new start," writes Fisher. "Mobility is made easier if community bonds are light." So might divorce and remarriage be made easier. We need to examine whether the image of Americans as a restless nation fits the facts and in what sense it might help to explain the greater number of intimate partnerships that Americans have. Much of the commentary on restlessness approvingly quotes Alexis de Tocqueville, the young French aristocrat who began a nine-month visit to the United States in 1831. His official task was to study the American penal system, but he traveled widely and took in everything he saw. Tocqueville wrote some of the most famous remarks on the subject of American restlessness, and his tone was both positive and negative. One month after he began his visit, he wrote in his diary, "A restless temper seems to me one of the distinctive traits of this people." On the positive side, a restless person may be quick to seize an opening, ready to make the next move, or primed for self-improvement. But Tocqueville's phrase for "restless temper," *l'inquiétude du caractère,* also suggests "disquietude," a state of worried unease. And this less flattering theme of anxiousness and apprehension also runs through writings on American restlessness. Tocqueville said of Americans that although they lived in happy circumstances, "a cloud habitually hung on their brow, and they seemed serious and almost sad even in their pleasures." The main reason, he wrote, was that they are "forever brooding over advantages they do not possess."

On the Move

Above all, whether for constructive or compulsive reasons, restlessness implies movement. George W. Pierson, a historian who in 1938 wrote a book on Tocqueville's travels, ended his career with a 1973 book entitled *The Moving American*. It is perhaps the most expansive treatment of the idea of restlessness. Pierson maintained that the central distinguishing feature of American character was what he called the "M-Factor": movement, migration, and mobility. He wrote:

> We Americans have taken what I shall call the "M-Factor" into our lives, into our public institutions, into our private and social psychology to such an extent that mobility has become an essential ingredient in the American way of life. Mobility has been something special here, something so different in degree as to approach a difference in kind. Our comparisons with Europe must therefore be in part contrasts as well as likenesses.

Has mobility really has been greater in the United States than in Europe, or is this just an example of Americans seeing themselves as they would like to be seen? Until recently, this was a very difficult question to answer. But researchers have now transferred to computer files the actual paper records of hundreds of thousands of people from the 1850, 1860, 1870, 1900, and 1910 censuses. It's possible to trace the same people across two or three censuses, yielding information on whether the places where they lived and the jobs that they held changed over time. These records can be compared to a similar British sample of 25,000 men followed from 1851 to 1881. The comparison shows that American men were much more likely to move from place to place in the second half of the nineteenth century than were British men. Two-thirds of American men changed their county of residence over a thirty-year period in the United States, compared to one-fourth of British men. Moreover, American men were much more likely to make long-distance moves: more than a third of their moves were over one hundred miles, compared to just 6 percent in Britain.

So Americans were indeed more likely to move from place to place. Were they more likely to move from job to job, bettering themselves in the process? Yes, if we compare the jobs of fathers and their sons. American sons were more likely than British sons to have a different occupation than their fathers. For instance, 80 percent of the American sons of men who were unskilled laborers—deliverers, stock clerks—

were able to move up to better jobs, such as printers or bakers, compared to 51 percent of the British sons. Unless British men were less mobile than other Europeans, which seems unlikely, we can conclude that the observations of visitors such as Tocqueville were correct: American mobility, geographic and occupational, was substantially higher than in Europe. Americans did move more from place to place and from occupation to occupation than their European counterparts.

However, this level of mobility began to decline after the 1920s, and by the second half of the twentieth century it was greatly diminished. Americans today do not move to new places or switch occupations as often as earlier generations did. What seems to have changed is the method people use to get ahead in life. In the old days, it required moving to a new town or switching jobs. Today, the better strategy for success is, first, to stay in one place and get a high school education (few high schools even existed in the nineteenth century) and then a college education. Then you may get a job in a large firm that has an internal ladder of positions that you can climb. You may make a move or two while you are doing this, but you are less likely to make a series of moves than were people in the past.

Nevertheless, Americans still move from place to place more than do the citizens in many other developed countries. The proportion of the population that changes residences within a year is about twice as great in the United States, Australia, Canada, and New Zealand (nations with an immigrant heritage and abundant land) as in Europe and Japan. Even when just state-to-state moves in America and their equivalent in Europe are considered, the difference remains. In fact, some of the writers who believe in American restlessness think that immigration is the heart of the matter. Everyone except African Americans and American Indians chose, or is descended from someone who chose, to move to the United States. The path of moving somewhere new, starting at the bottom, and working your way up is accepted, even taken for granted, in ways not found in most other countries. James M. Jasper, the author of *Restless Nation: Starting Over in America,* wrote:

> Americans have come to believe that migration and starting over are
> normal. Yet the norm, throughout the world, is to stay put, to heed the

demands of family, community, and identity. Less than 2 percent of the world's population today consists of people who have had the drive to migrate. We easily forget how unusual American restlessness is.

Starting over becomes something like a character trait that people inherit from their immigrant ancestors, perhaps not genetically but at least through a deep-seated influence on American culture.

To many observers, then, geographical mobility reflects the hold that the M-Factor has on the American psyche. There is another way, however, to explain the greater mobility in the United States, a way in which character counts for less and cost-benefit analysis counts for more. Economists will tell you that people migrate primarily because they do comparisons in their heads and conclude that their "utility," or overall well-being, will be greater at the destination than in their current communities. Consequently, areas with higher wages draw more migrants. Areas with more desirable climates and landscapes also draw migrants. So do areas where housing is relatively inexpensive. Economists would explain the greater geographical mobility of the United States not by proposing that Americans are inherently a nation of movers but rather by noting that the United States is a large country in which employment opportunities, climate, housing prices, and other such factors vary substantially from region to region. Some of these factors, such as housing prices, also vary greatly from central cities to their suburban and exurban rings, which encourages migration out of the city. This economic model fits the facts of modern movement well: it's consistent with the abandonment of central city neighborhoods for the suburbs and with the depopulation of the Northeast and upper Midwest, where factory jobs have declined, and the growth of the West and Southwest, where the job markets are stronger. Restlessness may be driven more by one's wallet than one's spirit.

Social Integration

No matter how it is driven, moving from one community to another could affect marriages because it disrupts social ties. Migration can separate people from friends and relatives who could help them through family crises. This line of thinking can be traced back to Émile Durkheim, one of the founders of modern sociology. In his 1897 book, *Suicide,* Durkheim argued that social integration—the strength of social ties—is beneficial to individuals in ways they may not realize. Individuals with a strong network of family and friends have others who care about them and will watch out for them, draw them into social groups, provide them with models of how to live one's life, and express disapproval if they deviate from accepted behavior. In contrast, individuals who are isolated from social support have fewer people encouraging them to behave in accepted ways. They are at risk of experiencing *anomie*—an isolated existence without accepted rules about how to live one's life. Durkheim showed that suicide rates were lower in Catholic countries than in Protestant countries. This was not because Catholics were happier, he claimed, but because the hierarchical Catholic Church integrated the individual better into society.

People who move out of a community tend to leave social ties behind and therefore are less integrated into society and more subject to anomie than people who stay put. If so, migrants may be at greater risk of suicide. To test this idea, Robert D. Baller and Kelly K. Richardson produced a detailed map of the United States in 1990, with each of its more than three thousand counties color-coded based on how many people had been living at different addresses five years earlier. The map shows that counties with many movers are concentrated in the western and mountain states and in Florida—the areas of the nation that have been experiencing the most in-migration in recent years. The lowest percentages of movers are in the upper Midwest—the Dakotas, Minnesota, Iowa, Nebraska—and in scattered clusters elsewhere. The authors then created a map of suicide rates for each county. If you lay one map next to the other, they look almost the same. In general, wherever the percentage of movers was high, so were suicides. The highest suicide rates were in the West and in central Florida, the very places that had seen the most people moving in.

But what about divorce? Do areas with lots of new residents have higher rates? Baller made another map, which he didn't publish but kindly sent to me, showing the percentage of men in each of the three thousand counties who were divorced in 2000. Sure enough, it looks like the migration map: wherever the percentage of new residents was high, so were the number of divorced men. Clusters of divorced men were most common in the West and in parts of Florida and least common in the upper Midwest. There was an exception in the West, and it proved the rule: one more or less rectangular area had relatively less suicide and divorce than its neighbors, fewer recent migrants, and, in addition, more people who belonged to a church. It was Utah. Its counties showed fewer movers, fewer suicides, and fewer divorced men than in all of its neighboring states. The obvious explanation is that the Church of Jesus Christ of Latter-Day Saints, the Mormon Church, with its strong family bonds and large church membership, provided a greater level of social integration to people in Utah. Divorce rates are lower among Mormons than among any other Christian or Jewish religious group.

These maps don't prove that migration raises the risk of divorce. It could be that the kinds of people who are likely to divorce for other reasons (perhaps they have more difficulty getting along with others in general) are also more likely to move. Historically, moving west was a way for a man to separate from his wife, whether she wanted a divorce or not. In the nineteenth century, Utah itself gained a reputation as a divorce haven because of liberal Mormon divorce practices at the time. Moreover, some of the divorced people in the West may have obtained their divorces in the states where they were born and only migrated afterward. Other married couples may have moved only after their marriages were already in trouble. In short, we could have cause and effect backward: migrants could be different kinds of people—more prone to marital breakups—than people who stay in one place. Even if they had stayed home, they might have gotten divorced more often.

Although we can't disentangle cause and effect with confidence, we can make some progress in thinking about it. For instance, let's take people who grew up in a family in which their parents divorced. They are at higher risk of divorce themselves no matter where they live. But we find that if they migrate, their chances of divorce are even greater, as if something about moving further raises their risk. We can also look at whether native, stay-at-home people who happen to live in high migrant-receiving areas, such as the Southwest, are themselves more likely to divorce than are people who live in areas where migrants are moving out. Are natives of Phoenix, in other words, more likely to divorce than natives of Fargo? The answer is yes, suggesting that the higher divorce rate in the Southwest isn't just due to the personal experience of migrating. Those who live in regions where they are surrounded by lots of migrants are more likely to divorce than those who live in regions with few migrants—as if there were something in the air that raised everyone's chances of divorcing in Arizona above the chances in North Dakota.

Regardless of the effects on adults, children's well-being could be affected by moves to new communities even if their parents do not divorce. When families move, children must adjust to new schools and find new friends. Good parents can compensate by helping their children with the adjustment process, but multiple moves still could be troublesome. In a rapidly growing Toronto suburb, students whose parents had recently moved into the area from elsewhere in Canada were less likely to complete high school and to graduate from college than were students who grew up in the area. Yet the difference was smaller for new students who reported receiving more support from their parents: those who talked about their feelings with their parents, had parents who knew where they were when they were away from home, and had fathers who participated more in the family did better. Migration sometimes caused problems, but supportive parents helped to ease them.

Megachurches are an attempt to solve the problem of low social integration in communities where people do not know each other and have no common history. They have been growing fastest in the suburbs of southern and western cities, the leading destinations for Americans who decide to migrate from one region of the country to another. The newer suburbs of these areas offer families affordable housing at the cost of a longer commute to work. As their populations grow, these suburbs struggle to add services fast enough to keep up, and megachurches can serve as instant community centers. The Prestonwood

Baptist Church in Plano, Texas, north of Dallas, has fifteen athletic fields, a 1950s-style diner, coffee shop, food court, student ministry center, outdoor prayer walk, chapel, sanctuary, and indoor commons. "We're not a large church," its executive pastor said. "We're a small town."

But Durkheim, should he have walked around the grounds of Prestonwood, might not have recognized it as a substitute for hometown solidarity. The essence of the old social ties was not merely associating with others but being bound to them in a web of social norms. Communities had codes of behavior and were prepared to enforce these norms on those who dared to deviate. The megachurch, however, is nondemanding. People join small groups—arts and crafts, business, fitness, movies—based on their common interests, not on their moral obligations to each other. There's no enforcement mechanism—a food court but no family court. To be sure, some of the small groups include Bible study and provide guidelines for living. And buried within all this activity is a religious message with strong views on truth and morality. It's questionable, however, how many members ever dig that deep. Will the average member of a megachurch in a rapidly growing area have a lower risk of divorce than a neighbor who does not have a religious affiliation? That's hard to say. At Willow Creek Community Church, one of the most famous megachurches, the message about divorce is nonjudgmental. At one service, the preacher said, "Mistakes are going to be made in [some] relationships that will lead to divorce. God knows that and He understands it." At another service, the head pastor said that "there is not an ounce of judgment in my spirit for those of you who are going through or who are recovering from a divorce in your family. . . . You matter to God more than you realize you do."

The megachurches also respond to another aspect of contemporary American mobility: the penchant for automobile travel even among those who do not change residences. Pierson railed against automobile-based irritants—to him at least—such as vacation travel ("in the hope of what it may bring, we will spend monies we have not got and tolerate discomforts no sane man would endure"), mobile homes ("be it ever so mobile, it's an emptier article"), and the supermarket ("that extraordinary flat-topped do-it-yourself store which car-minded Californians sold to the nation"). He would have been at once fascinated and appalled at the parking map on the Web site of Willow Creek, which draws about fifteen thousand people per week to its main campus: six color-coded lots plus a satellite lot with shuttle bus service for those who have trouble walking long distances. The atmosphere at the megachurches is unabashedly that of the automobile-dependent shopping mall. "Dude, where's the cinema?" joked Pastor McFarland. A pastor in Maryland said,

> The shopping center makes you feel comfortable; it makes you feel at home. There are clear instructions on where to go and what to do. We want our church to be equally as customer service oriented or equally as sensitive to the needs of all seekers, of all first time visitors who come here.

The idea is to market religion to suburbanites who think nothing of driving a half hour in search of a better place to shop—in this case, not for jeans but for spirituality. The idea is to orient the religious experience around the felt needs of the mobile, consumption-oriented suburbanite. The megachurch is where the car culture meets the quest culture.

Migration and Parental Control

Another kind of movement may contribute to having more partners: in the past half century, young adults have become much more likely to leave home before they marry. Until the 1950s, it was very uncommon for unmarried people in their twenties to head their own households; less than 5 percent did so. Before then, they either lived with their parents or were "boarders and lodgers," that is, single people who rented rooms and ate their meals in another family's home. Often, it was a home in which an older child had recently moved out, leaving a married couple with a free room. But by 1980 the numbers of young adults living on their own had increased greatly, and by 2000 nearly one-third of never-married adults in their twenties were heading their own households. Moreover, the size of the never-married young adult population—whether heading their own households or not—grew during this half century as the typical age at marriage rose.

Michael Rosenfeld calls this development the rise of the "independent life stage," a period of living apart from one's parents prior to marrying. He argues that young adults who live on their own have more freedom in choosing an intimate partner because it's more difficult for parents to influence their choices. Parents usually urge their children to choose someone from the same background as theirs—the same religion and race or ethnic group, for instance. With few exceptions, parents are less approving of a same-sex partnership than an opposite-sex one. They would rather see their children married than cohabiting. Said otherwise, parents urge their children to make conventional choices in the marriage market. But parents have less leverage over young adult children who are living independently. So independent young adults should be able to make less conventional choices.

It's possible to see whether this prediction is true by looking at information from the census. In addition to asking many questions about household and family, the census asks people whether they are living in the same state as five years ago. Couples in which at least one person has moved from out of state should be less conventional because they are farther away from at least one set of parents. That's what Rosenfeld finds. In fact, the less conventional the type of partnership, the greater are the chances that at least one partner has moved out of state. The least movement can be found in conventional, opposite-sex, same-race marriages: one or both partners had moved away from his or her home state 48 percent of the time. By comparison, one or both partners had moved away in 59 percent of interracial partnerships, 68 percent of same-sex partnerships, and 74 percent of interracial same-sex partnerships. The rise of the independent life stage, Rosenfeld maintains, is an important reason why interracial and same-sex partnerships are more common.

Unconventional partnerships are more likely to end in a breakup than are conventional ones. Cohabiting relationships are much more likely to end in a breakup, even if the couple has married in the meantime, than are partnerships begun as marriages. Marriages in which the partners are of different religions also have higher breakup rates than do marriages of people with the same religion, as do marriages of couples with different levels of education. We don't have reliable statistics on whether interracial partnerships and same-sex partnerships have higher breakup rates, but it is reasonable to assume they do, since they don't have as much social support. The general point is that the movement of unmarried young adults out of the family home—a phenomenon that barely existed a half century ago—may be leading them to form partnerships that have a higher risk of breaking up. If so, the independent life stage makes it more likely that they will have a series of intimate partners during their adult lives.

Restlessness and Culture

Restlessness, by now, could be part of Americans' personalities, whether they move around or not. Just by living in the United States, some observers say, people absorb the M-Factor as a character trait. W. I. Thomas, a pioneering sociologist who was writing in the 1920s at the same time that Ogburn was writing about cultural lag, proposed this law: "If men define things as real, they are real in their consequences." If people think something is true, then they act as if it's true, and it becomes true—like a self-fulfilling prophecy. In the current context, if enough Americans think their fellow citizens are restless, and if they keep telling each other that—as they keep telling me—then they may act more restless themselves.

The story people tell is that starting with the disaffected Protestants who sailed to the New World, American culture has been formed by those who value mobility, independence, and self-reliance. American culture was also shaped by the availability of seemingly endless, abundant land. A century ago, Frederick Jackson Turner, perhaps the most famous of all American historians, argued that the existence of the frontier helped produce character traits such as "that restless nervous energy; that dominant individualism, working for good and evil." American mythology has long celebrated the pioneer, the frontiersman, and the rugged individualist. Even after the frontier closed, the search for the new may have shifted to work life and personal life in what Fisher called "a new, permanently unsettled rhythm of creation and destruction."

Restlessness, then, may be part of Americans' cultural tool kit—a way you understand the actions of others or justify the decisions you make. But does it lead to a greater movement from one intimate partnership to another? Do people imagine a more fulfilling life with a different partner the way they may imagine a more prosperous life in a different place? That's the gist of the free advice I keep getting—we're like that; we just can't stay in one relationship. Maybe, but I'm skeptical. Even if restlessness is a character trait, it should be weaker now than it was in the past. Americans don't move from job to job or place to place as much as they did a century ago. The endless, unsettled frontier filled up in the twentieth century. Yet the phenomenon of multiple intimate partnerships increased sharply after the 1950s. The great growth of cohabiting relationships and the doubling of the divorce rate since then can't be tied to an increase in restlessness because there wasn't one. Rather, these trends reflect the spread of an individualistic view of family life that emphasizes personal growth. What we're experiencing is the rise of the newer, self-development-oriented kind of individualism, whereas restlessness is about the older, self-reliant, move-to-the-frontier form. What we're seeing is "Go quest, young man," not "Go west, young man."

Moreover, the supposed cultural trait of restlessness does not address family life directly. Instead it speaks to geography and economy. It refers to people's tendencies to take the risks of moving to a new place in search of economic opportunity and to their desires to move up the occupational ladder. It explains their zeal for technological innovation and their belief that the outmoded must give way to the new. Almost nowhere in the literature about mobility, however, does one find a direct statement that adults should (or should not) change partners or that they should (or should not) live in a particular family form. In contrast, two cultural influences I have discussed at great length in this book, American religion and law, directly address how people should live their family lives. All religious groups have explicit moral codes in this regard. Some value the father-headed, married-couple family above other forms on biblical grounds. Others accept all family forms because they value diversity and equality. All have doctrines about divorce and positions on same-sex partnerships. Similarly, the large and growing body of statutory law and court decisions regulates the way that individuals can go about forming and breaking partnerships and having children, and government policies are crafted with the express purpose of influencing family life.

The lack of a direct link between restlessness and family life means that its potential effect would require an additional degree of separation to work. In step 1, because you are steeped in American culture, you become restless about where you live and what you do for a living. Then, in step 2, you generalize that feeling to your marriage and become dissatisfied with it. It's a more complex, tenuous link. As a result, I prefer to think about the M-Factor today less in cultural terms than in cost-benefit terms. I view mobility as less of a character trait and more of a rational decision to improve the conditions of one's life, particularly for people who live in a large country with varying climates and topography and differentials in wages and employment opportunities. Moving allows people to find housing that they prefer: less expensive, larger, quieter, and with more open space; or, alternatively, more cosmopolitan and close to cultural amenities. Moving is also a way for young adults to avoid parental supervision. All this may make Americans appear restless. And all this can affect family stability. But I'm not convinced that the concept of restlessness as a cultural trait adds much to our understanding.

Consequently, if there is an effect of mobility on family life, I think it probably lies not in its influence on the American personality but in the disruption of social ties that geographic mobility can cause. Moving can indeed make the problem of social integration worse. It may remove people from the scrutiny and support of friends and family. It may require the movers to actively develop friendship networks in their new area of residence. If they cannot do so, it's possible that they or their children may be at higher risk for family breakup, school problems, or other unwanted events. This is the clearest pathway, I suggest, between the M-Factor and having a series of intimate partnerships.

Blue-Collar Blues/White-Collar Weddings

Until now, I have written this book mostly as if all Americans were alike in how they live their family and personal lives. I have done this deliberately, because I think that there is a shared American culture that influences nearly everyone and makes American family patterns different from those of other nations. By now, most books by sociologists like me would have rigorously analyzed American families from the perspective of the holy trinity of social science: class, race, and gender. It's an article of faith among my colleagues that these three basic divisions in American society must be emphasized in all studies. I feel no need to do so just for the sake of appearances. I have talked, of course, about gender—the breadwinner-homemaker marriage, the recent movement of married women into the workforce—because it's so central to family life. I have said less, however, about divisions in American society according to income, education, race, and ethnicity.

But these divisions matter. Social inequality—the differences in standard of living and economic opportunity—is more pronounced in the United States than in other Western countries. The gap between high-income and low-income families is wider. Most other Western governments tax the wealthy more and provide more assistance to low- and moderate-income families. This is a major difference between the United States and other countries, and it matters for family life. Low- and moderate-income families in the United States have less protection against the vagaries of the labor market. And it is among low- and moderate-income Americans that we have seen the greatest increase in the number of people who have multiple partnerships.

We need to look carefully, then, at the economic shock waves that have washed over American workers during the past several decades and at their likely connections to changes in family life. The main story line is as follows: During the past half century, the globalization of production (the movement of jobs overseas) and the automation of production (the use of machines and computers to perform jobs humans used to do) have jointly hit Americans without college educations hard. Their family lives appear to have changed as a result: they are more likely to live with partners without marrying them, to have their partnerships and marriages break up, and to have children outside of marriage. At the other end of the social spectrum, college-educated Americans have, by and large, benefited from globalization and automation, and their family lives have not changed as much. They show the same trends but in moderation. The result has been a growing social class divide in family patterns. Although other Western nations have also experienced these economic tremors, the effects on families are greater here because low- and moderate-income families have less protection against the winds of economic change.

The forces of globalization and automation can seem obscure, but it is possible to see them plainly at work. For instance, as I was writing a draft of this chapter in Miami, on leave from Johns Hopkins, I saw a huge freighter with "China Shipping Lines" painted on its hull motoring slowly toward the harbor with hundreds of trailer-truck-size containers stacked on its broad-beamed deck. In 2005 the port of Miami imported 155,664 tons of alcoholic beverages, 138,105 tons of clothing and textiles, 126,403 tons of refrigerated fruits and vegetables, 76,021 tons of nonalcoholic beverages, 62,682 tons of lumber and wood, 62,556 tons of furniture and other wood products, 57,459 tons of iron, steel, and other metal products, and 42,304 tons of paper. A half century ago, most of these goods would have been brewed, woven, sewn, grown, harvested, milled, built, or processed in the United States. The factories and farms that used to make these goods employed millions of American workers, most of whom did not have college degrees.

Some of the steel used to be milled at the giant Sparrows Point plant a half hour's drive from my Baltimore home. In the 1950s Bethlehem Steel, the owner of the plant, employed thirty thousand workers. Very few of them had gone to college. Yet with hard work they were able to earn decent wages—not enough to make them rich but enough to buy a home, perhaps with help from a Veterans Administration loan, and to marry, have children, and buy a car and the latest home appliances. They were blue-collar aristocrats, like the hundreds of thousands of workers on the assembly lines at Ford and General Motors who enjoyed comfortable if modest standards of living. The 1950s were a time when a young man could graduate from high school confident that he could find a job. (Young women in the 1950s worked part-time, if at all.) If he was fortunate enough to work at a company such as Bethlehem Steel or GM, he would get health insurance, sick leave, a pension plan, and paid vacations as well. A married couple could raise a family on that. But starting in the 1960s, jobs such as these began to move overseas. Today, fewer than 2,500 people are employed at Sparrows Point. New technologies enabled entrepreneurs in other countries to build smaller, more efficient plants that made dinosaurs of Sparrows Point and the mile-long line of blast furnaces along the Allegheny River in Pittsburgh. In 2004 the United States imported thirty-six million tons of steel but exported only eight million tons. In 2007 Toyota surpassed GM as the largest motor vehicle manufacturer in the world. The blue-collar aristocrats are gone.

Advances in communications and transportation now allow firms to bypass American workers in ways you never would expect. Suppose you order a new battery for your laptop online from an American computer company. Your order may be sent immediately to a computer in a warehouse in China, which will display the part number on its screen and print a shipping label. A shelf clerk will find the right part and box it. Hours later, the day's orders will be driven to an airport, where a jet from a delivery service such as Federal Express will be waiting to fly your battery to the United States. Two days after you placed your order, it will appear at your doorstep with an American return address. You are none the wiser.

As for automation, I can hear it when I call Amtrak to make a train reservation, and a perky voice answers by saying, "Hi, I'm Julie, Amtrak's automated agent," and continues to give me options until I yell "operator" several times and am finally connected to a human being. Julie could not function without a voice recognition system that depends upon fast, powerful computers and complex software that did not exist until about a decade ago. Before then, sales agents, most of whom did not have college degrees, answered the phones. At the same time, jobs for the well-educated people who design systems such as Amtrak's are increasing. The U.S. Bureau of Labor Statistics predicted that the number of jobs in computer systems, design, and related services will increase by 38 percent between 2006 and 2016, and the vast majority of these jobs will require bachelor's or advanced degrees.

Computer-based automation and communication have reduced the number of what economists call routine jobs—those that require some skill but not a college education. Think of bookkeepers, secretaries, call center workers. These are the kinds of jobs that someone with a high school degree could do. Since about 1990 these routine jobs have been disappearing so fast that the wages of Americans who perform them have been edging closer to the wages of the least-educated workers, who hold manual jobs such as waiters, janitors, and gardeners. Manual jobs, which serve the personal needs of others, can't be automated easily; your basic professional still needs people to take his lunch order, clean his office, and cut his lawn. But manual jobs don't pay well. Put another way, the middle is dropping out of the American labor market. People with college degrees can usually find well-paying professional or managerial jobs (computer programmers, business executives), but what's left for everyone else is a dwindling demand for routine work and a steady demand for low-paying manual work. This is the twenty-first-century economic reality that young adults must contend with as they try to establish their own family lives.

Pathways to Adulthood

Caught in the disappearing middle of the American economy are people who ended their education after getting their high school degrees, or perhaps took some college courses but never obtained a college degree. The wages of men without college degrees have fallen since they peaked in the early 1970s, and the wages of women without college degrees have failed to grow. In fact, high school–educated young men today may be the first generation in memory to earn less than their fathers did. By 1996, the average thirty-year-old husband with a high school degree earned 20 percent less than a comparable man in 1979.

Although young men are no longer expected to be the sole earners for their families, they still are expected to be the main earners. If they don't have steady jobs with decent pay, they simply aren't attractive marriage partners. A young woman might live with such a man, but she would be reluctant to marry him. In the Toledo study of young adults, most of whom did not have college degrees, about three times as many women as men said that their cohabiting partners needed to do better in the job market before they would consider marrying them. Men felt this pressure. The authors write:

> For example, Henry, a 33-year-old information systems manager, reflects: "Had I been . . . in a financial position where I was able to take care of myself and a family, then it might have moved things along quicker." Jamal, 27 years old, says, "What would make me ready? Knowing that I could provide. . . ." Victor, a 27-year-old male, states that "the male's financially responsible for like, you know, the household, paying the bills."

Increasingly, young adults who feel these financial worries are cohabiting rather than marrying. Young men who are out of school and working, but whose incomes are unstable—maybe they're working part-time or at a series of short-term jobs—are more likely to start a cohabiting relationship than are either men with steady, full-time earnings or men with little or no earnings. Living together seems to be emerging as the lifestyle choice for couples in which the men are doing well enough that they can envision marrying someday but not so well that they feel they can marry now. If the jobs were still there, they might be milling steel at Sparrows Point or telling callers to Amtrak whether their trains are on time. An unemployed twenty-nine-year-old man who was living with his girlfriend said, regarding what he needed to marry her, "I don't really know 'cause the love is there . . . trust is there. Everything's there except the money." A roofer said, "We feel when we get financially, you know what I'm saying, stable, then we will be ready." A woman who ended her cohabiting relationship without marrying explained what the issue was: "Money means, um . . . stability. I don't want to struggle; if I'm in a partnership, then there's no more struggling, and income-wise we were still both struggling."

Moreover, because they live in an era when the stigma of childbearing outside of marriage has faded, some of these cohabiting couples are willing to have children together even though they're not willing to marry. Since about 1990, almost all the growth in the percentage of children born to unmarried women has, in reality, been to women who are in cohabiting relationships. Currently, about one out of six American children are now being born to cohabiting couples. Few observers seem to have noticed this development, probably because it is invisible to government agencies (who treat cohabiting mothers as if they were lone mothers).

Many cohabiting couples, it must be said, are capable of doing a very good job of raising children. In parts of Europe, such as Scandinavia and France, there are many long-term cohabiting parents who maintain families that are little different from lasting marriages. But that's unusual in the United States, where cohabiting relationships are fragile and break up more often than marriages. As a result, children born to parents who are cohabiting face a far higher likelihood that their parents will separate than children born to married parents: more than half of those born to cohabiting parents will see their parents separate by the time they are nine, compared to 25 percent of those born to married parents. Only a minority of cohabiting relationships last long enough to provide a child with a stable home environment until adolescence. Moreover, when a cohabiting relationship breaks up, the former partners tend to form new relationships within a few years, some of which, in turn, do not last very long. Starting in a cohabiting relationship, consequently, increases the chances that young parents will eventually have two or three partnerships.

Among young adults who did not complete high school, one-third who give birth are lone parents. (Another third are cohabiting.) Given the low wages for the jobs available to young people without college educations, fewer of them see the possibility of marriage happening anytime soon. Few among them have faith that if they were to wait to have children, the future would unfold according to the conventional script—that staying in school until high school graduation or taking some college courses would pay off, that good jobs could be found, and that many years into the future they would find suitable spouses. They look at their neighborhoods and social networks and see few signs that following the conventional path of marriage and then child-bearing works. Nor do they think that a woman needs to be married to have a child. That's clear from the attitudes of low-income women in Boston, Chicago, and San Antonio whom I and other researchers studied. Seventy-nine percent agreed with the statement "A woman should have children if she wants to, even if she is not married." And 71 percent agreed that "a woman does not need to be married before having a child."

What many of the least educated do instead is follow a different path. With good jobs in short supply, what comes to the fore is their desire to have children. I don't think the poor have a greater absolute desire to have children than the affluent, but relative to the other major rewards adult life holds—meaningful and well-paying jobs, a fulfilling and long-lasting marriage—raising children is the reward they know they can get. So it becomes the reward that they are unwilling to postpone. In their study of women in low-income neighborhoods in the Philadelphia area, Kathryn Edin and Maria Kefalas wrote:

> Unlike their wealthier sisters, who have the chance to go to college and embark on careers—attractive possibilities that provide strong motivation to put off having children—poor young women grab eagerly at the surest source of accomplishment within their reach: becoming a mother.

It's not the case that all young unmarried women who have children deliberately plan their births. Without doubt, many pregnancies are completely unplanned. But some young women in sexual relationships are not taking any action to prevent pregnancy. Having a child is an outcome they are ambivalent about. Perhaps they don't want it to happen immediately, but they want it to happen soon. Nearly half the mothers in Edin and Kefalas's study said their pregnancies were neither fully planned nor fully unplanned, but rather somewhere in between.

Women in low-income neighborhoods perceive little cost to this strategy. For instance, they don't think having children early will hurt their chances of marrying later and they don't think it's embarrassing. These opinions reflect a cultural sea change since the mid-twentieth century, when having what was called an "illegitimate" child was shameful. Moreover, 44 percent in our study agreed that "it is not important for a woman to get married," a statement that would have seemed ludicrous to most poor women, as well as to affluent women, several decades ago. The set of circumstances many less-educated women see today makes postponing childbearing until marriage seem risky. Marriage is still valued symbolically—it is still a status that one very much wishes to attain someday. But you don't have to wait to have children until you attain it.

Among the college-educated, the picture is different. They are the winners in our globalized and automated economy: the managers who import the steel bound for the port of Miami, the engineers and programmers who give Julie her juice. Their skills—their ability to do analytic, abstract tasks such as designing new products or coordinating the activities of work groups—are in demand, and their earnings are growing faster than the earnings of people with less education. For them, the conventional life course still seems to provide its promised rewards. Most are able to find spouses first and to have children afterward, often several years after they marry. Their investments in education by and large yield successful careers—sometimes, for women, after a period of withdrawing from the paid workforce to raise young children. Marriage still retains practical advantages for them, in addition to its symbolic value. Marriage offers more protection than cohabitation to a woman who has concentrated on raising children, because if the couple breaks up, the wife can use the divorce laws to ask the court for a fair distribution of assets and income. Also, the higher level of enforceable trust in marriages (the lesser likelihood that either spouse will back out) reduces the risk of making long-term purchases together, such as houses, which require large outlays of cash and recoup their value only after many years of use.

Over the past few decades, the family lives of the college-educated have changed much less than among the people with less education. Consider the percentage of women who become lone mothers at some point during their mid-twenties to mid-thirties. It has doubled since 1965 for women with low to moderate levels of education. But it hardly changed among the well-educated: no change for well-educated white women since 1965 and no change since 1980 for well-educated African American women. What we are seeing is the emergence of two different ways of shooting the rapids of the transition to adulthood—the process of completing one's education, developing a career, having children, and finding a lasting, intimate partnership. Among the college-educated, we see a more orderly, predictable sequence of events, one that has fewer changes of partners. They typically finish college first and then take jobs. They may work for several years, investing in their careers, before they marry; the more education a woman has, the older she tends to be when she marries. They may live with a partner before marrying—nearly half of college-educated women under forty-five have been in a cohabiting relationship. But they don't have their first child until after they marry: nine out of ten college-educated women who give birth are married. It's waiting until they are married to have children that most distinguishes the transition to adulthood for the college-educated.

The sequence employed by the college-educated offers benefits: time to finish an advanced degree and start a career, a second parent to help raise the children, and a greater accumulation of assets before the children arrive. But it requires postponing childbearing into the mid- to late twenties, thirties, or even early forties. It is not an attractive strategy for people who have few assets and who do not see many successful models of marriage around them. The strategy that many young adults in the bottom third of the educational distribution, and some in the middle third, use is to have children earlier, sometimes in a cohabiting relationship, sometimes as a lone parent. Among high school–educated women, only six out of ten wait until after marriage to have their first child; among high school dropouts, only three or four out of ten wait. This path to adulthood is more disorderly. They may live with a partner while taking courses at a community college or at a technical school; they may have a child while still in school; they may have children with more than one partner; and they may not marry until five, ten, or fifteen years after they start to have children, if they marry at all.

Under current circumstances, then, the college-educated top third of the educational distribution, a group sometimes labeled the "middle class" or "upper middle class," tends to follow the conventional strategy in which you have children after marrying. In contrast, those who haven't completed high school tend to have children as lone parents or in cohabiting unions. Those who stopped their schooling after graduating from high school or who took a few college courses seem to be forging a middle ground, in which childbearing occurs in a mixture of settings. These young adults in the middle, neither poor nor prosperous, are developing family patterns that fit neither the image of the low-income mother living with her own mother and other kin nor the image of the married couple who postpone childbearing until every other step in the transition to adulthood has been completed.

The marriages that do form among the less-educated are precarious. Over the past two or three decades, the divorce rate has fallen for women with college educations while remaining steady or rising for women without college degrees. As a result, large differences now exist in the risk of divorce. According to one estimate, 34 percent of the first marriages of women without high school degrees will end in divorce or separation within five years—a very high breakup rate for just five years of marriage. The breakup rates are still substantial for the marriages of people in the middle: 23 percent for those who ended their education after high school, and 26 percent for those who took some college courses but don't have a degree. Among women with college degrees, on the other hand, just 13 percent will end in divorce or separation within five years. Marriages are much more stable among the college-educated than among the less-educated.

The tensions in the marriages of the non-college-educated reflect, in part, the declining job prospects that husbands face. A woman who had a job as a hotel desk clerk told Lillian B. Rubin six months after her husband lost his job as a welder:

We did okay for a while, but the longer it lasts, the harder it gets. . . .
I tell him maybe he has to get in a different line of work because maybe
they don't need so many welders anymore. But he just gets mad and tells
me I don't know what I'm talking about.

Her husband later told Rubin:

I can't go out and get one of those damn flunky jobs like my wife wants
me to. I've been working all my life, making a decent living, too, and I
got pride in what I do. I try to tell her, but she doesn't listen.

In fact, working-class couples, where the husband had a blue-collar
job and both spouses had a high school degree but no college degree,
reported the most stressed, least happy marriages of any group in a
recent national survey—worse than disadvantaged couples and much
worse than middle-class couples. The working-class wives said they
had taken jobs because the families needed the money, not to develop
careers, and many of them wanted to work fewer hours or not at all.
Many thought that the amount of housework and child care they did
was unfair compared to how much their husbands did. Husbands, for
their part, complained that their wives came home from work irritable
and tense and that their jobs interfered with the life of the family. Both
wives and husbands were more likely to say that they had problems in
their marriage because one of them got angry easily, was critical or
moody, or wouldn't talk to the other one. They were also more likely
to say that the thought of getting a divorce or separation had crossed
their minds or that they had discussed the idea with family members or
close friends.

Race and Marriage

The larger story for African Americans is a sharp decline in marriage
that is far greater than among other groups. The reasons for that
decline, and its implications for black families, have been a source of
debate and controversy. Some see the increase in lone-parent families

as the main cause of continuing poverty. Others claim that it is not the cause but rather the effect of poverty—the response to an increasingly unfavorable job market for workers without much education. This much we know for sure: in the 1950s, nearly nine out of ten African American women married at some point in their lives, but since then, their chances of marrying have dropped sharply. At current rates, only about two out of three black women will marry during their lifetimes. And their marriages are very fragile: 70 percent are projected to end in divorce or separation, a much higher percentage than among whites (47 percent). In sum, fewer African Americans marry, and those who do are very likely to have their marriages break up.

The decline of marriage among African Americans seems to have both economic and cultural roots. Economically, globalization and automation have sharply reduced the earnings prospects of African Americans without college educations—and African American young adults are only half as likely to have college degrees as are whites. It's more difficult today for a black man to earn the steady income that is still a requirement for marriage. The job market, however, isn't the whole story: Hispanic young adults are even less likely to have college degrees, and yet their marriage rates are higher. The rest of the story is the lesser role of marriage in African American culture and history. We've seen, for instance, how the black church places less emphasis on marriage than do the predominantly white mainline and conservative Protestant churches. To be sure, Americans of African descent have always married. Even when legal marriage was not allowed under slavery, many slaves married informally. In fact, until about 1950, African Americans tended to marry at younger ages than whites. Marriage is certainly part of African American family life. But compared to European American culture, the marriage-based family has always been less important compared to a larger family that includes grandparents, sisters and brothers, aunts, uncles, and cousins—what sociologists call the extended family. Within that extended family, ties among women—mothers, grandmothers, aunts, and sisters—have been most important for keeping daily family life going.

African Americans have reacted to the problems of the job market by increasingly relying on these woman-centered extended families rather than the family of husband, wife, and children. In these extended families, which may involve people in more than one household, female kin hold most of the authority over children and provide most of the supervision. Indeed, in some neighborhoods where it's common for teenagers to have children, grandmothers (who may only be in their late thirties or forties) are often the ones who actually raise the children. Although much has been written about the supposed weaknesses of extended families among African Americans, they may have an advantage in providing stable care to children in an era when parents go through many partners. If your grandmother is raising you, or even if she's only living in your household or down the block and helping out, she becomes a source of stability in your life. Black grandparents are much more likely than white grandparents to take on parentlike roles such as disciplining their grandchildren. One black grandmother described her role to Frank Furstenberg and me:

> I was always named "sergeant"—"Here comes the sergeant." I loved them. I *did* for them, and gave to them, so that they had an education, so that they had a trade. I went to school regularly to check on them; they didn't know I was coming.

Very few white grandparents would go to their grandchildren's school without telling them. If you have this type of presence in your life growing up, your mother's pursuit of intimate partners may take on less significance, and those partners' comings and goings may affect you less.

Kinship among whites, in contrast, centers on the marriage-based family of husband, wife, and children. Its strengths and weaknesses are the opposite of the woman-centered extended families of many African Americans. The marriage-based family tries to be self-sufficient. In practice, many young married couples with children receive occasional assistance from their parents. But married couples receive less help from other kin such as siblings, aunts, uncles, or cousins. Assistance tends to flow up or down the generations, yielding the image of a tall tree (parents and children and their children) with short branches (few sisters and brothers, aunts and uncles), which a sociologist once called the "beanpole family." In this marriage-centered form of kinship, assets or savings are passed from parents to children, rather than being spread through a broader network of kin.

A style of family life that relies so heavily on marriage, however, is a high-payoff, high-risk strategy in an era when many marriages end in divorce. The payoff for adults is that if their marriages remain intact, they can accumulate assets. Having a spouse may also help a person's mental and physical health—your spouse may be more likely than others to nag you to make an appointment for your annual physical exam. The payoff for children is having two parents to provide stable care and to earn enough money to fund everything from dance lessons to a college education. The risk for an adult woman occurs if she devotes so much time to child care that she works for pay only part-time or not at all for many years. If her husband later decides to leave the marriage, she may have a difficult time reentering the job market. (This is one reason why many wives work outside the home: they are hedging their bets.) The risk for children is that if the marriage ends, they may have no other family members to give them a sense of continuity and stability—white grandparents are more likely to live in Sun City and less likely to live down the block. So the effects of parents and partners moving in and out of their household may be greater.

Hispanics have substantially higher rates of marriage than do African Americans—so much higher, in fact, as to be puzzling to experts. Even though Hispanics as a group are economically disadvantaged compared to whites (and therefore should delay marriage), they tend to marry at younger ages than whites. Moreover, Hispanic marriages and cohabiting relationships are somewhat less likely to break up in the first five years than are white marriages and cohabiting relationships. But Hispanics are a diverse ethnic group, and it is mainly among the Mexican-origin population, who constitute about two-thirds of all Hispanics, that marriage occurs more quickly. Cuban Americans also have relatively high levels of marriage, but Puerto Ricans are similar to whites.

Some observers have suggested that Mexican Americans may place a high value on marriage. Perhaps they do, but what researchers have discovered is that much of the difference in marriage is due to recent immigrants. Mexican Americans born in Mexico have very high levels of marriage, but those born in the United States aren't much different from American-born whites. Moreover, it's common for Mexican immigrants to marry in Mexico and then come to the United States alone. Under the family reunification policies of the Citizenship and Immigration Services Agency (formerly the Immigration and Naturalization Service), a person still in Mexico who is married to a legal immigrant in the United States has a better chance of being allowed to immigrate. Continued immigration, then, is the main solution to the puzzle of why Hispanics seem more attached to marriage than their modest economic circumstances would imply. The children of immigrants tend to go about their family lives in ways that are more similar to other native-born Americans.

Given their lower levels of education, you might expect Hispanic and African American women to live with more partners during their lives than whites, but instead they live with fewer partners. Nationally, 16 percent of white women in their late thirties or early forties report that they have lived with three or more partners, compared to just 9 percent of Hispanics and African Americans. Among Hispanics, the lower figure results from the relatively large number of women who have had exactly one partnership (cohabiting or marital). Perhaps this is a reflection of the Catholic religious faith of most Hispanics, with its opposition to divorce and remarriage. Among African Americans, however, the lower percentage is driven by the greater number of women who reported never having had a live-in partner at all (14 percent, versus 4 percent for Hispanics and whites). This lifetime lack of partnerships may reflect the lower number of suitable spouses—or, as William Julius Wilson has called them, "marriageable men"—due to factors such as chronic unemployment, imprisonment, and higher mortality. The number of black women who are in the marriage market exceeds the number of marriageable black men in nearly every urban area.

The greatest amount of partnership turnover seems to be occurring among young adults whose incomes place them precariously above the poor—those who have high school degrees but no bachelor's degree. A majority of them are white. They're still trying to attain a middle-class lifestyle, including the two-parent family that's part of it. They try out more partnerships, end more partnerships, and try again. As a result, they have more partners during the years when they are raising children than do the poor or the wealthy. African American women, to be sure, have more children without partners. But they don't have as much movement subsequently of partners in and out of the home. Hispanics have more partnerships than African Americans but fewer breakups. So if you want a mental image of the typical woman who has several intimate partners while raising children, picture a white woman with a high school education.

What's in Common

It's easy, however, to exaggerate the differences in American family life across educational, racial, and ethnic lines. Americans have much in common, especially if you are looking at them from across the Atlantic Ocean, where marriage is, in general, less highly valued. Nearly all Americans have a similar view of marriage as the capstone experience of young adulthood. People tend to wait to marry until the other steps in the transition are accomplished, although the college-educated refrain from having children until they are married. For all, weddings have become public displays of the ability to assemble the parts necessary to build a marriage, such as finding steady employment, determining that you can live with your partner harmoniously, gaining confidence in his or her fidelity, and amassing enough money for a nice ceremony and reception. Everyone wants festive rather than "downtown" weddings to celebrate these achievements.

From the poorest to the most affluent, young adults seek companionship, emotional satisfaction, and self-development through marriage. African Americans, Hispanics, and whites all rate highly the emotional benefits of marriage. Money may be more important for the less affluent in deciding when to marry, but a relationship that promises an adequate income without personal fulfillment rarely leads to marriage. Consider Amber, a twenty-two-year-old white woman in San

Antonio. Amber was living with a man she was engaged to and already had a child with, but she said she was not ready to marry him:

> But I'm not ready to do that yet. I told him, we're not financially ready yet. He knows that. I told him by the end of this year, maybe. I told him that last year. Plus, we both need to learn to control our tempers, you could say. He doesn't understand that bills and kids and [our relationship] come first, not [his] going out and getting new clothes or [his] doing this and that. It's the kids, then us. He gets paid good, about five hundred dollars a week. How hard is it to give me money and help with the bills?

In this marriage-as-capstone story, Amber listed requirements for marriage that differ little from what better-off women would demand. She needed to be on sound financial footing before she would marry. But she also needed to be assured that her fiancé would treat her well. He must put his relationship with his wife ahead of running with his single male friends—a way of saying that a husband must place a priority on providing companionship and intimacy to his wife and must be sexually faithful. And both partners have to learn to control their tempers—a vague reference to the possibility that physical abuse exists in the relationship.

For Americans of Latin American descent, the major division in married life involves the norms of the old country versus the norms of the United States. In the three-city study, we observed some women who had been physically abused by their partners but who said they would stay with them despite the abuse. All were recent Mexican immigrants. For example, Guadalupe, who was twenty-seven years old when we first met her, married José when she was fifteen years old. On the surface, the couple led a fairly ordinary life: they had three children, José had a fairly stable low-paying job as a mechanic, and they lived in a small, well-kept house that they rented from one of their relatives. Guadalupe, however, made sure to schedule her interviews during the day, when José was not home. She flinched every time the phone rang. She often arranged to meet the ethnographer in places other than her home. After a year of interviews, one afternoon she disclosed to the ethnographer that José had physically abused her for many years and that her father had sexually abused her when she was a child. She mentioned that she wanted to leave José but could not because she is Catholic, she worried about her children, and her mother would not allow it. The next day, her mother called the ethnographer and said, "You are putting things in my daughter's head. You are making trouble for her and José. Leave her alone. She will stay with José. Do not call again." We did not observe any similar situations among second- or third-generation immigrants, nor among the poor black or white families we studied. First-generation Mexican immigrant women may also be more likely to tolerate infidelity than their daughters and granddaughters.

Many women with modest educations talk about love and companionship in terms little different from the middle-class romantic ideal. When they talked about what's important in a marriage, a quarter of the women in the Toledo study mentioned just financial issues (jobs, savings, house) and a quarter mentioned just relationship issues (needing more time in the relationship, the quality of the relationship, maturity, substance abuse, violence). But half mentioned both types of issues. Most commonly, then, young adults with low or moderate incomes will marry only when they are reasonably secure financially *and* have a partner with whom they can share love and companionship and from whom they can expect fair treatment and no abuse. Said otherwise, it's necessary for a couple to have their finances in order, but it's not sufficient, even among the poor. Edin and Kefalas, the authors of the Philadelphia-area study, concluded:

> The most fundamental truth these stories reveal is that the meaning of marriage has changed. It is no longer primarily about childbearing and childrearing. Now, marriage is primarily about adult fulfillment, it is something poor women do for themselves, and their dreams about marriage are a guilty pleasure compared to the hard task of raising a family.

This shift among poor women is part of a societywide trend toward a style of marriage in which personal emotional rewards are important.

The increasing importance of personal fulfillment as the basis for marital success has occurred across the board in the United States, among the poor as well as the affluent.

We can draw a similar lesson from a study in which researchers went to the maternity wards of hospitals in twenty cities and interviewed unmarried mothers within forty-eight hours of when they gave birth. They also interviewed fathers if they were present or could be found. Four out of five unmarried mothers were either living with or still romantically involved with the fathers at the time of the birth. Eager to learn which couples would marry and which would not, the researchers reinterviewed the mothers a year later. They found that the father's income during the year made a big difference: if fathers had earned $25,000 or more, the probability of marriage doubled. In addition, however, the answers that the mothers and fathers had given to questions about emotional support, asked just after the births, also strongly predicted being married a year later. Mothers and fathers were more likely to marry if they had said that their partner "is fair and willing to compromise when [they] have a disagreement," "expresses affection and love," "encourages or helps [him/her] do things that are important toward [him/her]," and does not criticize or insult the partner. In other words, mothers and fathers who felt that they were in the kind of relationship that provided emotional support (expressing affection and love) and opportunities for personal growth (i.e., encouragement to do things that are important to him or her) and had more egalitarian relationships (fair and willing to compromise) were more likely to marry. Even these urban couples, most of them with modest educations, were attracted to relationships that offered the rewards of the individualized marriage.

Or consider what happened when several thousand adults were asked to choose between pairs of statements about relationships. The interviewer said, "Next, we have some questions about the kind of relationship you would like with a spouse or partner. It doesn't matter whether you are now married or living with someone. For each pair of items on the card, which type of relationship would you prefer?" One pair of statements contrasted a more companionate relationship with a more distant relationship: "A relationship where the man and woman do most things in their social life together" versus "A relationship where the man and woman do separate things that interest them." People with less education were a bit *more* likely to say they preferred the companionate form: 80 percent of those who had not attended college chose this form versus 71 percent of those who had.

In short, the poor and near-poor have the same standards for marriage as the more educated and affluent. Too often we view the poor as if they have a different set of values than other Americans do. The classic example was anthropologist Oscar Lewis's description of a self-reproducing "culture of poverty" among the poor Puerto Rican families he studied in New York and on the island. By the time they were six or seven, Lewis claimed, individuals had absorbed a set of values that made them more "present-oriented" than "future-oriented"; that is, they lacked the middle-class virtue of being able to postpone gratification. Transposed to marriage, the culture of poverty would imply that poor people who are interested in marrying don't care about waiting until they are in a secure financial situation; rather, they care only about having enough money for the present—which, as we have seen, is not true. It would also suggest that they don't care about finding a partner with whom they can be compatible over a lifetime but rather prefer someone who is enjoyable to be with now. That also isn't true. When it comes to marriage, the poor and the near-poor are not mired in a culture of poverty; they are operating in the same twenty-first-century culture as the middle class.

Then why do college graduates marry more than people with less education? Because they get more material benefits from marriage. Those bus advertisements in Baltimore promise the low-income young adults to whom they are targeted that "marriage works," but it works better for the college-educated than it does for them. The college-educated can pool two decent incomes from occupations that have withstood, or even gained from, the restructuring of the American economy. Young adults on the college track seem to understand this: they are increasingly marrying one another rather then someone without a college degree. Decades ago, religion was a more important factor in who married whom: a Catholic college graduate was more likely to marry a Catholic high school graduate than to marry a college-educated Protestant. Now it's the other way around. Schooling has become the great sorting machine of the marriage market, and college graduates are separating themselves from the rest of the population. The winners in the new economy are marrying each other and consolidating their gains.

At the other extreme of the marriage market, people without high school degrees are separating themselves as well; fewer of them are marrying up than in the past, probably because they are not attractive to those with more education. They face uncertain economic prospects, largely in occupations that offer lower wages and fewer fringe benefits than before the restructuring of the economy. Moreover, individuals who are receiving social welfare benefits such as Temporary Assistance for Needy Families, or TANF, as the program most people think of as "welfare" is now called, food stamps, the EITC, or Medicaid may lose all or part of these benefits if they marry rather than cohabit. With fewer assets, lower-income couples also benefit less from the legal protections that marriage offers. When and if they marry, they face high odds of failure: a third of married people without high school degrees divorce or separate within five years, and an estimated 60 percent will eventually end their marriages in divorce.

In between are people with high school degrees. They are still trying to raise children as couples, still shooting for the American dream of marriage, kids, good jobs, and a home. Yet they are increasingly frustrated by the job market. Here you may find young men with stopgap jobs, the kind of short-term work with little stability and a limited future that may lead people to live together rather than marry. Here, too, money is important in determining which couples eventually marry, but it takes more than money for a couple to agree to marry.

As is usual in the United States, questions of class overlap with questions of race and ethnicity. African Americans have a cultural model of family life in which marriage is less prominent compared to ties to extended kin. Over the past several decades, they have responded to changing circumstances by withdrawing from marriage more than other groups have. A much higher percentage of births among African Americans occur to lone mothers. Marriage, if it occurs, comes later in life and is extraordinarily fragile. Hispanics come from a Catholic-influenced cultural tradition where marriage is central to childbearing and partnership. Immigrants from Mexico still display that centrality by marrying earlier and having lower divorce rates than most other Americans. But their children, raised in the United States, are similar to other native-born Americans in how they live their family and personal lives.

Despite these differences, all the major social groups in the United States have high levels of moving from partner to partner compared to Western Europeans. Even the most stable groups, such as the college-educated, go through partners at rates that exceed the rates in most other Western countries. By American standards, well-educated women have relatively fewer partnerships than other women, but by international standards they still have quite a few. While comparisons among people from different social classes or ethnic groups may grab the attention of Americans, the sheer speed at which the entire society goes through partnerships stands out to people living anywhere else.

8

Slow Down

Some of the Western Europeans I talk to about American family life are puzzled by the strength of the American attachment to marriage. In particular, what seems strange to them is our moral rhetoric about marriage, including the language of the administration of George W. Bush, the president who spoke of the "cultural, religious, and natural roots" of marriage and who proposed to protect its "sanctity" through a constitutional amendment. President Bush and his supporters did not invent this rhetoric; rather, they drew upon a long tradition of moralistic statements about marriage that peaked in the late nineteenth and early twentieth centuries. Think of Supreme Court justice Stephen Field in 1888 stating that marriage has "more to do with the morals and civilization of a people than any other institution," or President Theodore Roosevelt in 1905 decrying the effects of liberal divorce laws on the "sanctity of the marriage relation." Through most of American history, marriage was viewed in moral terms—specifically, Christian moral terms—and was seen as a fundamental building block of civil society. It is only in the twentieth century that such rhetoric faded. It was superseded in politics and legal affairs by morally neutral social scientific statements about the benefits of marriage and the costs of its decline. That's why the Moynihan Report linked the growth of single-parent families not to moral decline but rather to continued poverty and welfare dependency. That's why the key witnesses in civil suits about same-sex marriage have not been religious leaders but rather social scientists, who testify about the effects of same-sex parenthood on children's behavior.

It's possible that the moral rhetoric in support of marriage will once again fade from politics. But the American tradition of praising marriage will still exist. For one thing, the government will be handing out hundreds of millions of dollars for marriage promotion activities until at least 2010. The supporters of same-sex marriage will continue to press their case while their opponents seek to limit marriage to hetero-sexuals, and both sides will be praising their own visions of marriage. In addition, the loose-knit marriage movement of scholars, clinicians, and religious leaders will continue their public advocacy. Moreover, marriage will continue to be extolled in the pulpits and in the scrip-tures of the well-attended American churches, as it has been since colonial times. The promarriage message, in sum, is deeply embedded in American culture and history. The way it is expressed has varied over time, but it is still a stronger cultural force in the United States than in most other developed countries.

Which leads to another puzzle for foreign observers: If the United States is such a religious nation with so strong an attachment to mar-riage, why is there so much divorce? Americans are much quicker to abandon their marriages and cohabiting unions than are other West-erners. The answer is that divorce has long been part of the individual-istic side of American culture. Well before it was legal in Britain or France (except for few years during the French Revolution), divorce was legally available in America. The early settlers brought a reformed Protestantism that allowed divorce for adultery or desertion. While it has never endorsed divorce, American religion has long had an individ-ualistic component. It has emphasized the individual's direct relation-ship to God, personal faith rather than theology, and the expression of feelings. In the second half of the twentieth century, it incorporated the cultural theme of self-development: individuals were encouraged to search for a personally satisfying brand of spirituality, a quest that sometimes led them to seek self-development in their family lives as well. Religion taught that although divorce was unfortunate, churches would minister to divorced people and help them put their lives back in order.

The mixture of these cultural themes of marriage and individual-ism explains the American paradox of high rates of both marriage and divorce—and, by extension, the greater likelihood of having two, three, or more intimate partners, marital or cohabiting, during one's lifetime. What's more, Americans seem to carry both cultural models in their heads. It's not as though half of Americans value marriage and the other half are individualistic. Although observers sometimes try to divide the population into traditional conservatives and postmodern liberals, those labels are inaccurate, except perhaps at the extremes. When sociologist Alan Wolfe conducted interviews to learn whether middle-class Americans could be divided into "traditionalists" and "modernists" in their moral beliefs, he concluded that they could not. Rather, he found that many people seemed to hold both views at once, inconsistent as that may seem: "The divisions over the family do not take place between camps of people; instead, they take place within most individuals . . . middle-class Americans believe in both the traditional and the modern version of the family simultaneously."

The outcome is a society in which marriage is still valued, but an unhappy married couple is almost expected to divorce. It's a society in which cohabiting couples are expected to marry if they are happy and to break up if they are not. In short, it's a society in which there is a great deal of turnover in people's intimate partnerships.

The percentage of children experiencing three or more mother's partners today in the United States is probably higher than in any Western country at any time in the past several centuries. To be sure, it was common in the past for children to lose a parent, because many women died in childbirth and mothers and fathers commonly succumbed to disease. (In fact, as recently as 1900, an American child had a 25 percent chance that at least one of his or her parents would die before the child reached age fifteen.) During the twentieth century, death rates dropped sharply, but divorce and childbearing outside of marriage increased even faster. We know that a higher percentage of children live in lone-parent families today than a century ago. Moreover, cohabiting unions, with their quick turnover, did not become widespread until the 1970s. These newer sources of instability probably have more than compensated for the decline in parental deaths. In any case, what we see today is certainly the highest level of *voluntary* partnership turnover ever.

The Consequences of Continual Choice

In order to understand why this movement toward multiple partnerships has occurred, we need to step back and answer the larger question I posed at the beginning of this book: How can we make sense of the profound changes that have occurred in many facets of American family life during the last half century? Fundamentally, I believe, what has happened is that marriage and family life have become matters of personal choice to an extent that would have astounded Americans in the 1950s. The idea that you could choose to have a long-term sexual relationship outside of marriage and still be a respectable citizen would have seemed incredible. That people could skip from one live-in relationship to another, not because their partners were abusive or unfaithful but merely because that's what they wanted, would have horrified many people. That most married women would choose to work for wages would have seemed like an abandonment of home and children. That a woman could take a pill that would prevent her from becoming pregnant—and that hundreds of millions would choose to do so—would have seemed like science fiction.

Personal choice has become more important for several reasons. The first is a broad shift toward self-development, not just in family life but throughout American culture. Your task as an adult today is to develop your sense of self by making choices that let you grow and change as a person. A half century ago there were far fewer choices to make. You might take a job in the same factory where your father worked rather than choosing your own career; you had no choice but to marry if you wanted an intimate partner and children; and you faced considerable scorn and shame if you ended the marriage merely because it was unsatisfying. Today, your father's factory has moved to China, the paths to intimate partnerships are manifold, and your friends will understand and even sympathize if you tell them you're getting a divorce because your marriage isn't providing you with the personal growth you need.

The second cause is the movement of married women into the

workforce—a momentous change that has occurred in just the past half century. Some wives, especially those from blue-collar families, work for wages in order to stay ahead of the bill collectors. Others, particularly the college-educated, also work because of the satisfaction they get from their careers. In either case, it makes more sense today for women to postpone marriage—possibly while living with a partner—until they are confident they have established themselves in the labor market. Their work skills and job experience increase the choices they can make. Should they choose not to marry or to end a marriage, they are better able to support themselves than were women in the past.

The third cause is the flip side of the second: the sharp decline in the economic fortunes of young men without college educations. It has occurred over the past several decades as globalization and automation have reduced the number of routine jobs that used to be seen as men's work. As a result, high school–educated young men today may be the first generation of American wage earners to make less money than their fathers did. They are well aware of this depressing development, as are the young women they could marry. Increasingly, they are choosing cohabiting relationships until they feel financially secure enough to marry. And when they do marry, the tensions of tight family finances contribute to a very high rate of divorce.

The final cause is the technological breakthrough of the birth control pill, along with the IUD, injectables, implants, and other medical methods of contraception. We tend to take the pill, which was introduced in the early 1960s, for granted. We forget how radically it transformed intimate life. As late as the 1950s, sex, love, and marriage were bound together, because any young woman who had sex regularly had a high risk of getting pregnant and any couple in which the woman got pregnant was under heavy pressure to have a so-called shotgun wedding. Granted, condoms had long existed, and men had long practiced withdrawal, but these methods were unreliable for couples in long-term relationships. The pill removed the fear of pregnancy from sexual relationships for the first time in human history. It enabled couples to have loving, sexual relationships outside of marriage and even to have sexual relationships outside of love. The legalization of abortion nationwide following the 1973 *Roe v. Wade* decision further limited the risk of unwanted pregnancy. Without modern contraception and access to abortion, the growth of childless cohabiting relationships would have been much slower.

To some degree, all Western countries have experienced these cultural, economic, and technological changes, but they have been particularly pronounced in the United States. The trend toward greater personal choice resonates with the chords of American culture. Americans highly value striking out on their own and being responsible for their actions—the essence of the older, utilitarian individualism that can be traced back to Franklin and Emerson. Doing so means making choices in where and how you will live. Think of the story we tell ourselves about the M-Factor: Americans are always on the go, choosing to move up or choosing to move out. In addition, Americans value the quest for personal fulfillment—the core of the newer, expressive individualism. This quest can be seen in a vigorous religious life that, unnoticed by many, has embraced the spirituality of seeking. Today you must actively choose your faith, your church, and your beliefs, and if you aren't satisfied, you may leave and choose again. Forty-four percent of Americans have changed their religious affiliation from the religion in which they were raised (for example, from Catholic to Protestant or from Lutheran to Pentecostal). This quest for spiritual fulfillment reinforces the quest for personal fulfillment in one's family life. The seeker church and the seeker marriage both allow those whose preferences change to go elsewhere.

In addition, globalization and automation may have had greater effects on workers without college degrees in the United States than elsewhere. It's true that factory jobs have disappeared throughout the Western world. But other Western countries have more generous government benefits for low- and moderate-income families. As a result, less-educated workers and their families are better cushioned from the effects of the changing economy. In contrast, American social policy leaves workers at the mercy of the labor market to a greater extent. Both men and women are encouraged to depend on their jobs, rather than government, to make ends meet. The so-called welfare reform of the 1990s, for example, limited the number of years that a poor mother could receive cash assistance; she was told she had to work. Most Western nations place a floor under low-income families that is higher than in the United States.

Not surprisingly, given their shakier financial situations, less-educated individuals have more family transitions than do the better-educated. In fact, people with a history of multiple partners can be found in the greatest numbers among what's often called the "working class," a rough label that tells us little about what their lives are like. They are also called "blue-collar," stemming from an era when chambray-shirted men by the millions operated the machinery of America's manufactories while their wives remained at home. I think it's best to define this group by their education, because that's what seems to make the most difference in today's economy. Most of them have graduated from high school, which sets them apart from the least-educated. Many have taken courses at local colleges, and some even have two-year associate of arts degrees, but, crucially, they lack the four-year college degree that seems to be the ticket of entry into the vibrant sector of the American economy. A majority of them are white.

These individuals are still trying to live the American dream: they want a successful marriage and a comfortable lifestyle. But the foundation of their world is cracking as the work they used to do disappears into circuit boards and overseas assembly lines. They remember better times growing up; they may even have experienced better times themselves as adults. As the unemployed welder told Lillian Rubin: "I'm the only one in my whole family who was doing all right; I even helped my son go to college. I was proud of that; we all were. Now what do I do? It's like I have to go back to where I started. How can you do that at my age?" What's left are low-paying service jobs he and others like him consider beneath their dignity. The welder said, "Even she [his wife] doesn't think I should go sling hamburgers at McDonald's for some goddamn minimum wage."

A majority of high school–educated Americans are married when they have children. Their marriages, however, are fragile: nearly a quarter fail within five years. Moreover, high school–educated young adults are increasingly cohabiting rather than marrying while having a first child, due in part to the economic insecurity they face. The biggest increase in childbearing outside of marriage in recent years has come from cohabiting couples in their twenties, many with high school educations. Their cohabiting relationships are even more fragile than their marriages. Because so many mothers are partnered (either married or cohabiting) when they have children, because their partnerships break up at high rates, and because many who end one partnership find another, high school–educated adults are more likely to have a series of partners than are either less- or more-educated Americans.

Regardless of their educational level, Americans face a situation in which lifestyle choices, which were limited and optional a half century ago, are now mandatory: you *must* choose, again and again. The result is an ongoing self-appraisal of how your personal life is going, like having a continual readout of your emotional heart rate. Moreover, as bonds of neighborhood and community weaken, people's intimate relationships have become the main setting in which they develop a sense of meaning and identity. All of these factors create a heightened sensitivity to problems that arise in intimate relationships, and since some problems occur in almost every relationship, there often comes a time when the readout will plunge. When that occurs, people tend to question their relationships.

Combine this individualistic assessment of how one's marriage or cohabiting relationship is going with the distinctive American penchant for marriage, and the conditions are set for people to have multiple partnerships. Americans place a higher value on being married than do people in many other Western countries. That's apparent from the American battle over same-sex marriage, which the British and French avoided by passing national domestic partnership laws. In November 2008, California voters approved a ballot initiative, Proposition 8, that banned same-sex marriage, which had been legalized earlier in the year by the state supreme court. Within two weeks, tens of thousands of supporters around the nation attended rallies that condemned the initiative. This continuing struggle reflects the profound changes in the nature of American marriage. It evolved during the twentieth century from an institution focused on having children to a partnership focused on intimacy and companionship. Being married became an optional, though still highly regarded, status rather than a required role. But once that transformation had occurred, gay and lesbian couples could logically argue that they were just as entitled to official recognition of the intimate partnerships they chose as were heterosexual couples.

The increase in personal choice has brought important benefits. It has broadened the opportunity for wives to realize their full potential in paid employment as well as in the home. It has made marriage more egalitarian, with husbands and wives sharing more of the responsibilities for home and wage earning. For instance, it's no longer remarkable to see husbands who are caring for their kids while their wives work. In the 1950s, they would have been ridiculed as unmanly and meek. People would have wondered why they weren't capable of earning enough to support their families. Today men are freer to choose to do child care and to be more involved in their children's daily lives. The increase in personal choice has also made marriage more democratic: decision making is now based on negotiation and bargaining rather than solely on the husband's preferences. Gone are the days when husbands could beat their wives with little fear of prosecution, demand sex at any time, or decide to sell their wives' property. Most people view all of these changes positively.

Some conservative Protestant groups, it is true, still argue that wives should submit to their husbands' will, but even among them marriage has become more egalitarian and democratic in practice. Joyce Meyer, a leading television preacher and popular author, tells mothers that working outside the home when their children are small is not a good idea, but she adds, "I believe that if you have to do it, God will cover you and your children." She did it, she confesses, and her children turned out okay. And if both spouses work outside the home, she says, they should share the laundry and household duties. She advises that if the couple cannot agree on a major purchase, they probably should not make it. She says of her relationship with her husband, "On relatively unimportant things Dave and I sort of take turns. On major ones the final call is his." Yet her example of deferring to Dave's wishes is to ask him to teach her to play golf rather than to remain angry at him for spending so much time at it. Yes, in Meyer's world the woman at the end of the day must yield to her husband's preferences, but you wonder how many major final calls Dave gets. Fifty years ago, his predecessors got more of them.

Nevertheless, along with benefits, the increase in personal choice has brought costs. Making choices about important aspects of one's life can be difficult and anxiety-provoking. What career to pursue, where to live, whether to marry, whether to have children, whether to end a marriage—it's hard to answer questions such as these. Change may be liberating, but it can also be stressful. Stability may be constraining, but it can also be comfortable. The accumulated weight of decision after decision can wear on people. The continual self-monitoring—*How am I feeling? Am I getting what I need from my job and my marriage?*—creates a bias toward altering that job or that marriage because there are so many opportunities to decide that it's unsatisfactory.

In addition, children and adolescents must deal with the changes their parents decide to make. Those who experience a series of parental partnerships seem to be more likely to act out, be delinquent, or have a baby. We can't rule out the possibility that partnership turnover is merely an indicator of other underlying family or personal problems, such as an irritable temperament or a tendency toward depression, that could be passed genetically from parents to children. These tendencies might both cause adults to have trouble staying in long-term relationships and cause their children to have behavior problems. But as best as we can tell from research studies, some of which have looked for genetic effects, genes are far from the whole story. Children seem to be influenced by their family environments as well as their genes. Perhaps children find it difficult to adjust to repeated changes in the caregivers and partners of caregivers in their households. Perhaps some short-term boyfriends preoccupy their mothers while providing little support to the children. Or perhaps it's just too hard to cope with complex households in which each child may have different parents and parents have children living elsewhere. What may matter for children, then, is not simply the kind of family they live in but how stable that family is.

How important is this problem? In the study of young adolescents I did with Paula Fomby, for each partner who had entered or left the household, the odds that the adolescent had stolen something, skipped school, gotten drunk, or done something similar rose by 12 percent. Yet most of the adolescents, even those who experienced several transitions of partners in and out, didn't report much of this kind of delinquent behavior. So partnership turnover raised the risk of delinquent behavior, but most children who experienced it didn't become delinquents. Think of it as though having a series of partners raises the risk that your children will catch an illness that is going around, although no matter how many partners you have, your children are still unlikely to catch it. If the illness is bad enough, you might not want to raise the risk, modest as it may be. On the other hand, if the risk is acceptably low and changing partners is important, you might go ahead.

This is the kind of social problem that is serious and worthy of our attention but not calamitous. And this is just the kind of problem that American social and political debates seem to have no language for. Too often, debates about social issues play out in a sequence in which someone stakes out an extreme position that receives a great deal of media attention, someone else stakes out a position at the other extreme, and then news coverage lurches back and forth between the extremes as if there were no middle. This sequence has occurred in debates about the effects of divorce on children, with a prominent clinical psychologist arguing that divorce is a disaster for most children, after which another psychologist argued that the effects of divorce are an illusion and really it's all about children's peer groups and the genes that parents transmit to their children. Neither assertion is true for the effects of divorce, and I strongly suspect that neither is true for the effect of experiencing a series of partners. The latter effect is not strong enough to alter the lives of all children whose parents have multiple partners, but even if only a minority have their lives altered, that's still a lot of children.

I'm not suggesting that we roll back the principle of personal choice. I don't think we could if we tried. It's a central component of the more individualistic society we live in—part of what we might call the postmodern condition. The modern era began with the industrial revolution and the mass movement from the farm to the city, and it ended soon after the 1950s. Its last years were a time of full employment and seemingly secure factory work, confidence in the future, and the Pax Americana. It was the high point of the breadwinner-homemaker family. Those conditions, however, changed dramatically in the last third of the twentieth century. The result is today's postmodern era, when people without college educations find it difficult to get good jobs, when factory work is moving overseas or into computer chips, when people lack confidence in the future, and when American dominance in foreign affairs has declined. It's a time of questioning rather than complacency, a time when individuals are uncertain how their lives will turn out. As a result, it's also a period when people reflect on where to take their lives rather than mechanically following established pathways. Unless we see a reversal of this transformation, we are unlikely to go back to the modern era and its ubiquitous male-breadwinner families.

Coping with the Costs of Individualism

The introduction of modern life had its costs, too. Max Weber, writing in the early 1900s, recognized that a new administrative form—the bureaucracy—would be necessary in complex, modern societies. But he also perceived that bureaucracies could trap people in an alienating and rigid "iron cage." The task of twentieth-century society, he realized, was to minimize the unwanted effects of bureaucracy while learning to live with the costs that remain. To a great extent, we have done so. While people still complain about the IRS or the phone company, by and large we have been able to protect our private lives from the worst effects of bureaucracy and have benefited from its efficiencies. It's hard to imagine, for instance, how people could receive their Social Security checks without a government bureaucracy or get the interest on their savings accounts without a large financial industry.

Similarly, the task of twenty-first-century society is to minimize the unwanted effects of individualism while learning to live with the costs that remain. How best to go about this mission is not obvious. In the realm of the family, the marriage movement argues that we should focus

our efforts almost entirely on promoting and defending marriage—
and not just any kind of marriage, to be sure, but rather a marriage that
is centered on a mother and a father raising their biological children.
That type of family, the movement argues, is optimal for bringing up
children. I would agree that, at its best, the two-parent family is hard to
beat for child rearing. Stable, low-conflict families with two biological
or adoptive parents provide better environments for children, on average, than do other living arrangements. The problem is that most people see marriage in a different light these days. They view it as a private
relationship centered on the needs of adults for love and companionship. The postmodern, relationship-based view of marriage has carried
the day.

The marriage movement would like to reverse this development—
to rebuild the levees that crumbled under the flood tide of individualism. That is unlikely to happen. The newer meaning of marriage is
deeply rooted in the personal choice–based culture of the current day.
The increases in divorce, cohabiting relationships, single parenting,
and stepfamilies are likely to stay with us unless we somehow return to
the 1950s—a very unlikely prospect. We could see some modest rever-
sals; divorce, for instance, seems to have declined among the college-
educated. But our current family patterns reflect fundamental changes
in the ways we make a living and think about our lives. I would argue
that, as a result, we should not rely on marriage promotion as our only
strategy for reducing the costs of individualism in family life.

Yet the message of our political and moral leaders of late has been
almost exclusively "Get married." That's the essence of the position
taken by the defenders of heterosexual marriage, some of whom want
to amend the Constitution to protect their vision of marriage. It was an
important part of the message from Congress to welfare recipients: find
a job, and if you still can't support your family, find a husband. The
"Get married" message is also implicit in the demands of gay activists
for same-sex marriage. But the message hasn't been particularly effective: the United States has just experienced the most sustained period
of promarriage rhetoric in a century, and yet little increase in marriage
has occurred.

I grant that if an unmarried couple has just had a child together, their relationship is good, and they wish to marry, then helping them to establish a durable marriage is worthwhile—assuming we know how to do so. A new birth, some observers suggest, constitutes a "magic moment" in the lives of unmarried couples when government and private agencies could take action to help them marry. The magic moment, it turns out, is closer to the magic millisecond: although a large majority of unmarried couples say at the time of the birth that their chances of marrying are good, very few marry in the first few years of their children's lives. Whether government-supported efforts to help them get married and stay married will be effective remains to be seen.

If we think that Americans' pattern of going quickly from partner to partner is problematic for children and that the "Get married" message is insufficient, what else could we do about it? No Western society would challenge the right of unmarried people to form romantic relationships whenever they wish with whomever they choose. Nor should this happen: we don't want a cohabitation tax or marriage police. Instead, I suggest supplementing the marriage message with this new message: *Slow down.* Don't rush into having children with a boyfriend/girlfriend or a partner you've recently started living with. If you are already single and raising children, choose your next live-in partner or spouse carefully. Introduce your partner gradually to your kids, and don't try to make him an instant parent.

The "slow down" message, in other words, implies that we should focus not only on Americans' tendency to end relationships too quickly—the most common critique—but also on their tendency to start relationships too quickly. It's easier to start a live-in partnership than in the past because of the acceptability of cohabiting. Indeed, a majority of people today start their partnerships by simply living together. You needn't marry, and you needn't even make a conscious decision—you can just drift into a cohabiting relationship by spending a night or two a week together, then three or four, and then seven. The risks are low, since you can leave the relationship easily if you are unhappy with it. If there are no children involved, these relationships are private matters best left to the partners. But in some cohabiting relationships one or both partners may have children from previous relationships. If the mother brings her children with her, as is usually the case, their presence creates an instant stepfamily-like situation. Some of the men in these households, however, are primarily romantic partners whom no one in the household sees as real stepfathers and who don't become involved with the children. A majority of them will be gone within a year or two; in the interim, they occupy the time and affection of the mothers, sometimes to the detriment of the children. Other men, in contrast, are seriously involved with the mothers and take on the stepparent role. If the partnership lasts, they can become important figures in their stepchildren's lives. If the partnership doesn't last, however, the children will have to adjust to another loss.

If the male partner has children from previous relationships, they are likely to be living with a former partner, to whom he may be paying child support. The mother in the new partnership typically is raising her children in the household, but she may be receiving money or diapers from a former partner. As a result, the lives of the children living in the household can vary greatly: one child may have a devoted nonresident father who sees her regularly, another child who has no contact with her father jealously watches her half sister go away for weekends with her dad, and a third child—from the new partnership—has both of her parents in the household. One child may have health insurance coverage through her father's job and see a pediatrician regularly, while another child has no coverage and sees emergency room doctors only when she is seriously ill. The inequalities among children in the same household can be stark. What drives these complex families is early childbearing, either as a lone parent or in a partnership that quickly breaks up, soon followed by new partnerships, nearly all of which begin as cohabiting relationships rather than marriages. Competent and creative parents may be able to deal with this complexity, but in general it is not in the best interests of the children involved.

Not all cohabiting relationships with children are complex. Some consist of a couple who have had children together but have no prior children. They may be committed to each other and waiting for the right time to marry. Others may have children and be in long-term, stable cohabiting relationships that seem like substitutes for marriage, as is more common in Western Europe. Still others may not be so committed but may live together simply because it's the most practical way to care for a new baby. They may want to share expenses and parenting responsibilities for the moment, but they may not be ready to make a long-term commitment. Describing the range of cohabiting relationships is a bit like hitting a moving target. Cohabitation is only a few decades old and is still evolving in both the United States and Europe. Perhaps the more stable, marriage-substitute version will someday be as widespread here as in France or Sweden. For now, however, cohabiting relationships are a major contributor to the speed at which American parents and children experience multiple partnerships.

Suppose that a cohabiting relationship (or a marriage) has ended after the couple has had a child together and, as is typical, the woman keeps the child with her and begins living as a lone mother. What's the message we should give to her? Marriage advocates might urge her to find a new partner and get married. But a marriage would not necessarily be in the best interests of her child. We know that children living with married stepparents don't do better, on average, than children living with lone parents, and children living with cohabiting stepparents may do even worse. In part, that's because some of the new men with whom lone mothers start partnerships, while good enough in the mothers' eyes to cohabit with, are problematic as husbands due to persistent employment problems, violence toward women, or substance abuse. A marriage to one of them would have a high likelihood of soon ending in divorce. In fact, children's interests are not served by bringing a male partner into the household unless the relationship endures; otherwise they must adjust to another transition as the partner exits. I would speculate that, in general, a child in a lone-parent family who sees a partner move into her household and then soon move out would have been better off had her mother not started the partnership.

Said otherwise, the slow-down message shifts the focus from promoting marriage to supporting stable care arrangements for children. I suggest that we advise lone parents to take their time in finding partners and to be confident that a relationship will last before they bring a stepparent into their home. We should urge them to choose carefully and deliberately so that their subsequent partnerships, if any, have the greatest chance of enduring. Some stepfamilies do work well, but they tend to be assembled carefully over time. Successful stepfathers gradually insert themselves into their stepchildren's lives. They tend to hang back at first and then carefully ramp up their involvement. Consequently, we should avoid encouraging a mother to quickly marry the man she is seeing, because we may undermine a stepfamily by rushing it.

One way of slowing the process would be to provide lone mothers with sufficient resources so that they wouldn't feel pressured by financial worries to find new partners quickly. I am not suggesting that women today are making decisions about live-in relationships based primarily on finances, or that men are seeking these relationships primarily by offering money. But if a car payment is overdue or the lights are about to be turned off, a lone mother may be more inclined to escalate a relationship to the cohabiting stage if the man offers to help with the bills, even if she is uncertain about his long-term suitability. If she had more income or savings, she could take more time to search for men who have the potential for long-term partnerships, and she could more easily avoid exposing her children to live-in relationships that are unlikely to last.

There are political barriers, however, to providing cash assistance to low-income families. Many Americans view cash assistance as inconsistent with strongly held values such as personal responsibility and self-reliance. The welfare reform law of 1996 was popular because it tied cash assistance to working for pay. Any increase in assistance to lone mothers would need to be consistent with the ethic of personal responsibility or it would have little chance of being enacted by Congress or state legislatures. Moreover, if legislators thought a new program discouraged marriage (as by providing lone mothers with benefits that reduced the incentive to marry), many would oppose it.

Is it possible for the government to provide mothers with assistance that would allow them to take their time finding good partners while also being consistent with values such as personal responsibility and marriage? Perhaps. Take child support payments, for example. Most people think that absent fathers have a responsibility to support their children and that mothers have a right to receive that support. When a lone mother signs up for TANF, she must identify the father, or fathers, of her children. A state government agency tries to collect support payments from the fathers, and if the agency is successful, it keeps most of the money and shares it with the federal government. It gives the mother $50 at most. This system provides little incentive for mothers to cooperate or for fathers to pay.

Now consider an experiment that began in Wisconsin in 1997. A state agency randomly selected a group of TANF recipients to whom they would give all of the child support payments they could collect from the fathers. The federal and state governments kept nothing; every dollar was passed to the parents. Although no one was thinking about the effects of this change on living arrangements, it did have an effect: by 2004, mothers in the experiment were less likely to have cohabited with men (other than the fathers of their children), but they were just as likely to have married. The extra income may have allowed some mothers to avoid live-in relationships with men who might have helped them financially in the short term but were not good candidates for marriage. These are the kind of short-term relationships that often do not benefit the children in the household. If the lesson is that state agencies should pass through more child support payments to mothers receiving welfare, the nation may be about to follow it. In 2006, when Congress reauthorized the welfare reform legislation, it changed the rules concerning child support payments to encourage states to increase the share that is given to the mothers. The new rules make it less costly for states to increase the amount they pass through. One can hope that many states will use this new rule to increase the percentage of child support receipts that they provide to mothers.

Sociologist Myra Marx Ferree has recently proposed that workers be allowed to draw down a small portion of their Social Security accounts in order to pay for family or medical leave. Such leave would allow a parent to stay home with a young child and still receive some income. It would also be available, of course, to married parents. She suggests that for every twenty quarters of earnings covered by the Social Security system, workers should be allowed to use one quarter. As with child support payments, Social Security benefits are viewed by Americans as income to which recipients are entitled. The widespread myth is that Social Security benefits merely return to retired Americans the wages they paid in Social Security taxes while working (when in reality today's workers are paying the taxes that support today's recipients). Ferree's proposal could provide benefits to parents, lone or partnered, that would not be perceived as undermining personal responsibility or discouraging marriage.

The Wisconsin experiment is just that: one experiment in one state. We don't know whether the outcomes would transfer to the nation's welfare population. And we can say even less about whether increases in child support payments would reduce hasty living-together relationships among more affluent lone mothers. Moreover, Ferree's intriguing Social Security scheme is just a proposal at this point; many people might oppose allowing workers to spend some of their benefits before retirement. I therefore can't say confidently that social programs could reduce the comings and goings of partners without discouraging marriage or running afoul of American values. Yet it may be possible to make some modest progress. The general idea is that when lone mothers have more resources, they may avoid short-term relationships, and their children may benefit from the stable single-parent care they receive and from their mothers' more deliberate choices of new partners.

Speeding up the Clock

One may wonder how, if marriage was such a central part of American family life, it could have lost its near monopoly in just a half century. If it was such a strong institution, so dominant in our culture, how could it have gone from a requirement to an option? Let me suggest two answers. First, marriage was always a more fragile accomplishment than it seemed. Although some religious doctrines hold it to be the "natural" setting for sexual relationships, it is not natural in an evolutionary sense. We marry not because of what's in our genes but in spite of what's in our genes. In evolutionary terms, women and men are probably attracted to pair bonding during the phase of their lives when they have young children in need of care, but they are probably not attracted to lifelong monogamous relationships—especially in a low-birth-rate era when such a short period of married life is spent with small children at home. Rather, lifetime marriage has always been a social creation that needed enforcement from family, religion, and law.

From family came the influence of parents and other kin. Before industrialization, when a young man's best hope for a prosperous life was often to inherit his father's farm, he would be reluctant to disobey his parents' wishes about whom to marry. Today, when young adults typically leave home to forge their own careers, parental control is weaker. People who move out of their home state, you'll remember, are more likely to be in interracial or same-sex unions—the kinds of unconventional unions that parents might not approve of. From religion came the influence of the organized church. After European religious authorities decided a few hundred years ago that marriage needed formal approval, church bodies sanctified marriage and limited divorce. They did so at least until recently; now most denominations reluctantly accept divorce, allow it, and minister to people going through its traumatic consequences. You'll recall that the Catholic Church now issues more than fifty thousand annulments per year in the United States. From law came restrictions on the rights and responsibilities that women and men in unmarried relationships had toward each other and toward their children. Think of Peter Stanley, whose children were nearly taken from him by Illinois authorities in 1972 after the death of their mother and his unmarried partner left him a "legal stranger" to his offspring. In sum, marriage's vulnerability was hidden until the 1960s by strong institutional support. By the early twenty-first century, much of that support had been swept away.

Second, marriage was designed for an environment of scarcity. Its pragmatic purpose was to increase the chances that adults could feed and clothe themselves and raise children who would live to adulthood. Until recently, a person needed a reliable partner of the opposite sex in order to accomplish these requirements. A man needed a woman to bear children, breast-feed them, and help raise them, all the while tending to a vegetable garden or the farm animals. A woman needed a man to perform the hard labor of growing crops or building a barn.

Both parents needed children to help with daily tasks, which they did from a young age. Marriage was not designed for a time when young adults could start intimate partnerships but delay having children and then stop having them after only one or two. Infant and childhood deaths were so common in the past that to raise two children to adulthood a woman might need to give birth to four or five. Marriage was also not designed for intense, intimate bonds. People were too busy securing the daily necessities to luxuriate in a lifetime of emotional openness, personal growth, and shared leisure. Only when a rising tide of prosperity lifted most marriages above the subsistence level did these objectives come to the fore. And then, like a ship designed for a lighter load of love, marriage foundered under the weight of husbands' and wives' enormous emotional expectations.

As lifetime marriage declined—its support system eroded and its pragmatic purpose imperiled by prosperity—a newer style of family life developed. It offers multiple ways to travel from adolescence to adulthood, and it accommodates further changes well into middle age. It allows for living with a partner or having a child without marrying, for easily ending cohabiting relationships, and, with a bit more effort, for ending marriages. To be sure, marriage still endures as a symbol of attaining a successful life; indeed, the sentiment in favor of marriage appears to be stronger in the United States than in much of the developed world. But it is a different kind of marriage. No longer the first step into adulthood, it is often the last—one that is taken after finishing school, starting a career, living with a partner, and possibly having children. No longer required, it is an optional part of adult life. Yet so prestigious is marriage that if people get divorced, they tend to try again, usually by starting a cohabiting relationship that will either dissolve or lead to a remarriage.

The result is that we have sped up the hands on the relationship clock. We have more turbulence in our family lives, more changes of partners and parents, than any other nation. This unprecedented rapidity reflects a cultural contradiction between marriage and individualism that most Americans carry around in their heads. It is as if we each use two lenses to view family life and shift between them unaware, like an automatic camera effortlessly adjusting its focus from close-up to panoramic views of the same scene. One view emphasizes the desirability of marriage and, by extension, stable long-term relationships. The other emphasizes self-development and causes people to end relationships that no longer provide the benefits they think they need. The cycling back and forth we do between these two views whirls the American merry-go-round of partnership after partnership faster than anywhere else in the Western world.

Appendix: Charts

These charts compare the family patterns of Americans with other Westerners. I refer to them in the notes, mostly in Chapter 1. For Charts 1 to 14, I have relied most heavily on life tables published in Andersson and Philipov 2002. These authors used a consistent method to compare ten Western countries that participated in the Fertility and Family Surveys (FFS). The countries were Austria, Finland, Belgium (Flanders, the Dutch-speaking region, and the Brussels Capital Region), France, the former West Germany, Italy, Norway, Spain, Sweden, and the United States. The authors did not include data on other Western countries in the FFS, most notably Canada and New Zealand.

Some figures estimated from FFS data for Canada and New Zealand can be found in Heuveline, Timberlake, and Furstenberg 2003. I have used two other sources: Lapierre-Adamcyk, Le Bourdais, and Marcil-Gratton 1999, and Statistics Canada 1997.

Neither Australia nor Great Britain participated in the FFS. For Australia, I have used statistics from de Vaus 2004. I have used a variety of sources for Great Britain, including Haskey 1999, Kiernan 2002, Office of National Statistics 2005, and Shaw 1999. These non-FFS figures for Australia and Great Britain are not strictly comparable to the FFS estimates of Andersson and Philipov and should be seen as the closest available estimates. Where I judged that no comparable estimate for Australia, Great Britain, Canada, or New Zealand existed, I have left the chart blank. And in some cases, Andersson and Philipov were themselves unable to calculate estimates for all ten countries.

Charts 9, 10, and 11 are based on special, unpublished tabulations that Jeffrey Timberlake provided to me at my request, based on the data files and programs he had prepared for analyzing FFS data for

Heuveline, Timberlake, and Furstenberg 2003. I am grateful to Professor Timberlake for providing these data.

Charts 12 and 13 are based on published tabulations from the 1995 National Survey of Family Growth (which was the American component of the FFS) and from the life table estimates in Andersson and Philipov.

Chart 14 is based on statistical tabulations I produced from the 2002 National Survey of Family Growth. This survey was the successor to the 1995 NSFG, which was the American survey in the FFS.

Chart 15, a Moran scatterplot map of high- and low-divorce areas in the United States, was kindly provided by Robert Baller. I thank Professor Baller for this contribution.

Chart 1. Median age at first
marriage for women

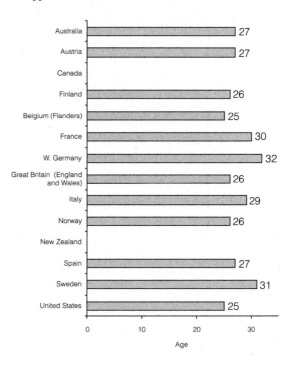

Age

Chart 2. Percent ever married
by age forty for women

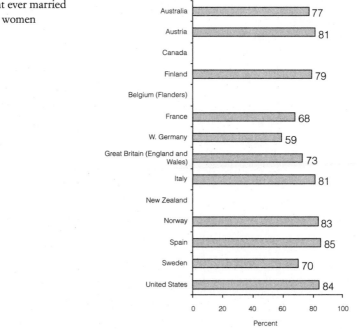

Percent

Chart 3. Percentage of marriages ending in separation or divorce within five years of marriage

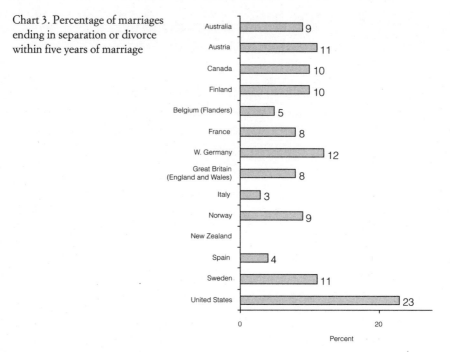

Chart 4. Percentage of cohabiting relationships disrupted after five years

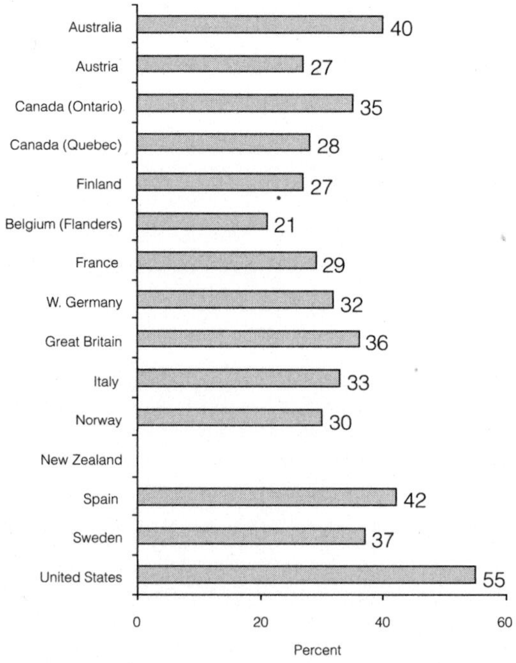

Chart 5. Percentage of children
who experience the dissolution
of their parents' intimate
partnership (married or
cohabiting) by age fifteen

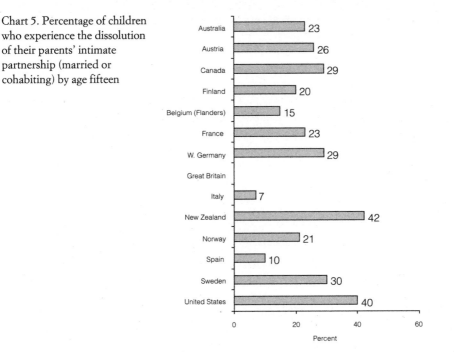

Chart 6. Percentage of children
seeing a new partner enter their
home within three years of a
parental disruption (from either
a marriage or a cohabiting
relationship)

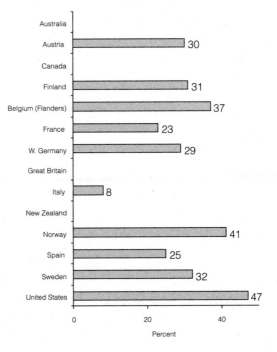

Chart 7. Percent who have spent
time as a lone parent by age
thirty

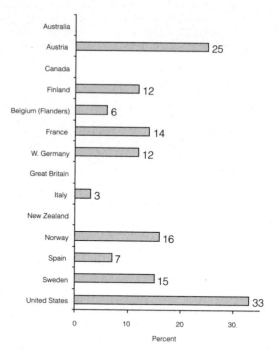

Chart 8. Percentage of children
born to lone parents who have
experienced a new parental
partner entering their home
by age three

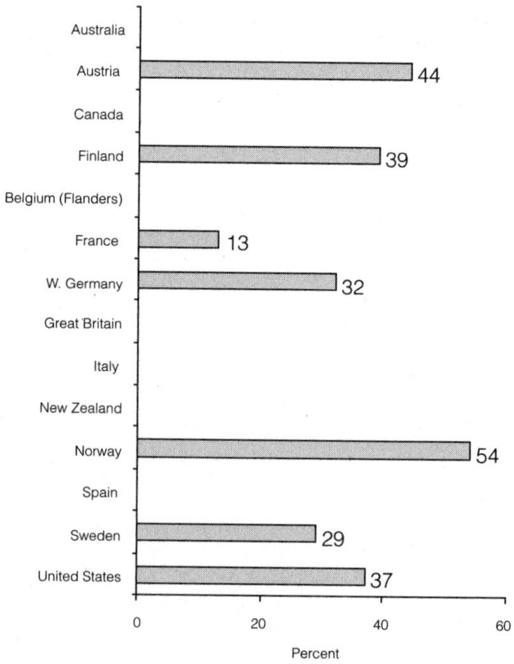

Chart 9. Percentage of women who had experienced three or more coresidential partnerships by age thirty-five, for all women over age thirty-five at the time of the Fertility and Family Survey interviews

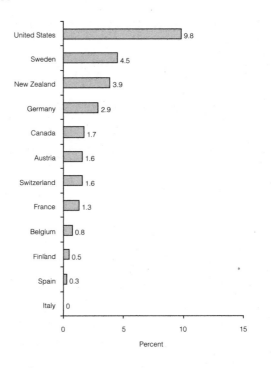

Chart 10. Percentage of children experiencing three or more maternal coresidential partnerships by age fifteen for all children over age fifteen at the time of the Fertility and Family Survey interviews

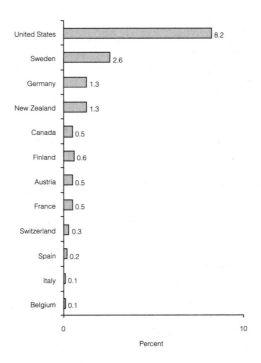

Chart 11. Percentage of children experiencing exactly two maternal coresidential partnerships by age fifteen for all children over age fifteen at the time of the Fertility and Family Survey interviews

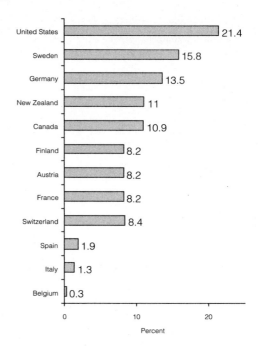

Chart 12. Percentage of marriages ending in separation or divorce in fifteen years

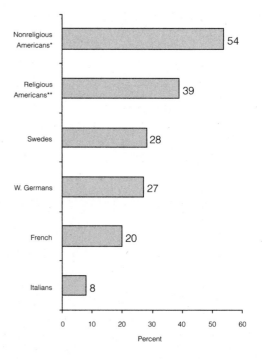

*Religion "not at all" important
**Religion "very" important

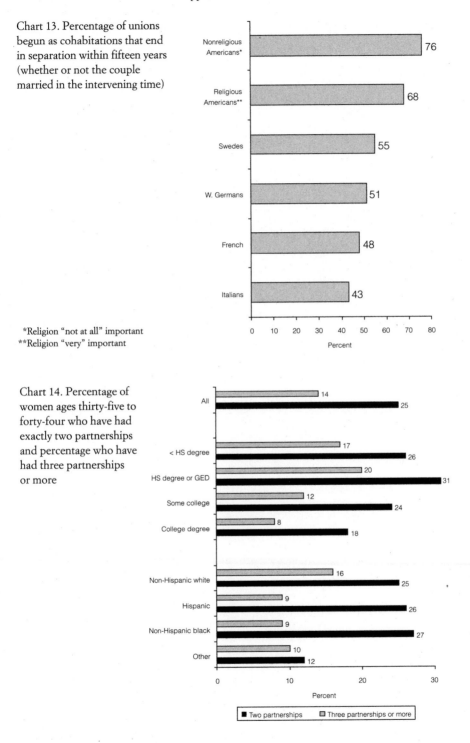

Chart 13. Percentage of unions begun as cohabitations that end in separation within fifteen years (whether or not the couple married in the intervening time)

Nonreligious Americans* — 76
Religious Americans** — 68
Swedes — 55
W. Germans — 51
French — 48
Italians — 43

*Religion "not at all" important
**Religion "very" important

Percent

Chart 14. Percentage of women ages thirty-five to forty-four who have had exactly two partnerships and percentage who have had three partnerships or more

All — 14 / 25
< HS degree — 17 / 26
HS degree or GED — 20 / 31
Some college — 12 / 24
College degree — 8 / 18

Non-Hispanic white — 16 / 25
Hispanic — 9 / 26
Non-Hispanic black — 9 / 27
Other — 10 / 12

Percent

■ Two partnerships   ▨ Three partnerships or more

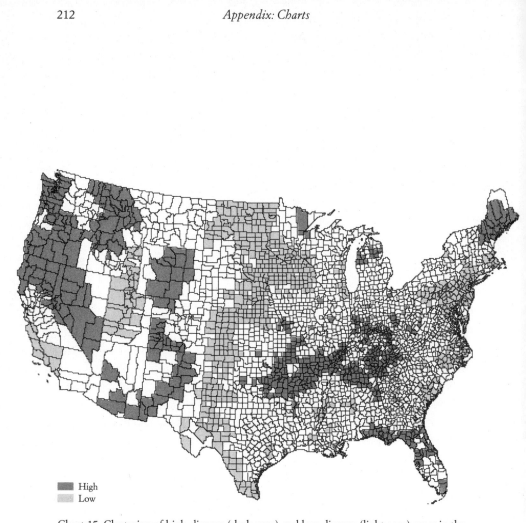

High
Low

Chart 15. Clustering of high-divorce (dark gray) and low-divorce (light gray) areas in the United States in 2000, by county

Notes

Introduction

3   I was stunned to read, buried in a footnote: Heuveline, Timberlake, and Furstenberg 2003, p. 57.

4   The percentage of people who are projected to marry: Goldstein and Kenney 2001.

4   At current rates, nearly half of all American marriages: Raley and Bumpass 2003.

5   Simply put, some children seem to have difficulty: Fomby and Cherlin 2007. See also Osborne and McLanahan 2007. I will review the evidence on serial partnerships and children more fully in Chapters 1 and 8.

9   Each is part of the cultural tool kit: Swidler 2001.

Chapter 1. How American Family Life Is Different

13 On Valentine's Day: My description of the rally draws upon Kellams 2005. Governor Huckabee's radio address was aired on November 27, 2004; retrieved November 22, 2005, from http://www.arkansas.gov/governor/media/radio/text/r11272004.html.

14 In 2004, it had the third-highest per capita rate of marriage: U.S. Bureau of the Census 2007.

14 Yet six of the ten states with the highest divorce rates: The ten states in order of divorces per person in 2004 are Nevada; Arkansas; Wyoming; Alabama and West Virginia (tied); Idaho; Kentucky, Oklahoma, and Tennessee (three-way tie); and New Mexico.

14 That's why Arkansas stands out: U.S. Bureau of the Census 2004. Median age at marriage: U.S. Bureau of the Census 2005a; percent Catholic: Glenmary Research Center 2005.

15 more than half of first births in Sweden: Thomson and Hoem 1998.

16 Instead, demographers use the "life table" method: Here's how the life table method works. Imagine a woman who marries this year. Suppose that every year

in the future her risk of divorce will be the same as the risk of people who have been married for exactly that many years in the recent past. By calculating these annual risks from people's recent experience, demographers can obtain an estimate of her probability of getting a divorce in the future if (and this is the big if) her future experience is similar to that of married people in the recent past. For each FFS country, then, we identify all of the people in the survey who have ever married. Then we calculate the fraction who told the interviewer that they divorced in their first year of marriage. That's the divorce risk for year one. Then, for everyone whose marriage lasted at least one year, we calculate the fraction who told the interviewer they divorced during their second year. That's the risk for year two. We repeat that calculation for all those who made it through at least two years, then all who made it through at least three, then at least four, and so forth. Then we cumulate all of these risks in a mathematical formula and obtain the estimated lifetime risk of divorce for our imaginary newlywed. In practice, the procedure is a bit more complicated than this. For instance, Andersson and Philipov 2002 use only responses concerning the six years prior to the survey, to avoid reliance on people's memories of events that occurred many years ago. For more information on life tables, see Preston, Heuveline, and Guillot 2001.

16 Here are some comparisons: Charts that graphically show the results can be found starting on page 203. The charts are referred to by number in the notes that follow. I have relied most heavily on life tables published in Andersson and Philipov 2002. These authors used a consistent method to compare ten Western countries, including the United States, that participated in the Fertility and Family Surveys (FFS). They did not include three other Western countries in the FFS: Australia, Canada, and New Zealand. Some figures estimated from FFS data for these three countries can be found in Heuveline, Timberlake, and Furstenberg 2003. Great Britain, unfortunately, did not participate in the FFS. I have used a variety of non-FFS sources for figures from Great Britain, where available, as well as for Canada, Australia, and New Zealand. However, these non-FFS figures could differ somewhat from the figures that have been estimated from the FFS.

16 Americans marry and cohabit for the first time sooner: The figures on median age at marriage (the age at which half of all young women who will ever marry have done so) come from Andersson and Philipov 2002, Table 7. See Chart 1. The figures on median age at first partnership of either kind (marital or cohabiting) come from Andersson and Philipov 2002, Table 6.

16 A higher proportion of Americans marry at some point: The percentages are from Andersson and Philipov 2002, Table 7. See Chart 2.

17 For technical reasons, all of these forecasts are likely to be somewhat lower: In a period when ages at marriage are rising, as has been the case recently, the life table method and similar projections cannot distinguish whether people are merely waiting longer before marrying or whether they are forgoing marriage.

In this situation, estimates tend to be too low. See Dworak-Winkler and Engel-hardt 2004.

17 If we consider both marital and cohabiting relationships: The percentages are from Andersson and Philipov 2002, Table 6.

17 Other English-speaking countries are more similar to the United States: For instance, the British Office of National Statistics estimates that 73 percent of women would ever marry at the rates prevalent in the mid-1990s; the Australian Institute of Family Studies estimates that 77 percent of women would ever marry; and Canadian demographers estimate approximately 60 percent outside of Quebec and only about 40 percent in Quebec. The median age at marriage (the age at which half of all marriages will have occurred) was estimated to be about four years higher in Britain and about two years higher in Australia than in the United States. See de Vaus 2004; Shaw 1999; Le Bourdais and Lapierre-Adamcyk 2004, p. 942.

17 Marriages and cohabiting relationships in the United States are far more fragile: The percentages of marriages that end in separation or divorce within five years are from Andersson and Philipov 2002, Table 27, for continental Europe and United States; de Vaus 2004, Table 15.1 (the figure is for divorces only); Haskey 1999, Figure 5 (the figure is for divorces only); and Statistics Canada 1997. See Chart 3. The percentages of cohabiting relationships that are disrupted after five years are from Andersson and Philipov 2002, Table 24; Kiernan 2002 for Great Britain; de Vaus 2004; and Lapierre-Adamcyk et al. 1999. See Chart 4.

17 Because of these fragile partnerships: The percentage of children born to mari-tal or cohabiting parents (combined) who see their parents' union break up by age fifteen is from Andersson and Philipov 2002, Table 33; Heuveline et al. 2003, Table 1, for Canada and New Zealand; and de Vaus 2004, Table 11.2. See Chart 5. The percentage of children born to cohabiting parents (only) who experience a breakup is from Andersson and Philipov 2002, Table 34; and Heuveline et al. 2003, Table 1, for Canada and New Zealand. The percentage of children born to married parents (only) who experience a breakup is from Andersson and Philipov 2002, Table 35; and Heuveline et al. 2003, Table 1, for Canada and New Zealand. The statement that children born to married parents in the United States are more likely to experience parents' breakup than chil-dren born to cohabiting parents in Sweden is from Heuveline et al. 2003, p. 57.

18 After their breakups, American parents are more likely to repartner: The percent-ages of children seeing a new partner in their homes within three years of breakup are from Andersson and Philipov 2002, Table 43. See Chart 6. The percentages of children who spend time in stepfamilies (specifically, with a mother and stepfa-ther) are from Andersson and Philipov 2002, Table 45; Andersson 2002, Table 7; and Heuveline et al. 2003, Table 2, for Canada and New Zealand. Only the New Zealand figure (9 percent) approaches the U.S. figure (10 percent).

18 American women become parents at an earlier age and are much more likely to spend time as lone parents: The percentages on age at parenthood are from

Andersson and Philipov 2002, Table 8. The percentages on time spend as lone parents are from Andersson and Philipov 2002, Table 11. See Chart 7. The percentages on children experiencing a new parental partner are from Andersson and Philipov 2002, Table 36. See Chart 8.

19 So more lone-parent families started, and more ended: The English-speaking countries have more lone-parent families than do the continental European nations. Canada has more lone parents than most European countries but still fewer than the United States. Great Britain and New Zealand approach the American level of lone-parent families. Information is lacking on rates of partnering among lone parents. Heuveline et al. 2003; Office of National Statistics 2005.

19 What all these statistics mean: I thank Jeffrey Timberlake and Patrick Heuveline for providing the unpublished tabulations cited in this paragraph and the following one. For the percentages of women in each country who had three or more live-in partners, see Chart 9. You might wonder whether the United States is different because of its greater percentage of nonwhites and Hispanics or its larger poor population. Actually, having a series of partnerships seems to be more common among whites who don't identify as Hispanic than among Hispanics or African Americans. It is true, however, that the non-college-educated have a greater number of partnerships than do the college-educated. See Chapter 7 for a discussion of variations in the American pattern.

19 The percentage of children who experienced three or more mother's partners: Unpublished tabulations by Timberlake and Heuveline. See Chart 10.

20 The number of children who experienced exactly two parental partnerships: Unpublished tabulations by Timberlake and Heuveline. See Chart 11.

20 Children who experience a series of transitions: Wu and Martinson 1993; Wu and Thomson 2001.

20 Studies in other countries: Cockett and Tripp 1994; Woodward et al. 2001.

20 A group of American researchers followed more than a thousand children: Cavanagh and Huston 2006. The data are from the NICHD Study of Early Child Care and Youth Development. See also an article examining transitions in romantic (although not necessarily coresident) relationships: Osborne and McLanahan 2007.

21 We know, for example, that some of the seeming effects of divorce: Cherlin et al. 1991.

21 Rather, emotional problems increase comparably for both groups: O'Connor et al. 2000. Paula Fomby and I looked at this question another way. If what's happening is merely that parents are passing along traits that lead to difficulties, then, we reasoned, children who are acting out or delinquent should be more likely to have parents who acted out or were delinquent when *they* were children. Once that's taken into account, there should not be an effect on children of experiencing a series of partnerships. We examined the records of a twenty-year national study that followed women beginning when they were teenagers. Most of the women became mothers during the study. We found that even after we

took into account whether the mothers had, when they were teenagers, used drugs, shoplifted, stolen something, or had early sexual intercourse, their children still had more behavior problems and admitted to more delinquency if their mothers had had more partners. Our study suggests that experiencing a series of partnerships may be, at least in part, a true cause of children's difficulties. See Fomby and Cherlin 2007. We did not, however, find any greater difficulties among African American children who experienced a series of partnerships. A possible reason is the greater role that other family members such as grandmothers and aunts typically play in their upbringing. Black grandparents are more likely to take on a parentlike role toward their grandchildren than are white grandparents. Their stable presence could insulate children from the consequences of having parents' partners move in and out of the home. See McLoyd et al. 2000; Cherlin and Furstenburg 1992. Other studies similar to Fomby and Cherlin 2007 have, however, found similar effects for blacks and whites: see Osborne and McLanahan 2007.

21 The breakup of a marriage usually produces a short-term crisis: Hetherington and Kelly 2002; Wallerstein et al. 2000.

21 When Frank Furstenberg and I began to study stepfamilies: See, for example, Cherlin and Furstenberg 1994.

22 But children whose parents have remarried: Coleman et al. 2000.

22 Their levels of behavior problems: Hetherington and Clingempeel 1992.

22 the addition of a stepparent increases stress: Coleman et al. 2000.

22 But in some respects, such as school achievement: Raley et al. 2005.

22 Children living with a mother and her cohabiting partner: Brown 2006; Raley et al. 2005.

23 If children are being raised by parents who have chronic open conflict: Amato 2005.

24 All are being affected by the globalizing economy: In fact, a recent article reports that globalization has had nearly the same effects on government social welfare spending and on workers' fringe benefits (pensions, sick leave, unemployment insurance) in Western Europe as in non-European Western countries such as the United States. Brady et al. 2005.

24 To use Swidler's metaphor: Swidler 1986, 2001.

24 In the kit are sets of tools I will call cultural models: Social scientists often use the technical term "cultural schema" instead of "cultural model." See DiMaggio 1997.

25 In a similar vein, Karla B. Hackstaff: Hackstaff 1999.

25 Seventy-six percent agreed: These are the weighted responses of the main respondents to wave 2 of the National Survey of Families and Households, conducted from 1992 to 1994. I tabulated the results from the public use data set distributed by the University of Wisconsin–Madison with funding from the National Institutes of Health.

25 When a journalist interviewed sixty people: Paul 2002.

25 A twenty-year-old Puerto Rican mother said: Edin and Kefalas 2005, p. 120.

26 Seventy-six percent responded: Cherlin 1999b.

26 In fact, over the past few decades, people have become *more* disapproving: My calculations from online data from the General Social Survey, National Opinion Research Center, University of Chicago.

27 In his weekly radio address two days before the senatorial debate: President's radio address, June 3, 2006; retrieved June 5, 2006, from http://www .whitehouse.gov/news/releases/2006/06/ 20060603.html.

27 $150 million per year for research and demonstration projects: Roberts 2006.

27 He told reporters he expected the measure to pass: Struck 2004.

28 A British legal scholar, John Eekelaar, wrote: Eekelaar 2006, p. 440.

28 Fewer Americans agreed: Inglehart et al. 2004. Interviews were conducted in Australia and New Zealand in 1995.

28 But the literature on the cultural model of individualism: See, e.g., Lasch 1978; Bellah et al. 1985; Putnam 2000.

28 Robert Bellah and his colleagues: Bellah et al. 1985.

28 The great German social theorist Max Weber, in a classic book: Weber 2002.

29 You develop your own sense of self: See Giddens 1991; Beck and Beck-Gernsheim 2002; Beck et al. 1994.

30 The World Values Survey asked about expressive individualism: Inglehart and Baker 2000.

30 The answers to these questions suggest: Inglehart and Baker 2000; Baker 2005.

30 Even among married couples, we have seen: Whitehead 1997.

33 Such a distinctive cultural climate: Ronald Inglehart, the director of the World Values Surveys, and Wayne E. Baker wrote that although the United States does rank high among nations in self-expressive (i.e., individualistic) values, "the United States is a deviant case, having a much more traditional value system than any other advanced industrial society." I think that *traditional* is not quite the right word to describe these values, but the point is that in no other highly expressive society is cultural support for marriage so strong. See Inglehart and Baker 2000, p. 31.

34 For instance, Americans are more likely to agree: Inglehart et al. 2004.

34 This is evident at the many "seeker churches": Sargeant 2000.

34 And it is visible in the religious self-help sections: Osteen 2004; Beale et al. 2004.

34 In other words, being a parent rather than being a spouse: Carbone 2000.

35 constitutional amendments passed in more than half of the states: Peterson 2006; National Council of State Legislatures 2006.

Chapter 2. The Historical Origins of the American Pattern, 1650–1900

36 In 1857, a New England woman: For this account, I draw upon Hartog 2000 and Ganz 1997.

36 "I told him decidedly that I should leave him forever": Ganz 1997, p. 257, quoting from Abby's statement in the *New York Tribune* after the trial.

37 By the 1850s, judges and juries followed an unwritten law: Hartog 2000.

38 "That man was made for God": Hartog 2000, p. 232.

39 an 1849 Connecticut "omnibus clause": Phillips 1988, p. 442.

40 *Boston Quarterly Review* and *Continental Monthly:* Both quotations are taken from Lantz et al. 1977.

40 In the famous phrase of historian John Demos: Demos 1970.

41 laws forbidding people to live alone: Flaherty 1967, pp. 178, 177.

41 An observer in Hertfordshire, England: Butler 1990, p. 19.

41 First, they gave an important but subtle boost: LeBeau 2000.

42 The Bible tells us that Paul said: 1 Corinthians 7.

42 Luther rejected this position: Witte 1997.

42 It was part of what Luther called the "earthly kingdom": Witte 1997, p. 51.

43 As historian Nancy Cott writes: Cott 2000, p. 12.

43 In 1641, the Massachusetts Bay Colony: Pleck 1987.

44 By 1700, levels of church membership: Butler 1990.

45 Immigrants brought religious traditions: Butler et al. 2003.

45 Still, by 1776 only 17 percent: Finke and Stark 1992.

45 A witness at the event wrote: Gillis 1985, p. 45.

45 A British historian claimed: Stone 1990.

45 A woman described to a British folklorist the ritual: Gillis 1985, p. 198, citing William Rhys Jones, "A Besom Wedding in the Ceiriog Valle," *Folk-Lore* 34 (1928): 153–54, and T. Gwynn Jones, *Welsh Folklore and Folk Customs* (Woodbridge: D. S. Brewer, 1979), p. 155.

46 Up to one-fifth of the rural population of Britain: Gillis 1985, p. 219.

46 An Anglican minister in eighteenth-century Maryland: Grossberg 1985, p. 68.

46 A form of bigamy was also common: Hartog 2000.

46 In addition, slaves organized themselves into families: Gutman 1976a.

46 "Clairissa your affectionate Mother and Father": Gutman 1976b.

47 Slave kinship patterns: Herskovits 1990.

47 Getting married was more of a process: Bledsoe 1990.

48 He became the crucial intermediary: Cott 2000. Seymour Martin Lipset (1996) also wrote about the "moralism" of the Protestant sects in the colonies, the importance of marriage in their framework, and the existence of divorce.

48 For instance, Hendrik Hartog wrote: Hartog 2000, p. 29.

48 Even as recently as the early 1900s: Phillips 1988, pp. 517–18.

49 Indeed, he never divorced anyone: Phillips 1988.

49 The willful deserter: Phillips 1988, p. 47, quoting Luther from *On Marriage Matters* (1530).

49 "Frequently something must be tolerated": Witte 1997, p. 67.

49 He also acted as counsel: Kingdon 1995.

49 Nevertheless, the seed of divorce was planted: Phillips 1988; Rheinstein 1972.

50 This breathtaking statute: Although after the 1917 Bolshevik Revolution in Russia, unilateral divorce was allowed.

50 In 1816, after the fall of Napoleon: Phillips 1988.

51 This persistent difference: Mahoney 2000.

51 "atmosphere of moral belligerence": Cott 2000.

52 In 1888, for instance, Supreme Court justice Stephen Field: Hartog 2000, p. 261.

52 To the Mormons, the issue was one of religious freedom: For a description of the Mormon position, see Thornton 2005.

52 "a blot on our civilization": Cott 2000, pp. 118, 119.

53 Many states followed with laws forbidding: Cott 2000.

53 Similarly, in the late 1800s: Cott 2000, p. 87.

53 In a high-profile Kansas case: Passet 2003, p. 135.

54 By the end of the century: Grossberg 1985, pp. 70–71.

55 Fifteen percent of Americans: U.S. Bureau of the Census 1975.

55 The mass-circulation newspapers: Starr 2004.

55 Historian John Gillis: Gillis 1985.

56 When Sanger was indicted in 1914: Chesler 1992.

56 Entrepreneurs started firms to produce and distribute: McLaren 1978.

56 A 1920 law outlawing contraception and abortion: Accampo 2003.

56 In 1899, he published a novel: Teitelbaum and Winter 1985.

56 In 1783, Frederick the Great of Prussia: Glendon 1989, p. 174, citing Heinrich Dörner, *Industrialisierung und Familienrecht* (Berlin: Dunker and Humblot, 1974), p. 59.

57 Some French writers offered similar arguments: Phillips 1988.

57 By the end of the Civil War: Speth 1982.

57 In 1800, judges gave custody to fathers: Mason 1994.

58 Despite the new marital property laws: Basch 1979.

58 Even as late as the 1950s: Hartog 2000.

58 husbands retained the right to hit them: Pleck 1987.

58 Between 1776 and 1850: Finke and Stark 2005.

58 According to one estimate, the number of black Baptists: Lincoln and Mamiya 1990.

59 A million Bibles: Butler 1990, pp. 270–80.

59 For instance, Charles Grandison Finney: Charles Grandison Finney, *Lectures on Revivals of Religion* (1835; Cambridge, MA: Harvard University Press, 1960), pp. 9–10, quoted in Finke and Stark 2005, p. 92.

59 Illustrations of camp meetings: See, for example, the engraving in Finke and Stark 2005, p. 106.

59 By 1850, the Methodists were the largest denomination: Finke and Stark 2005.

60 The passage of Connecticut's "omnibus clause": Rheinstein 1972.

60 "An Indiana divorce": Blake 1962. The quotation from the *Times* editorial is on p. 116.

60 Its place was secure until the 1970s: Nevada still, however, has the highest number of divorces per person of any state, as I noted in Chapter 1.

60 Between 1865, the first year for which good statistics exist: Cherlin 1992.

61 President Theodore Roosevelt wrote in a message to Congress: O'Neill 1967. Roosevelt is quoted on pp. 245–46.

61 "It is not perceived": O'Neill 1967, p. 256.

61 "Divorce was not a right": Hartog 2000, p. 84.

Chapter 3. The Rise of the Companionate Marriage, 1900–1960

63 The diary of Isabella Maud Rittenhouse: Seidman 1991, pp. 48–50.

64 Historian Elaine Tyler May: May 1980, p. 158.

64 "It is simply impossible": *Cole v. Van Riper,* 44 58 (Ill. 1867), as quoted in Hartog 2000, p. 292.

65 Allowing such suits would be unwise: *Thompson v. Thompson,* 218 611 (U.S. 1910), quoted at pp. 617–18.

65 So the Supreme Court left the domestic harmony: Olsen 1955.

65 A training bulletin: Siegel 1996, p. 2171.

66 Social scientists saw no need to study family violence: O'Brien 1971.

66 "All the time I am planning": Quoted in Seidman 1991, p. 49.

66 In 1900, 40 percent of Americans: U.S. Bureau of the Census 1975, 2005b. By "worked outside the home," I mean in the "labor force," that is, all people who work for pay outside the home or are looking for such work.

68 Theodor van de Velde: Van de Velde 1930. The four cornerstones quotations are from p. 6 and the table is on pp. 218–21 of the revised edition.

68 By the 1920s, according to historian Stephanie Coontz: Coontz 2005, p. 214.

69 The law resulted in about fifteen hundred women: Cott 2000.

70 American tax law also encouraged: Carasso and Steuerle 2005.

70 Maternity leave benefits: Gauthier 1996.

70 A 1939 law even required: De Luca 2005.

70 In contrast, British policies: Pedersen 1993.

71 "A girl who hasn't a man in sight": Sidonie M. Gruenberg, quoted in Weiss 2000, p. 23.

71 Only about 5 percent: O'Connell and Moore 1980.

72 They stayed high throughout the 1950s baby boom: Cherlin 1992.

72 But, as we know, the birth rate and the divorce rate: In 1920, for instance, the average woman in the United States had 3.3 children, compared to 3.1 in Britain and 2.7 in France. National Institute of Demographic Studies 2007.

73 By 1906 the figure had reached half: Finke and Stark 2005.

73 In much of Europe just the opposite had occurred: Gill 2001.

73 According to a 1950 survey: The British figure is from Gill 1999.

73 Secularization, many experts think: Bruce 2001.

74 But the proponents of the competition explanation: The most thorough treatment of competition theory is in Stark and Finke 2000. See also Roof 1999 and Butler 2004.

74 Consistent with this theory, old-line denominations: Finke and Stark 2005.

74 "spirituality of dwelling": Wuthnow 1998; Roof 1999.

74 "Homes and congregations": Wuthnow 1998, p. 36.

75 The suburban churches offered a standard package: Edgell 2006.

75 By 1961 the National Council of Churches: May 1988, p. 151.

75 Moreover, the Catholic Church maintained its prohibition: Westoff and Jones 1979.

76 By the end of the baby boom: Curry et al. 1977.

76 Perhaps one in three marriages: See Cherlin 1992.

76 *The Power of Positive Thinking:* Peale 1952.

77 "I couldn't possibly get along without you": Peale 1952, pp. 50–51.

77 As for men, Peale tells the story: Peale 1952, pp. 40–41.

77 Another man, Bill, was passed over: Peale 1952, pp. 134–37.

78 The leading sociological theorist Talcott Parsons argued: Parsons and Bales 1955; Becker 1991.

79 When he appeared five minutes late: Peale 1952, pp. 96–99.

80 When the economy expanded in the postwar years: See Easterlin 1980.

82 *The Feminine Mystique:* Friedan 1963.

82 "marriage penalty": Budig and England 2001.

82 A few articles in monthly magazines: Meyerowitz 1994.

82 A 1954 article in *Reader's Digest:* McCormick 1954, p. 55.

84 According to historian Jessica Weiss: Weiss 2000, p. 115.

84 "Marriages built upon the shifting sands": D'Emilio and Freedman 1988. Sanger is quoted in Seidman 1991, p. 76.

85 "It is unlikely": Quoted in Weiss 2000, p. 146.

Chapter 4. The Individualized Marriage and the Expressive Divorce, 1960-2000

87 The author of "Love vs. Privacy": Lobsenz 1977.

87 "Time for Yourself": Jacoby 1980.

88 The result was a transition: Cherlin 2004.

88 Francesca Cancian pinpointed it: Cancian 1987.

89 As a result, their minds were freed: For an application of this theory to European birth rates, see Lesthaeghe and Surkyn 1988.

89 The proportion of them with college degrees: Between 1950 and 1970, the percentage of people aged twenty-five to thirty-four with bachelor's degrees or more education doubled from about 7.5 percent to about 15 percent. U.S. Bureau of the Census 2006b, Table 2.

91 Just 8 percent of couples: Bumpass 1990; Bumpass, Sweet, and Cherlin 1991.

91 By 1970, 49 percent of women: U.S. Bureau of the Census 2005a.

92 AFDC recipients typically combined: Edin and Lein 1997.

93 They tend to spend less time doing housework: Bittman et al. 2003.

93 In *Griswold*: *Griswold v. Connecticut,* 381 479 (U.S. 1965).

93 *Eisenstadt*: *Eisenstadt v. Baird,* 438 405 (U.S. 1972).

94 One important case involved Peter and Joan Stanley: *Stanley v. Illinois,* 405 645 (U.S. 1972).

95 Justice Lewis F. Powell Jr. wrote: *Weber v. Aetna Casualty & Surety Co.,* 406 164 (U.S. 1972).

95 In Germany, for example: Glendon 1989, p. 268, quoting the 1896 code.

96 "expressive divorce": Whitehead 1997.

96 In fact, a legal historian claims: Friedman 2004.

96 Allen described how he and his wife: Allen 1999. The performance was origi-
    nally recorded in 1964.

96 "no-fault divorce": Glendon 1987.

97 A marriage begun around 1980: Cherlin 1992.

97 In England, France, and Germany: Glendon 1987.

· 97 And after the feminist movement made wife beating: Schneider 2000.

98 More important, nearly all the increase: Bumpass and Lu 2000; Kennedy and
    Bumpass 2007.

98 Although the percentage of young adults who were married: Bumpass and Lu
    2000; Bumpass, Sweet, and Cherlin 1991. On the percentage of remarriages that
    begin as cohabiting relationships, see Smock 2000.

99 In 1995, for example, 59 percent: Bumpass and Lu 2000.

99 A cohabiting relationship may be all: Oppenheimer 2003.

99 Cohabiting couples raise children: U.S. Bureau of the Census 2003.

99 "It began by attrition": Manning and Smock 2005, p. 995.

100 In fact, it's rare enough: Heuveline and Timberlake 2004.

100 In some European nations: Kiernan 2002.

100 About 60 percent of American children: Kennedy and Bumpass 2007.

100 Overall, children living in cohabiting families: Smock and Manning 2004.

100 They are more likely to be expelled: Nelson et al. 2001; Manning and Lamb
    2003.

100 For instance, cohabiting parents spend more money: DeLeire and Kalil 2005.

101 The appeals court ruled: *People v. Liberta,* 474 N.E. 2nd 567 (N.Y. 1984). See
    also Ryan 1995.

102 The act included funds: Manegold 1994.

102 Mexican immigrant men: Hirsch 2003.

102 Legal scholar Sanford Katz: Katz 2000, p. 621.

103 "Over the past century, marriage has steadily become": Coontz 2005, p. 301.

103 The percentage of the American population that belonged: Finke and Stark
    2005.

104 the United States is one of the most religious countries: Inglehart et al. 2004.

104 61 percent of Americans said yes: Italy and Canada were the next highest at 48 percent. Much farther down the list were Great Britain at 30 percent and France at 28 percent. The Irish, who went to church in large numbers, apparently didn't think they learned as much: only 27 percent agreed that their churches gave adequate answers to the problems of family life. At the bottom of the list, at 15 percent, was Denmark. Inglehart et al. 2004.

104 In the mid-twentieth century, American Protestantism: Ammerman 2005.

105 They did not interpret the Bible's words literally: Butler et al. 2003.

105 They accounted for about 25 percent: Finke and Stark 2005.

105 By and large, they interpreted the Bible: Butler et al. 2003.

105 Many would also accept the label "evangelical": Woodberry and Smith 1998. Within these designations are internal divisions between, for example, Pentecostalists, who believe that God is continually revealed to individuals through healing powers, prophecy, and speaking in tongues, and fundamentalists, who believe that all of God's revelation is in the Bible. "Conservative Protestant" seems to be the preferred overall descriptor today, whereas "fundamentalist," except in reference to specific beliefs about God's revelations, is now considered something of an epithet.

105 At midcentury, Catholics comprised about 20 percent: Finke and Stark 2005.

105 No less a public figure than Norman Vincent Peale: Meyer 1988.

105 Numerically, the major religious trend: Finke and Stark 2005. Among the conservative groups, Southern Baptists continued their upward trajectory, while new, smaller denominations such as the Assemblies of God and the Pentecostal Assemblies of the World grew rapidly.

105 By the 1990s, nearly as many Americans: Sherkat and Ellison 1999.

106 "Spirituality," writes Wuthnow: Wuthnow 1998, p. 2. Other authors have also described the transformation of American religion in which personal growth and self-expression have become more prominent. Religious historian Jon Butler (2004) wrote that rather than fading away, religion remains "commonplace but also transformed in modern American history." Sociologist Alan Wolfe (2003) described a similar change. Wolfe himself relied on other scholars of the sociology of religion, such as Wuthnow (1988) and Wade Clark Roof (1999), who have written about the increasing emphasis on the individual's spiritual journey. All have noted how American religion increasingly incorporates the therapeutic ethic of the counseling session, the support group, or the twelve-step program. See also Bellah et al. 1985.

106 "This church has a class where you can ask": Roof 1999, p. 25.

106 "We want the church to look like a mall": Mahler 2005, p. 33.

107 They placed less emphasis on the Church as an institution: D'Antonio et al. 2001.

109 Since then, mainline churches have been more likely: Wilcox 2002.

109 The Catholic priests, despite their church's formal opposition: Edgell 2006.

109 Instead they show what one observer called: Wilcox 2004.

109 In an article in *Christianity Today:* Instone-Brewer 2007.

109 As for welcoming divorced people: Wilcox 2004.

109 But in addition, conservative Protestant churches: Ammerman 2005; Edgell 2006.

110 Nevertheless, Pilgrim Baptist has programs for divorced congregants: Edgell 2006.

110 Joseph Tamney tells of the experience of Iris: Tamney 2002.

110 The result is that a separated or divorced adult: Edgell 2006.

110 Catholics who have remarried: Hout 2000.

111 And the percentage of Catholics who thought: D'Antonio et al. 2001.

111 These include problems that rendered one spouse: Lawrence G. Wrenn, quoted in Vasoli 1998, p. 76.

111 The number of annulments grew enormously: Wilde 2001. Annulments have risen far more in the United States than in other countries with large Catholic populations. Of course, the divorce rate is higher in the United States, so one might expect a de facto divorce procedure to increase faster there. But even accounting for the difference in divorce risks, the American rate of annulments is about twice as high as in any other country. In Canada, for instance, about 10 out of every 100 Catholics who divorced in 1995 obtained an annulment, compared to 23 out of 100 in the United States. Wilde argues that annulments are more common in the United States because divorce and remarriage were dealt with more severely until recently. From 1886 to 1976, any Catholic in the United States (unlike in any other country) who remarried after a civil divorce without first obtaining an annulment was automatically excommunicated from the Church. Once the conditions for annulments were liberalized in the 1970s, many Catholics rushed to obtain one.

This line of reasoning, however, does not explain why annulment rates have remained high since then. I would suggest that the reason is the greater religious activity of American Catholics, who, like American Protestants, attend church more regularly and look for religious guidance more often than do their coreligionists in other countries. Wilde notes that annulments have risen only in countries with sizeable numbers of both Catholics and Protestants, which, she argues, suggests that annulments may be a marketing strategy for attracting parishioners and retaining those who might otherwise leave. (In fact, nearly 20 percent of American Catholics who remarry do leave the Church; see Hout 2000.) She focuses on five such countries, in addition to the United States: Canada, Great Britain, the Netherlands, Australia, and Germany. Annulments have risen in all five, which supports her theory. But nowhere has the rise been as sharp and as sustained as in the United States. According to the 2000 World Values Surveys, Catholics in the United States attend church more often and are more likely to say that God is very important in their lives than are Catholics in the other five countries—often by sizeable margins. Sixty-eight percent of American Catholics, according to my calculations from the 2000 World Values Survey data, say they attend church at least monthly, compared to 48 percent of German Catholics, 44 percent of Canadian Catholics, 44 percent of Dutch Catholics, 39 percent of British Catholics, and 38 percent of Australian Catholics. And 61 percent of American Catholics say that God is very important in their lives, compared to 42 percent of Canadian Catholics, 26 percent of Australian Catholics, 20 percent of British Catholics, 11 percent of German Catholics, and 12 percent of Dutch Catholics. American Catholics, in other words, are more religiously active than are Catholics in other mixed-religion Western countries. Consequently, more of them care about obtaining an annulment should they wish to remarry.

111   In fact, the differences in divorce rates: Two different analyses of data from a five-year national study of married couples found no statistically significant difference in the risk of divorce among mainline Protestants, conservative Protestants, Catholics, and Jews. See Lehrer and Chiswick 1993; Call and Heaton 1997.

111   During the first fifteen years after marrying: Bramlett and Mosher 2002.

112   Another survey question, "Currently, how important is religion in your daily life?": See Chart 12 for the figures in this sentence and the next paragraph on the United States and Sweden. The estimates for Americans who say religion is "very important" or "not at all important" are from Bramlett and Mosher 2002. The estimates for Western Europe (which are for all the adults in each country, regardless of their attitude toward religion) are from Andersson and Philipov 2002, Table 27. A comparison of rates of dissolution of *cohabiting* unions (whether or not the couple married before breaking up) shows the same pattern. Seventy-six percent of cohabiting unions break up within fifteen years among Americans who say religion is "not important," compared to 68 percent among Americans who say religion is "very important," 55 percent among all Swedes, 51 percent among all West Germans, 48 percent among all French, and 43 percent among all Italians. See Chart 13.

113   Abortion, for instance, was legal: Reagan 1997.

113   Rather than being a traditional concern: Gordon 1990.

Chapter 5. The American Way of Marriage

117   But in 1993, after the couples appealed: *Baehr v. Lewin,* 74 Haw. 530, 852 P.2d 44 (1993).

117   Defense of Marriage Act: Public Law 104–199.

118   That social scientists rather than, say, religious leaders: Cott (2000, p. 207) writes, "The government's stake in marriage and divorce in the late twentieth century was economic far more than it was moral."

118   Still, Eggebeen spoke of the importance of marriage: *Baehr v. Miike* trial transcript, September 11, 1996, p. 42.

118 In contrast, Pepper Schwartz: The first quotation is from the trial transcript, September 16, 1996, p. 59, and the second is from pp. 61–62.

120 The Vermont Supreme Court ruled: *Baker v. Vermont,* 864 A.2nd 744 (1999).

120 "Civil marriage," the majority wrote: *Goodridge v. Department of Public Health,* 440 Mass. 309 (2003).

121 President Bush announced that he would support: "President's Statement on the Sanctity of Marriage Senate Vote," 2004, retrieved November 19, 2005, from http://www.whitehouse.gov/news/releases/2004/07/20040714-7.html.

121 At the announcement, he said: See "President Calls for Constitutional Amendment to Protect Marriage," 2004, retrieved June 13, 2006, from http:// www .whitehouse.gov/news/releases/2004/02/20040224-2.html.

121 After the amendment failed in Congress: National Council of State Legislatures 2008.

121 In at least eight of these states: For example, the 2004 Michigan amendment banning same-sex marriage states "the union of one man and one woman in marriage shall be the only agreement recognized as a marriage or similar union for any purpose." The Michigan attorney general ruled that the amendment allows Michigan cities to continue existing employee benefits for domestic partners of city employees but prohibits them from offering any new benefits. Retrieved August 8, 2006, from http://www.ag.state.mi.us/opinion/datafiles/ 2000s/op10247.htm.

121 In 2008 Massachusetts was joined by Connecticut: The best summary of each state's position can be found in National Council of State Legislatures 2008.

122 One British gay man said: Weeks et al. 2001, p. 193; see also Eekelaar 2003 and Fassin 2001.

122 In 2004 Britain legalized "civil partnerships": Cowell 2005.

122 "with hardly a murmur of protest": See Chapter 1.

123 France enacted a somewhat different form: Martin and Théry 2001. The PACS does not provide all of the legal benefits of marriage. Even when children are present, there is no provision requiring one partner to support the other after dissolution, and judges are reluctant to award joint custody.

123 The more contentious issue in Western Europe: Glendon 2006.

123 This "symbolic order" of family life: Fassin 2001.

123 Nor did it allow them to adopt children: Martin and Théry 2001.

123 And France is not alone: Andersson et al. 2006; "Gay Couples Win Partnership Rights," accessed August 8, 2006, from www.swisspolitics.org; Baetens and Brewaeys 2001.

123 "A woman shall not be provided with treatment services": Human Fertilisation and Embryology Act 1990, Section 13.5; retrieved August 11, 2007, from http:// www.opsi.gov.uk/acts/acts1990/Ukpga_19900037_en_1.htm.

123 In 2006 the minister of health announced: Henderson 2006.

124 "despite a nationwide shortage of sperm donors": Foster 2006.

124   Access to assisted reproduction in the United States: "Developments in the Law" 2003.

124   The Sperm Bank of California: "About Us," retrieved August 8, 2006, from http://www.thespermbankofca.org/about.html.

124   "lesbian baby boom": Patterson 1995.

124   They are now beginning to write about gay male partners: Stacey 2006.

124   In most states, adoption laws do not cover same-sex parents: Fisher 2003.

124   The parent's partner then adopts: Schacter 2000.

125   By 2005, 75 percent of married women with school-age children: U.S. Bureau of the Census 2007, Table 584.

125   When asked, "Do you approve": National Opinion Research Center, General Social Surveys, retrieved November 15, 2005, from http://webapp.icpsr.umich .edu/GSS. Tabulations by the author.

125   The "Moynihan Report": Rainwater and Yancey 1967.

126   Its first section included these "findings": Personal Responsibility and Work Opportunity Reconciliation Act of 1996, Public Law 104–193, Section 101.

126   "Healthy Marriage Initiative": U.S. Department of Health and Human Services, Administration for Children and Families, http://www.acf.hhs.gov/ healthymarriage, retrieved November 9, 2005.

126   $150 million per year for promoting marriage: Roberts 2006.

126   Advocates of promoting marriage stressed: Ooms 2002.

127   Similar programs for middle-class couples: Ooms 2005.

127   The government agency leading the Healthy Marriage Initiative: Dion 2005.

127   The proposed changes, advocated by a prestigious legal institute: American Law Institute 2002.

127   "The state," they wrote: Institute for American Values and Institute for Marriage and Public Policy 2006. See also Wilson 2006.

128   Britain probably comes closest: Smart 2000.

128   "It is not for the state to decide": From a 1998 Home Office report, "Supporting Families: A Consultation Document," p. 30, quoted in Smart 2000, p. 381.

128   "There is something fundamentally different": Horn 2002. Horn was assistant secretary of health and human services for children and families.

128   The British policy priority: There is considerable support in Germany for the marriage-based family in which mothers play the major role in raising children. After the reunification of West and East Germany, the federal government sharply cut back programs in the East that had supported employed mothers, such as a shortened workweek with full pay, a day off once a month for household tasks, and virtually free child care. (See Rudd 2000.) Still, compared to the United States, Germany's support for employed mothers is substantial. Its family allowances are in the middle range of generosity compared to other Western countries. Moreover, its paid maternity and child care leaves can be used by unmarried women, potentially eroding its support for marriage. (See Gauthier 1996.) It does not rely as heavily on the market to support parents as does the United States.

129 That may be why far fewer Americans: See Chapter 1.

130 Each week in Houston: Symonds 2005; Blumenthal 2006.

130 His 2004 book, *Your Best Life Now:* Wyatt 2006.

130 "Quit dwelling on those disappointments": Osteen 2004, p. 178. The quotation about King David is from p. 48; the quotation "He doesn't wink" is from p. 176.

131 "applied Christianity": Meyer 1988, p. 260, quoting Peale from his book *The Art of Living.*

131 Amazon.com's helpful concordance: Amazon.com provides a concordance for the one hundred most frequently used words in some of its best-selling books. I accessed this concordance on October 7, 2005. Amazon has since taken it down.

132 *BusinessWeek* reported in 2005: Symonds 2005.

132 "Sadly, a quick review": Warren 2002, pp. 177–78. The quote "This is more than a book" is from p. 9 (emphasis in the original). The quote "Christianity is not a religion" is from p. 183.

133 The enormous appetite of the American public: Osteen 2007. For the report about Osteen's book deal, see Wyatt 2006.

134 "The meaning of [divine] guidance": Wuthnow 1998, p. 101.

135 The roughly fifty thousand churches: Ammerman 2005.

135 "dizzying diversity of institutions that make up": McRoberts 2003, p. 142. The Baptist churches (such as the National Baptist Convention, USA, Inc.) remain numerically dominant, accounting for nearly half of all black congregants today. The Methodist churches (such as the African Methodist Episcopal Church) account for about 18 percent. Yet much as in white Protestant churches, the real growth in the twentieth-century black church occurred among Pentecostal groups (such as the Church of God in Christ), which by the end of the century were about as numerous as the Methodists. See Lincoln and Mamiya 1990.

135 "enduring institutions": Berry and Blassingame 1982.

135 "Church and household at times overlapped": Gilkes 1995, p. 188.

135 Some black churches have an informal position of "church mother": Lincoln and Mamiya 1990.

136 The nineteen-page index: Lincoln and Mamiya 1990.

136 "The head of the household, male or female": "Changing Church Confronts the Changing Black Family" 1993.

136 Although the meaning of marriage has changed: Goldstein and Kenney 2001.

137 "having a good marriage and family life": Thornton and Young-DeMarco 2001.

137 Rather than being natural, marriage was described: See, for example, Tiger and Fox 1971.

137 You'll recall the economist Gary Becker: Becker 1991.

138 One benefit that marriage still provides: Cherlin 2000. See also Portes and Sensenbrenner 1993.

138 As a result, marriage lowers the risk: In the language of economic theory, marriage lowers the transaction costs of enforcing agreements between the partners. See Pollak 1985.

138 It allows you to spend more time: Caregivers can make "relationship-specific investments" with less worry. See England and Farkas 1986.

139 62 percent agreed in a survey: Whitehead and Popenoe 2001.

140 "While marriage is losing much of its broad public and institutional character": Whitehead and Popenoe 2001.

140 "do-it-yourself biography": Beck and Beck-Gernsheim 2002.

140 The 2002 Toledo study: Smock et al. 2005.

140 "Um, we have certain things": Smock et al. 2005, p. 690.

141 According to the recollections of Detroit-area women: Whyte 1990.

141 The contemporary wedding, as Rebecca Mead puts it: Mead 2007, p. 11. A small literature on contemporary weddings and honeymoons is developing in North America and Europe, and it treats them as occasions of consumption and celebrations of romance. See R. Bulcroft et al. 2000; K. Bulcroft et al. 1997; Ingraham 1999; Otnes and Pleck 2003; Boden 2003; Howard 2006; Mead 2007.

142 A home health care aide said: Smock et al. 2005, p. 689.

142 There's one other explanation: Ogburn 1964.

Chapter 6. The M-Factor

144 "Uniquely, in the culture of the United States": Fisher 1999, p. 4. The subsequent quotation ("America has always signaled") is from p. 23.

145 "A restless temper seems to me": Pierson 1938, p. 118.

145 "a cloud habitually hung on their brow": Tocqueville 1994, 2:136.

146 "We Americans have taken what I shall call the 'M-Factor' ": Pierson 1973, p. 29.

146 The comparison shows that American men: Ferrie 2005.

146 American sons were more likely: Ferrie 2005. Nor was this difference due solely to the number of men who grew up on farms and moved to cities; the difference held even when men who left or moved into farming were excluded.

147 The proportion of the population that changes residences within a year: Long 1991; Greenwood 1997.

147 Even when just state-to-state moves: Krueger 2000.

147 "Americans have come to believe": Jasper 2000, p. 11.

148 Economists would explain the greater geographical mobility: Greenwood 1997.

149 In his 1897 book, *Suicide:* Durkheim 1951.

149 To test this idea, Robert D. Baller and Kelly K. Richardson: Baller and Richardson 2002.

149 Baller made another map: See Chart 15.

150 Divorce rates are lower among Mormons: Lehrer and Chiswick 1993.

150 Moreover, some of the divorced people in the West: Jasper 2000.

151 Those who live in regions where they are surrounded by lots of migrants: Glenn and Shelton 1985.

151 Migration sometimes caused problems: Hagan et al. 1996.

151 They have been growing fastest in the suburbs of southern and western cities: The best set of figures, although still of questionable representativeness, comes from a survey of 153 megachurches by the Hartford Institute of Religion Research. Retrieved January 3, 2006, from http://hirr.hartsem.edu/org/ faith_megachurches_research.html.

152 "We're not a large church": Brown 2002.

152 At Willow Creek Community Church: Sargeant 2000, pp. 83, 104.

152 Pierson railed against automobile-based irritants—to him at least: Pierson 1973, pp. 65, 115, 128.

153 "The shopping center makes you feel comfortable": Sargeant 2000, pp. 106–7.

154 Michael Rosenfeld calls this development: Rosenfeld 2007. The figures are for 1990.

155 Cohabiting relationships are much more likely to end: Smock and Manning 2004.

155 Marriages in which the partners are of different religions: Bumpass, Martin, and Sweet 1991; Lehrer and Chiswick 1993.

155 "If men define things as real": Thomas 1923.

156 "that restless nervous energy": Frederick Jackson Turner, *The Frontier in American History* (New York: Henry Holt and Company, 1920), quoted in Pierson 1973, p. 233.

156 "a new, permanently unsettled rhythm of creation and destruction": Fisher 1999, p. 3.

Chapter 7. Blue-Collar Blues/White-Collar Weddings

160 In 2005 the port of Miami imported: Statistics retrieved December 13, 2005, from http://www.miamidade.gov/portofmiami/port_statistics.asp.

160 Some of the steel used to be milled: Reutter 2001; Connelly 2007. On steel imports and exports, see U.S. Bureau of the Census 2007, Table 997. On the demand for computer specialists, see U.S. Bureau of Labor 2007. On motor vehicle sales, see Bradsher 2007. See also LeMasters 1975.

161 Suppose you order a new battery: This sequence of events is described in Fallows 2007.

162 The U.S. Bureau of Labor Statistics predicted: U.S. Bureau of Labor Statistics 2007.

162 Since about 1990 these routine jobs have been disappearing: Autor et al. 2006.

162 The wages of men without college degrees: Ellwood and Jencks 2004b; Richer et al. 2003.

163 By 1996, the average thirty-year-old husband: Levy 1998.

163 "For example, Henry": Smock et al. 2005.

163 Young men who are out of school and working: Oppenheimer 2003.

163 An unemployed twenty-nine-year-old man: Smock et al. 2005, p. 687.

164 Currently, about one out of six American children: Official government statistics show only that in the 2000s a little over a third of all children were born to unmarried mothers. But the U.S. government's statistical agencies don't differentiate between unmarried mothers who are cohabiting and those who are truly living without partners. Other surveys show that by the early 2000s, about half of the unmarried women who gave birth were cohabiting.

164 As a result, children born to parents who are cohabiting: Kennedy and Bumpass 2007.

165 That's clear from the attitudes: Cherlin et al. 2008.

165 "Unlike their wealthier sisters": Edin and Kefalas 2005, p. 46.

166 Women in low-income neighborhoods perceive little cost: Just 20 percent of the women in our three-city study agreed with the statement "Having children when a woman is single hurts her chances of later getting married," and just 19 percent agreed that "having a child without being married is embarrassing for a woman." Cherlin et al. 2008.

167 But it hardly changed among the well-educated: Ellwood and Jencks 2004b.

167 They may work for several years: Martin 2004.

167 It's waiting until they are married: Kennedy and Bumpass 2007.

167 Among high school–educated women: Kennedy and Bumpass 2007.

168 Marriages are much more stable among the college-educated: Martin 2006; Raley and Bumpass 2003.

169 "We did okay for a while": Rubin 1994, pp. 121–22.

169 The working-class wives said: Amato et al. 2007.

170 At current rates, only about two out of three black women: Goldstein and Kenney 2001.

170 And their marriages are very fragile: Martin 2006; Raley and Bumpass 2003.

170 African American young adults are only half as likely to have college degrees: Among people ages twenty-five to twenty-nine, 34 percent of whites and 17 percent of African Americans have four-year college degrees. U.S. Bureau of the Census 2006a.

170 In fact, until about 1950, African Americans tended to marry: Cherlin 1992.

171 Indeed, in some neighborhoods: Burton 1990.

171 "I was always named 'sergeant' ": Cherlin and Furstenberg 1992.

171 In practice, many young married couples with children: Almost one-third of American parents give gifts of $500 or more to one of their adult children per year (McGarry and Schoeni 1995).

172 "beanpole family": Bengtson et al. 1990.

172 Having a spouse may also help: There is a large literature that suggests that marriage is beneficial to adults' health and well-being. The question is whether marriage makes people healthier and happier or whether healthier and happier people are the ones who are most likely to marry and to stay married. See Waite and Gallagher 2000.

172 Hispanics have substantially higher rates of marriage: Oropesa et al. 1994.

172 Even though Hispanics as a group are economically disadvantaged: Oropesa and Landale 2004. By "whites" I mean people who identified as whites but did not identify as Hispanic in surveys.

172 Moreover, Hispanic marriages and cohabiting relationships: Raley and Bumpass 2003.

172 Cuban Americans also have relatively high levels: Oropesa and Landale 2004.

173 Mexican Americans born in Mexico: Raley, Durden, and Wildsmith 2004.

173 Nationally, 16 percent of white women: Author's estimates from the 2002 National Survey of Family Growth. The women were age thirty-five to forty-four. High school graduates tend to have the most partnerships, followed closely by high school dropouts. Both groups have a higher number of partnerships, on average, than do the college-educated. See Chart 14. These differences held in further statistical analyses. I estimated three sets of regression equations, each of which included indicators of education, Hispanic ethnicity, race, age, and religious attendance. The first was a Poisson regression model based on the number of partners; the second was a logistic regression model based on having had three or more partners versus having had two or fewer; and the third was a logistic regression model based on having had two or more partners versus having had one or none. The results of all three were very similar: women with more education had significantly fewer partners, with high school graduates who did not attend college having the highest level. Hispanics and African Americans had significantly fewer partners than non-Hispanic whites; women who attended religious services at least once a month had significantly fewer partners than did women who attended less often; and older women had significantly more partners.

173 "marriageable men": Wilson 1987.

173 The number of black women who are in the marriage market: The lifetime lack of partnerships also could reflect a different definition of what counts as living with someone. The ethnographic accounts in the three-city study of low-income families suggest that an African American woman may be more likely than a white or Hispanic woman to define a man who spends most of his time at her house as a friend rather than a live-in partner. Whether a person views herself or himself as living with a partner is a subjective decision that can vary from person to person or from group to group. I thank Linda Burton for this insight.

176 First-generation Mexican immigrant women: Hirsch 2003.

176 "The most fundamental truth these stories reveal": Edin and Kefalas 2005, p. 136.

177 We can draw a similar lesson: Carlson et al. 2004.

178 People with less education: Author's tabulations from General Social Survey, 1972–2000 Cumulative Codebook, retrieved December 11, 2005, from http://webapp.icpsr.umich.edu/GSS.

178 The classic example was anthropologist Oscar Lewis's description: Lewis 1965.

179 Schooling has become the great sorting machine: Kalmijn 1991.

179 At the other extreme of the marriage market: Schwartz and Mare 2005.

179 When and if they marry: Raley and Bumpass 2003.

180 Even the most stable groups: Recall that the highest mid-1990s estimate of the proportion of women who live with three or more partners by age thirty-five elsewhere in the Western world was 4.5 percent, in Sweden. In the 2002 United States survey, there were 501 women who had graduated from college and were between the ages of thirty and thirty-five. Eleven percent of them had already lived with three or more partners, according to my tabulations.

Chapter 8. Slow Down

181 That's why the Moynihan Report: Rainwater and Yancey 1967.

183 "The divisions over the family": Wolfe 1998, pp. 110–11.

183 In fact, as recently as 1900: Uhlenberg 1980.

183 We know that a higher percentage of children live: Ellwood and Jencks 2004a.

186 Forty-four percent of Americans have changed their religious affiliation: Pew Forum on Religion and Public Life 2008.

187 "I'm the only one in my whole family": Rubin 1994, p. 122. The subsequent quote is from the same page.

189 Joyce Meyer: Meyer 2000, pp. 193, 69.

190 Fifty years ago, his predecessors got more of them: Wilcox 2004 makes a similar argument.

191 In the study of young adolescents: Fomby and Cherlin 2007.

191 This sequence has occurred in debates: Cherlin 1999a. The two psychologists are Judith S. Wallerstein and Judith Rich Harris. See Wallerstein et al. 2000; Harris 1998.

192 Unless we see a reversal of this transformation: On the transformation, see Beck and Beck-Gersheim 2002; Giddens 1992.

192 "iron cage": Weber 2002.

193 Stable, low-conflict families: For a recent review, see Amato 2005.

194 The magic moment: Center for Research on Child Well-Being 2007.

196 They may want to share expenses and parenting responsibilities: Reed 2006.

196 We should urge them to choose carefully and deliberately: I am focusing on heterosexual partnerships, but the same principle would apply to lesbian and gay male partnerships.

198 In 2006, when Congress reauthorized the welfare reform legislation: The federal government will waive its share of the first $100 for one child and $200 for two or more children. Consequently, a state that used to give the federal government 65 percent of what it collected would save $65 on the first $100 it provided to a mother. See Justice 2007.

198 Sociologist Myra Marx Ferree: Ferree 2007. The benefit rate would be equivalent to the median benefit currently being paid to retired workers.

199 The general idea is that when lone mothers: However, notwithstanding the Wisconsin results, they may also avoid marriage; experiments with income supplements in other states and Canadian provinces have produced inconsistent effects on marriage. See, for example, Harknett and Gennetian 2003.

Bibliography

Accampo, Elinor A. 2003. "The Gendered Nature of Contraception in France: Neo-Malthusianism, 1900–1920." *Journal of Interdisciplinary History* 34:235–62.

Allen, Woody. 1999. *Standup Comic.* Los Angeles: Rhino Entertainment.

Amato, Paul R. 2005. "The Impact of Family Formation Change on the Cognitive, Social, and Emotional Well-Being of the Next Generation." *The Future of Children* 15, 2:75–96.

Amato, Paul R., Alan Booth, David R. Johnson, and Stacy J. Rogers. 2007. *Alone Together: How Marriage in America Is Changing.* Cambridge, MA: Harvard University Press.

American Law Institute. 2002. *Principles of the Law of Family Dissolution: Analysis and Recommendations.* Philadelphia: American Law Institute.

Ammerman, Nancy Tatom. 2005. *Pillars of Faith: American Congregations and Their Partners.* Berkeley: University of California Press.

Andersson, Gunnar. 2002. "Children's Experience of Family Disruption and Family Formation: Evidence from 16 FFS Countries." *Demographic Research* 7:343–63.

Andersson, Gunnar, Turid Noack, Ane Seierstad, and Harald Weedon-Fekjær. 2006. "The Demographics of Same-Sex Marriage in Norway and Sweden." *Demography* 43:79–98.

Andersson, Gunnar, and Dimiter Philipov. 2002. "Life-Table Representations of Family Dynamics in Sweden, Hungary, and 14 Other FFS Countries: A Project of Descriptions of Demographic Behavior." *Demographic Research* 7:67–145.

Autor, David H., Lawrence F. Katz, and Melissa Kearney. 2006. "The Polarization of the U.S. Labor Market." *American Economic Review* 96:189–94.

Baetens, P., and A. Brewaeys. 2001. "Lesbian Couples Requesting Donor Insemination: An Update of the Knowledge with Regard to Lesbian Mother Families." *Human Reproduction* 7:512–19.

Baker, Wayne E. 2005. *America's Crisis of Values: Reality and Perception.* Princeton, N.J.: Princeton University Press.

Baller, Robert D., and Kelly K. Richardson. 2002. "Social Integration, Imitation, and the Geographic Patterning of Suicide." *American Sociological Review* 67:873–88.

Basch, Norma. 1979. "Invisible Women: The Legal Fiction of Marital Unity in Nineteenth-Century America." *Feminist Studies* 5:346–66.

Beale, Lucy, Sandy G. Couvillon, and Edna C. Brown. 2004. *Christian Family Guide to Losing Weight.* New York: Alpha Books.

Beck, Ulrich, and Elisabeth Beck-Gernsheim. 2002. *Individualization: Institutionalized Individualism and Its Social and Political Consequences.* London: Sage Publications.

Beck, Ulrich, Anthony Giddens, and Scott Lash. 1994. *Reflexive Modernization: Politics, Tradition and Aesthetics in the Modern Social Order.* Cambridge: Polity Press.

Becker, Gary S. 1991. *A Treatise on the Family.* Enlarged ed. Cambridge, MA: Harvard University Press.

Bellah, Robert, Richard Madsen, William M. Sullivan, Ann Swidler, and Steven M. Tipton. 1985. *Habits of the Heart: Individualism and Commitment in America.* Berkeley: University of California Press.

Bengtson, Vern L., Carolyn J. Rosenthal, and Linda M. Burton. 1990. "Families and Aging: Diversity and Heterogeneity." Pp. 263–87 in *Handbook of Aging and the Social Sciences,* 3rd ed., edited by R. H. Binstock and L. K. George. New York: Academic Press.

Berry, Mary Frances, and John W. Blassingame. 1982. *Long Memory: The Black Experience in America.* New York: Oxford University Press.

Bittman, Michael, Paula England, Liana Sayer, Nancy Folbre, and George Matheson. 2003. "When Does Gender Trump Money? Bargaining and Time in Household Work." *American Journal of Sociology* 109:186–214.

Blake, Nelson Manfred. 1962. *The Road to Reno: A History of Divorce in the United States.* New York: Macmillan.

Bledsoe, Caroline. 1990. "Transformations in Sub-Saharan African Marriage and Fertility." *Annals of the American Academy of Political and Social Science* 501:115–25.

Blumenthal, Ralph. 2006. "A Preacher's Credo: Eliminate the Negative, Accentuate Prosperity." *New York Times,* March 30.

Boden, Sharon. 2003. *Consumerism, Romance, and the Wedding Experience.* Hampshire: Palgrave Macmillan.

Bradsher, Keith. 2007. "Toyota Tops GM in Sales for First Time," *New York Times,* April 24.

Brady, David, Jason Beckfield, and Martin Seeleib-Kaiser. 2005. "Economic Globalization and the Welfare State in Affluent Democracies." *American Sociological Review* 70: 921–48.

Bramlett, Matthew D., and William D. Mosher. 2002. "Cohabitation, Marriage, Divorce and Remarriage in the United States." U.S. National Center for Vital and Health Statistics.

Brown, Patricia Leigh. 2002. "Megachurches as Minitowns." *New York Times,* May 9.

Brown, Susan L. 2006. "Family Structure Transitions and Adolescent Well-Being." *Demography* 43:447–61.

Bruce, Steve. 2001. "The Social Process of Secularization." Pp. 249–63 in *The Black-*

well Companion to the Sociology of Religion, edited by R. K. Fenn. Oxford: Blackwell.

Budig, Michelle, and Paula England. 2001. "The Wage Penalty for Motherhood." *American Sociological Review* 66:204–25.

Bulcroft, Kris, Richard Bulcroft, Linda Smeins, and Helen Cranage. 1997. "The Social Construction of the North American Honeymoon, 1880–1995." *Journal of Family History* 22:462–90.

Bulcroft, Richard A., Kris Bulcroft, Karen Bradley, and Carl Simpson. 2000. "The Management and Production of Risk in Romantic Relationships: A Postmodern Paradox." *Journal of Family History* 25:63–92.

Bumpass, Larry L. 1990. "What's Happening to the Family? Interactions Between Demographic and Institutional Change." *Demography* 27:483–98.

Bumpass, Larry L., and Hsien-hen Lu. 2000. "Trends in Cohabitation and Implications for Children's Family Contexts in the United States." *Population Studies* 54:19–41.

Bumpass, Larry L., Teresa Castro Martin, and James A. Sweet. 1991. "The Impact of Family Background and Early Marital Factors on Marital Disruption." *Journal of Family Issues* 12:22–42.

Bumpass, Larry L., James A. Sweet, and Andrew J. Cherlin. 1991. "The Role of Cohabitation in Declining Rates of Marriage." *Journal of Marriage and Family* 53:338–55.

Burton, Linda M. 1990. "Teenage Childbearing as an Alternative Life-Course Strategy in Multigenerational Black Families." *Human Nature* 1:123–43.

Butler, Jon. 1990. *Awash in a Sea of Faith: Christianizing the American People.* Cambridge, MA: Harvard University Press.

———. 2004. "Jack-in-the-Box Faith: The Religion Problem in Modern American History." *Journal of American History* 90:1357–78.

Butler, Jon, Grant Wacker, and Randall Balmer. 2003. *Religion in American Life: A Short History.* New York: Oxford University Press.

Call, Vaughn R., and Tim B. Heaton. 1997. "Religious Influence on Marital Stability." *Journal for the Scientific Study of Religion* 36:382–92.

Cancian, Francesca M. 1987. *Love in America: Gender and Self-Development.* Cambridge: Cambridge University Press.

Cancian, Maria, and Daniel R. Meyer. 2006. "Effects of the Full Child Support Pass-Through/Disregard on Marriage and Cohabitation." Madison: Institute for Research on Poverty; retrieved September 24, 2006, from http://www.irp.wisc .edu/ research/childsup/csde/ publications/cancian-meyer-choi-i.pdf.

Carasso, Adam, and Eugene Steuerle. 2005. "The Hefty Penalty on Marriage Facing Many Households with Children." *The Future of Children* 15:157–75.

Carbone, June. 2000. *From Partners to Parents: The Second Revolution in Family Law.* New York: Columbia University Press.

Carlson, Marcia, Sara McLanahan, and Paula England. 2004. "Union Formation in Fragile Families." *Demography* 41:237–61.

Cavanaugh, Shannon E., and Aletha C. Huston. 2006. "Family Instability and Children's Early Problem Behavior." *Social Forces* 85:551–81.

Center for Research on Child Well-Being. 2007. "Parents' Relationship Status Five Years After a Non-Marital Birth"; retrieved February 6, 2008, from http://www.fragilefamilies.princeton.edu/briefs/ResearchBrief39.pdf.

"Changing Church Confronts the Changing Black Family." 1993. *Ebony* 48 (August):94–98.

Cherlin, Andrew J. 1992. *Marriage, Divorce, Remarriage.* Revised and expanded ed. Cambridge, MA: Harvard University Press.

———. 1999a. "Going to Extremes: Family Structure, Children's Well-Being, and Social Science." *Demography* 36:421–28.

———. 1999b. "I'm O.K., You're Selfish." *New York Times Magazine,* October 17, 44–46.

———. 2000. "Toward a New Home Socioeconomics of Union Formation." Pp. 126–44 in *The Ties That Bind: Perspectives on Marriage and Cohabitation,* edited by L. J. Waite, C. Bachrach, M. Hindin, E. Thomson, and A. Thornton. New York: Aldine de Gruyter.

———. 2004. "The Deinstitutionalization of American Marriage." *Journal of Marriage and Family* 66:848–61.

Cherlin, Andrew, Caitlin Cross-Barnet, Linda M. Burton, and Raymond Garrett-Peters. 2008. "Promises They Can Keep: Low-Income Women's Attitudes Toward Motherhood, Marriage, and Divorce." *Journal of Marriage and Family* 70:919–33.

Cherlin, Andrew J., and Frank F. Furstenberg Jr. 1992. *The New American Grandparent: A Place in the Family, a Life Apart.* Cambridge, MA: Harvard University Press.

———. 1994. "Stepfamilies in the United States: A Reconsideration." *Annual Review of Sociology* 20:359–81.

Cherlin, Andrew J., Frank F. Furstenberg Jr., P. Lindsay Chase-Lansdale, Kathleen E. Kiernan, Philip K. Robins, Donna Ruane Morrison, and Julien O. Teitler. 1991. "Longitudinal Studies of the Effects of Divorce on Children in Great Britain and the United States," *Science* 252:1386–89.

Chesler, Ellen. 1992. *Woman of Valor: Margaret Sanger and the Birth Control Movement in America.* New York: Simon and Schuster.

Cockett, M., and J. Tripp. 1994. *The Exeter Family Study.* Exeter: University of Exeter.

Coleman, Marilyn, Lawrence H. Ganong, and Mark Fine. 2000. "Reinvestigating Remarriage: Another Decade of Progress." *Journal of Marriage and Family* 62:1288–307.

Connelly, Allison. 2007. "15 Days for Sparrows Point." *Baltimore Sun,* June 21.

Coontz, Stephanie. 2005. *Marriage, a History: From Obedience to Intimacy, or How Love Conquered Marriage.* New York: Viking.

Cott, Nancy F. 1977. *The Bonds of Womanhood: "Women's Sphere" in New England, 1780–1835.* New Haven: Yale University Press.

———. 2000. *Public Vows: A History of Marriage and the Nation.* Cambridge, MA: Harvard University Press.

Cowell, Alan. 2005. "Gay Britons Signing Up as Unions Become Legal." *New York Times,* December 5.

Curry, Robert, Alan Gilbert, and Lee Horsely. 1977. *Churches and Churchgoers: Patterns of Church Growth in the British Isles Since 1700.* Oxford: Clarendon Press.

D'Antonio, William V., James D. Davidson, Dean R. Hoge, and Katherine Meyer. 2001. *American Catholics: Gender, Generation, and Commitment.* Walnut Creek, CA: Altamira Press.

DeLeire, Thomas, and Ariel Kalil. 2005. "How Do Cohabiting Couples with Children Spend Their Money?" *Journal of Marriage and Family* 67:286–95.

De Luca, Virginie. 2005. "Restoring the Notion of Family in France: Pronatalist and Pro-family Propaganda in Schools and Army Barracks (1920–1940)." *Population-E* 60:11–36.

D'Emilio, J., and E. B. Freedman. 1988. *Intimate Matters: A History of Sexuality in America.* New York: Harper and Row.

Demos, J. 1970. *A Little Commonwealth: Family Life in Plymouth Colony.* Oxford: Oxford University Press.

de Vaus, David. 2004. "Diversity and Change in Australian Families: Statistical Profiles." Australian Institute of Family Studies, Melbourne.

"Developments in the Law—the Law of Marriage and Family." 2003. *Harvard Law Review* 116:1996–2122.

DiMaggio, Paul. 1997. "Culture and Cognition." *Annual Review of Sociology* 23:263–87.

Dion, Robin. 2005. "Healthy Marriage Programs: Learning What Works." *Future of Children* 15:139–56.

Durkheim, Émile. (1897) 1951. *Suicide: A Study in Sociology.* Glencoe, IL: Free Press.

Dworak-Winkler, Maria, and Henriette Engelhardt. 2004. "On the Tempo and Quantum of First Marriages in Austria, Germany, and Switzerland: Changes in Mean Age and Variance." *Demographic Research* 10:231–64.

Easterlin, Richard A. 1980. *Birth and Fortune: The Impact of Numbers on Personal Welfare.* New York: Basic Books.

Edgell, Penny. 2006. *Religion and Family in a Changing Society.* Princeton, NJ: Princeton University Press.

Edin, Kathryn, and Maria J. Kefalas. 2005. *Promises I Can Keep: Why Poor Women Put Motherhood Before Marriage.* Berkeley: University of California Press.

Edin, Kathryn, and Laura Lein. 1997. *Making Ends Meet: How Low-Income Single Mothers Survive Welfare and Low-Wage Work.* New York: Russell Sage Foundation.

Eekelaar, John. 2003. "The End of an Era?" *Journal of Family History* 28:108–22.

———. 2006. "Empowerment and Responsibility: The Balance Sheet Approach in the Principles and English Law." Pp. 433–45 in *Reconceiving the Family: Critique on the American Law Institute's Principles of the Law of Family Dissolution,* edited by Robin F. Wilson. New York: Cambridge University Press.

Ellwood, David T., and Christopher Jencks. 2004a. "The Spread of Single-Parent Families in the United States Since 1960." Pp. 26–65 in *The Future of the Family,* edited by D. P. Moynihan, T. Smeeding, and L. Rainwater. New York: Russell Sage Foundation.

———. 2004b. "The Uneven Spread of Single-Parent Families: What Do We Know? Where Do We Look for Answers?" Pp. 3–118 in *Social Inequality,* edited by K. M. Neckerman. New York: Russell Sage Foundation.

England, Paula, and George Farkas. 1986. *Households, Employment, and Gender: A Social, Economic, and Demographic View.* New York: Aldine de Gruyter.

Fallows, James. 2007. "China Makes, the World Takes." *The Atlantic,* July/August, 48ff.

Fassin, Eric. 2001. "Same Sex, Different Politics: 'Gay Marriage' Debates in France and the United States." *Popular Culture* 13:215–32.

Ferree, M. M. 2007. "An American Roadmap? Framing Feminist Goals in a Liberal Landscape"; retrieved December 13, 2008, from http://www.ssc.wisc.edu/~mscaglio/2006documents/Marx_Ferree_2007_American_Utopia.pdf.

Ferrie, Joseph P. 2005. "The End of American Exceptionalism? Mobility in the United States Since 1850." *Journal of Economic Perspectives* 19:199–215.

Finke, Roger, and Rodney Stark. 2005. *The Churching of America 1776 to 2005: Winners and Losers in Our Religious Economy.* New Brunswick, NJ: Rutgers University Press.

Fisher, Allen P. 2003. "Still 'Not Quite as Good as Having Your Own'? Toward a Sociology of Adoption." *Annual Review of Sociology* 29:335–61.

Fisher, Philip. 1999. *Still the New World: American Literature in a Culture of Creative Destruction.* Cambridge, MA: Harvard University Press.

Flaherty, David H. 1967. *Privacy in Colonial New England.* Charlottesville: University Press of Virginia.

Fomby, Paula, and Andrew J. Cherlin. 2007. "Family Instability and Child Well-Being." *American Sociological Review* 72:181–204.

Foster, Kate. 2006. "Scottish Health Boards Fund IVF for Lesbians." *Scotland on Sunday,* August 11.

Friedan, Betty. 1963. *The Feminine Mystique.* New York: W. W. Norton.

Friedman, Lawrence M. 2004. *Law in America: A Short History.* New York: Modern Library.

Ganz, Melissa J. 1997. "Wicked Women and Veiled Ladies: Gendered Narratives of the McFarland-Richardson Tragedy." *Yale Journal of Law and Feminism* 9:255–303.

Gauthier, Anne H. 1996. *The State and the Family: A Comparative Analysis of Family Policies in Industrialized Countries.* Oxford: Clarendon Press.

Giddens, Anthony. 1991. *Modernity and Self-Identity.* Stanford, CA: Stanford University Press.

———. 1992. *The Transformation of Intimacy.* Stanford, CA: Stanford University Press.

Gilkes, Cheryl Townsend. 1995. "The Storm and the Light: Church, Family, Work, and Social Crisis in the African-American Experience." Pp. 177–98 in *Work, Fam-*

ily, and Religion in Contemporary Society, edited by Nancy Ammerman and Wade Clark Roof. New York: Routledge.

Gill, Robin. 1999. *Churchgoing and Christian Ethics.* Cambridge: Cambridge University Press.

———. 2001. "The Future of Religious Participation and Belief in Britain and Beyond." Pp. 279–91 in *The Blackwell Companion to the Sociology of Religion,* edited by R. K. Fenn. Oxford: Blackwell.

Gillis, John R. 1985. *For Better or Worse: British Marriages, 1600 to the Present.* Oxford: Oxford University Press.

Glendon, Mary Ann. 1987. *Abortion and Divorce in Western Law.* Cambridge, MA: Harvard University Press.

———. 1989. *The Transformation of Family Law: State, Law, and Family in the United States and Western Europe.* Chicago: University of Chicago Press.

———. 2006. "Family Law in a Time of Turbulence." Pp. 3–28 in *International Encyclopedia of Comparative Law,* vol. 4: *Persons and Families,* edited by M. A. Glendon. Tübingen: Mohr Siebeck.

Glenmary Research Center. 2005. "Ten States with Lowest Percentage Catholic, 2000 and 1990"; retrieved November 23, 2005, from www.glenmary.org.

Glenn, Norval D., and Beth Ann Shelton. 1985. "Regional Differences in Divorce in the United States." *Journal of Marriage and Family* 47:641–52.

Goldstein, Joshua R., and Catherine T. Kenney. 2001. "Marriage Delayed or Marriage Forgone? New Cohort Forecasts of First Marriage for U.S. Women." *American Sociological Review* 66:506–19.

Gordon, Linda. 1990. *Woman's Body, Woman's Right: Birth Control in America.* Revised and updated ed. New York: Penguin Books.

Greenwood, Michael J. 1997. "Internal Migration in Developed Countries." Pp. 647–721 in *Handbook of Population and Family Economics,* vol. 1B, edited by M. R. Rosenzweig and O. Stark. Amsterdam: Elsevier.

Grossberg, Michael. 1985. *Governing the Hearth: Law and the Family in Nineteenth-Century America.* Chapel Hill: University of North Carolina Press.

Gutman, Herbert G. 1976a. *The Black Family in Slavery and Freedom, 1750–1925.* New York: Pantheon Books.

———. 1976b. "Durability on the Plantation." *New York Times,* September 23.

Hackstaff, Karla B. 1999. *Marriage in a Culture of Divorce.* Philadelphia: Temple University Press.

Hagan, John, Ross MacMillan, and Blair Wheaton. 1996. "New Kid in Town: Social Capital and Life Course Effects of Family Migration on Children." *American Sociological Review* 61:368–85.

Harknett, Kristin, and Lisa A. Gennetian. 2003. "How an Earnings Supplement Can Affect Union Formation Among Low-Income Single Mothers." *Demography* 40:451–78.

Harris, Judith Rich. 1998. *The Nurture Assumption.* New York: Free Press.

Hartog, Hendrik. 2000. *Man and Wife in America: A History.* Cambridge, MA: Harvard University Press.

Haskey, John. 1999. "Divorce and Remarriage in England and Wales." *Population Trends* 95:18–23.

Henderson, Mark. 2006. "Fathers Are Out of the Picture as Lesbians Get IVF." London *Times,* August 11.

Herskovits, M. J. 1990. *The Myth of the Negro Past.* Boston: Beacon Press.

Hetherington, E. Mavis, and Glenn Clingempeel. 1992. "Coping with Marital Transitions." *Monographs of the Society for Research in Child Development* 57.

Hetherington, E. Mavis, and John Kelly. 2002. *For Better or for Worse: Divorce Reconsidered.* New York: W. W. Norton.

Heuveline, Patrick, and Jeffrey M. Timberlake. 2004. "The Role of Cohabitation in Family Formation: The United States in Comparative Perspective." *Journal of Marriage and Family* 66:1214–30.

Heuveline, Patrick, Jeffrey M. Timberlake, and Frank F. Furstenberg Jr. 2003. "Shifting Childrearing to Single Mothers: Results from 17 Western Countries." *Population and Development Review* 29:47–71.

Hirsch, Jennifer S. 2003. *A Courtship After Marriage: Sexuality and Love in Mexican Transnational Families.* Berkeley: University of California Press.

Horn, Wade. 2002. "YES: Healthy Marriages Provide Numerous Benefits to Adults, Children and Society." *Insight on the News* (March 18); retrieved November 9, 2005, from http://www.insightmag.com.

Hout, Michael. 2000. "Angry and Alienated: Divorced and Remarried Catholics in the United States." *America,* December 16, pp. 10–12.

Howard, Vicki. 2006. *Brides, Inc.: American Weddings and the Business of Tradition.* Philadelphia: University of Pennsylvania Press.

Inglehart, Ronald, and Wayne E. Baker. 2000. "Modernization, Cultural Change, and the Persistence of Cultural Values." *American Sociological Review* 65:19–51.

Inglehart, Ronald, Miguel Basáñez, Jaime Díez-Medrano, Loek Halman, and Ruud Luijkx. 2004. *Human Beliefs and Values: A Cross-Cultural Sourcebook Based on the 1999–2002 Values Surveys.* Mexico City: Siglo Veintiuno Editores.

Ingraham, Chrys. 1999. *White Weddings: Romancing Heterosexuality in Popular Culture.* New York: Routledge.

Institute for American Values and Institute for Marriage and Public Policy. 2006. "Marriage and the Law: A Statement of Principles"; retrieved September 6, 2008, from http://www.americanvalues.org/html/mlawstmnt2.html.

Instone-Brewer, David. 2007. "What God Has Joined." *Christianity Today,* October.

Jacoby, Susan. 1980. "Time to Yourself: Must It Threaten Your Marriage?" *McCall's,* April, 95ff.

Jasper, James M. 2000. *Restless Nation: Starting Over in America.* Chicago: University of Chicago Press.

Justice, Jan. 2007. "State Policy Regarding Pass-Through and Disregard of Current Month's Child Support Collected for Families Receiving TANF-Funded Cash

Assistance"; retrieved July 13, 2007, from http://www.clasp.org/publications/pass
_through_2007june01.pdf.

Kalmijn, Matthijs. 1991. "Shifting Boundaries: Trends in Religious and Educational
Homogamy." *American Sociological Review* 56:786–800.

Katz, Sanford N. 2000. "Individual Rights and Family Relationships." Pp. 621–35 in
Cross Currents: Family Law and Policy in the United States and England, edited by
S. N. Katz, J. Eekelaar, and M. Maclean. Oxford: Oxford University Press.

Katz, Sanford N., John Eekelaar, and Mavis Maclean. 2000. *Cross Currents: Family
Law and Policy in the United States and England.* Oxford: Oxford University Press.

Kellams, Laura. 2005. "Huckabees Say 'I Do' to Covenant Marriage." *Arkansas
Democrat-Gazette,* February 15.

Kennedy, Sheela, and Larry L. Bumpass. 2007. "Cohabitation and Children's Living
Arrangements: New Estimates from the United States." Working Paper no.
2007-20. Madison, WI: Center for Demography and Ecology.

Kiernan, Kathleen E. 1999. "Cohabitation in Western Europe." *Population Trends* 96
(summer):25–32.

———. 2002. "The State of European Unions: An Analysis of FFS Data on Partnership Formation and Dissolution." Pp. 57–76 in *Dynamics of Fertility and Partnership in Europe: Insights and Lessons from Comparative Research,* vol. 1, edited by
M. Macura and G. Beets. New York: United Nations.

Kingdon, Robert M. 1995. *Adultery and Divorce in Calvin's Geneva.* Cambridge, MA:
Harvard University Press.

Krueger, Alan B. 2000. "From Bismarck to Maastricht: The March to European Union
and the Labor Contract." *Labor Economics* 7:117–34.

Lantz, Herman, Martin Schultz, and Mary O'Hara. 1977. "The Changing American
Family from the Preindustrial to the Industrial Period: A Final Report." *American
Sociological Review* 42:406–21.

Lapierre-Adamcyk, Évelyne, Céline Le Bourdais, and Nicole Marcil-Gratton. 1999.
"Vivre en couple pour la première fois: la signification du choix de l'union libre au
Québec et en Ontario." *Cahiers Québécois de Démographie* 28:199–227.

Lasch, Christopher. 1978. *The Culture of Narcissism: American Life in an Age of
Diminishing Expectations.* New York: W. W. Norton.

LeBeau, Bryan. 2000. *Religion in America to 1865.* Edinburgh: Edinburgh University
Press.

Le Bourdais, Céline, and Évelyne Lapierre-Adamcyk. 2004. "Changes in Conjugal
Life in Canada: Is Cohabitation Progressively Replacing Marriage?" *Journal of Marriage and Family* 66:929–42.

Lehrer, Evelyn L., and Carmel U. Chiswick. 1993. "Religion as a Determinant of Marital Stability." *Demography* 30:385–404.

LeMasters, E. E. 1975. *Blue-Collar Aristocrats: Life-styles at a Working-Class Tavern.*
Madison: University of Wisconsin Press.

Lesthaeghe, Ron, and Johan Surkyn. 1988. "Cultural Dynamics and Economic Theories of Fertility Change." *Population and Development Review* 14:1–45.

Levy, Frank. 1998. *The New Dollars and Dreams: American Incomes and Economic Change.* New York: Russell Sage Foundation.

Lewis, Jane. 2001. "Debates and Issues Regarding Marriage and Cohabitation in the British and American Literature." *International Journal of Law, Policy and the Family* 15:159–84.

Lewis, Oscar. 1965. *La Vida: A Puerto Rican Family in the Culture of Poverty, San Juan and New York.* New York: Random House.

Lincoln, C. Eric, and Lawrence H. Mamiya. 1990. *The Black Church in the African American Experience.* Durham, NC: Duke University Press.

Lipset, Seymour M. 1996. *American Exceptionalism: A Double-Edged Sword.* New York: W. W. Norton.

Lobsenz, Norman. 1977. "Love vs. Privacy." *McCall's,* August, 46ff.

Long, Larry H. 1991. "Residential Mobility Differences Among Developed Countries." *International Regional Science Review* 14:133–47.

Mahler, Jonathan. 2005. "The Soul of the New Exurb." *New York Times Magazine,* March 27.

Mahoney, James. 2000. "Path-Dependence in Historical Sociology." *Theory and Society* 29:507–48.

Manegold, Catherine S. 1994. "Quiet Winners in House Fight on Crime: Women." *New York Times,* August 25.

Manning, Wendy D., and Kathleen A. Lamb. 2003. "Adolescent Well-Being in Cohabiting, Married, and Single-Parent Families." *Journal of Marriage and Family* 65:876–93.

Manning, Wendy D., and Pamela J. Smock. 2005. "Measuring and Modeling Cohabitation: New Perspectives from Qualitative Data." *Journal of Marriage and Family* 67:989–1002.

Martin, Claude, and Irène Théry. 2001. "The PACS and Marriage and Cohabitation in France." *International Journal of Law, Policy and the Family* 15:135–58.

Martin, Steven P. 2004. "Women's Education and Family Timing: Outcomes and Trends Associated with Age at Marriage and First Birth." Pp. 79–118 in *Social Inequality,* edited by K. M. Neckerman. New York: Russell Sage Foundation.

———. 2006. "Trends in Marital Dissolution by Women's Education in the United States." *Demographic Research* 15:537–60.

Mason, Mary Ann. 1994. *From Fathers' Property to Children's Rights: The History of Child Custody in the United States.* New York: Columbia University Press.

May, Elaine Tyler. 1980. *Great Expectations: Marriage and Divorce in Post-Victorian America.* Chicago: University of Chicago Press.

———. 1988. *Homeward Bound: American Families in the Cold War Era.* New York: Basic Books.

McCormick, Elsie. 1954. "That Amazing Secretarial Shortage." *Reader's Digest,* February, pp. 53–56.

McGarry, Kathleen, and Robert F. Schoeni. 1995. "Transfer Behavior in the Health and Retirement Study." *Journal of Human Resources* 30 (supp.):S184–S226.

McLaren, Angus. 1978. *Birth Control in Nineteenth-Century England.* New York: Holmes & Meier.

McLoyd, Vonnie C., Ana Mari Cauce, David Takeuchi, and Leon Wilson. 2000. "Marital Processes and Parental Socialization in Families of Color: A Decade Review of Research." *Journal of Marriage and Family* 62:1070–93.

McRoberts, Omar M. 2003. *Streets of Glory: Church and Community in a Black Urban Neighborhood.* Chicago: University of Chicago Press.

Mead, Rebecca. 2007. *One Perfect Day: The Selling of the American Wedding.* New York: Penguin.

Meyer, Donald. 1988. *The Positive Thinkers: Popular Religious Psychology from Mary Baker Eddy to Norman Vincent Peale and Ronald Reagan.* Revised ed. Middletown, CT: Wesleyan University Press.

Meyer, Joyce. 2000. *Help Me—I'm Married!* New York: Warner Books.

Meyerowitz, Joanne. 1994. "Beyond the Feminine Mystique: A Reassessment of Postwar Mass Culture, 1946–1958." Pp. 229–62 in *Not June Cleaver: Women and Gender in Postwar America, 1945–1960,* edited by J. Meyerowitz. Philadelphia: Temple University Press.

National Council of State Legislatures. 2008. "Same Sex Marriage"; retrieved November 2, 2008, from http://www.ncsl.org/programs/cyf/samesex.htm.

National Institute of Demographic Studies (France). 2007. "Indice synthétique de fécondité (Period Total Fertility Rate)"; retrieved May 16, 2007, from http://www.ined.fr/fr/pop_chiffres/pays_developpes/conjoncture/un_indicateur.

Nelson, Sandi, Rebecca L. Clark, and Gregory Acs. 2001. "Beyond the Two-Parent Family: How Teenagers Fare in Cohabiting Couple and Blended Families." Washington, D.C.: The Urban Institute; retrieved December 8, 2005, from http://www.urban.org/UploadedPDF/anf_b31.pdf.

O'Brien, John E. 1971. "Violence in Divorce Prone Families. *Journal of Marriage and Family* 33:692–98.

O'Connell, Martin, and Maurice Moore. 1980. "The Legitimacy Status of First Births to U.S. Women Aged 15–24, 1939–1978." *Family Planning Perspectives* 12:16–25.

O'Connor, Thomas G., Avshalom Caspi, John C. DeFries, and Robert Plomin. 2000. "Are Associations Between Parental Divorce and Children's Adjustment Genetically Mediated? An Adoption Study." *Developmental Psychology* 36:429–37.

Office of National Statistics (United Kingdom). 2005. "Child Population: 23% Dependent Children Living in Lone Parent Family in 2001"; retrieved November 24, 2005, from http://www.statistics .gov.uk/cci/nugget.asp?id=716.

Ogburn, William F. 1964. "Cultural Lag as Theory." Pp. 86–95 in *William F. Ogburn on Culture and Social Change: Selected Papers,* edited by O. D. Duncan. Chicago: University of Chicago Press.

Olsen, Robert B. 1955. "Husband and Wife: Personal Tort Actions Between Spouses: Statutory Construction." *Michigan Law Review* 53:1192–95.

O'Neill, William L. 1967. *Divorce in the Progressive Era.* New York: New Viewpoints.

Ooms, Theodora. 2002. "Marriage and Government: Strange Bedfellows?" Center for Law and Social Policy.

———. 2005. "The New Kid on the Block: What Is Marriage Education and Does It Work?" Center for Law and Social Policy.

Oppenheimer, Valerie K. 2003. "Cohabiting and Marriage During Young Men's Career-Development Process." *Demography* 40:127–49.

Oropesa, R. S., and Nancy S. Landale. 2004. "The Future of Marriage and Hispanics." *Journal of Marriage and Family* 66:901–20.

Oropesa, R. S., Daniel T. Lichter, and Robert N. Anderson. 1994. "Marriage Markets and the Paradox of Mexican American Nuptiality." *Journal of Marriage and Family* 56:889–907.

Osborne, Cynthia, and Sara McLanahan. 2007. "Partnership Instability and Child Well-Being." *Journal of Marriage and Family* 69:1065–83.

Osteen, Joel. 2004. *Your Best Life Now: 7 Steps to Living at Your Full Potential.* New York: Warner Faith.

———. 2007. *Become a Better You: 7 Keys to Improving Your Life Every Day.* New York: Free Press.

Otnes, Cele C., and Elizabeth H. Pleck. 2003. *Cinderella Dreams: The Allure of the Lavish Wedding.* Berkeley: University of California Press.

Parsons, Talcott, and Robert F. Bales. 1955. *Family, Socialization, and the Interaction Process.* New York: Free Press.

Passet, Joanne E. 2003. *Sex Radicals and the Quest for Women's Equality.* Urbana: University of Illinois Press.

Patterson, Charlotte J. 1995. "Families of the Lesbian Baby Boom: Parents' Division of Labor and Children's Adjustment." *Developmental Psychology* 31:115–23.

Paul, Pamela. 2002. *The Starter Marriage and the Future of Matrimony.* New York: Random House.

Peale, Norman Vincent. 1952. *The Power of Positive Thinking.* New York: Prentice-Hall.

Pedersen, Susan. 1993. *Family, Dependence, and the Origins of the Welfare State: Britain and France, 1914–1945.* Cambridge: Cambridge University Press.

Peterson, Kavan. 2006. "Seven More States Ban Gay Marriage, but Ariz. Bucks Trend"; retrieved January 3, 2007, from http://stateline.org.

Pew Forum on Religion and Public Life. 2008. "U.S. Religious Landscape Survey"; retrieved April 14, 2008, from http://religions.pewforum.org/reports.

Phillips, Roderick. 1988. *Putting Asunder: A History of Divorce in Western Society.* Cambridge: Cambridge University Press.

Pierson, George W. 1938. *Tocqueville and Beaumont in America.* New York: Oxford University Press.

———. 1973. *The Moving American.* New York: Knopf.

Pleck, Elizabeth. 1987. *Domestic Tyranny: The Making of American Social Policy Against Family Violence from Colonial Times to the Present.* New York: Oxford University Press.

Pollak, Robert A. 1985. "A Transaction Costs Approach to Families and Households." *Journal of Economic Literature* 23:581–608.

Portes, A., and J. Sensenbrenner. 1993. "Embeddedness and Immigration: Notes on the Social Determinants of Economic Action." *American Journal of Sociology* 98:1320–50.

Preston, Samuel H., Patrick Heuveline, and Michel Guillot. 2001. *Demography: Measuring and Modeling Population Processes.* Malden, MA: Blackwell.

Putnam, Robert D. 2000. *Bowling Alone: The Collapse and Revival of American Community.* New York: Simon and Schuster.

Rainwater, Lee, and William L. Yancey. 1967. *The Moynihan Report and the Politics of Controversy.* Cambridge, MA: MIT Press.

Raley, R. Kelly, and Larry L. Bumpass. 2003. "The Topography of the Divorce Plateau: Levels and Trends in Union Stability in the United States After 1980." *Demographic Research* 8:245–59.

Raley, R. Kelly, T. Elizabeth Durden, and Elizabeth Wildsmith. 2004. "Understanding Mexican-American Marriage Patterns Using a Life-Course Approach." *Social Science Quarterly* 85:872–90.

Raley, R. Kelly, Michelle L. Frisco, and Elizabeth Wildsmith. 2005. "Maternal Cohabitation and Educational Success." *Sociology of Education* 78:144–64.

Reagan, Leslie J. 1997. *When Abortion Was a Crime: Women, Medicine, and Law in the United States, 1867–1973.* Berkeley: University of California Press.

Reed, Joanna M. 2006. "Not Crossing the 'Extra Line': How Cohabitors with Children View Their Unions," *Journal of Marriage and Family* 68:1117–31.

Reutter, Mark. 2001. "Shadow of Steel's Lost Empire," *Baltimore Sun,* October 19.

Rheinstein, Max. 1972. *Marriage Stability, Divorce, and the Law.* Chicago: University of Chicago Press.

Richer, Elise, Abby Frank, Mark Greenberg, Steve Savner, and Vicki Turetsky. 2003. *Boom Times a Bust: Declining Employment Among Less-Educated Young Men.* Washington, DC: Center for Law and Social Policy; retrieved July 13, 2004, from http://www.clasp.org/DMS/Documents/1058362464.08/Boom_Times.pdf.

Roberts, Paula. 2006. "Update on the Marriage and Fatherhood Provisions of the 2006 Federal Budget and the 2007 Budget Proposal." Washington, DC: Center for Law and Social Policy; retrieved June 13, 2006, from http://www.clasp.org/publications/marriage_conference.pdf.

Roof, Wade Clark. 1999. *Spiritual Marketplace: Baby Boomers and the Remaking of American Religion.* Princeton, NJ: Princeton University Press.

Rosenfeld, Michael J. 2007. *The Age of Independence: Interracial Unions, Same-Sex Unions, and the Changing American Family.* Cambridge, MA: Harvard University Press.

Rubin, Lillian B. 1994. *Families on the Fault Line.* New York: HarperCollins.

Rudd, Elizabeth C. 2000. "Reconceptualizing Gender in Postsocialist Transformation." *Gender & Society* 14:517–39.

Ryan, Rebecca M. 1995. "The Sex Right: A Legal History of the Marital Rape Exemption." *Law and Social Inquiry* 20:941–1001.

Sargeant, Kimon Howland. 2000. *Seeker Churches: Promoting Traditional Religion in a Nontraditional Way.* New Brunswick, NJ: Rutgers University Press.

Schacter, Jane S. 2000. "Constructing Families in a Democracy: Courts, Legislatures, and Second-Parent Adoption." *Chicago-Kent Law Review* 75:933–50.

Schneider, Elizabeth M. 2000. "The Law and Violence Against Women in the Family at Century's End: The US Experience." Pp. 471–94 in *Cross-Currents: Family Law and Policy in the United States and England,* edited by Sanford N. Katz, John Eekelaar, and Mavis Maclean. Oxford: Oxford University Press.

Schwartz, Christine R., and Robert D. Mare. 2005. "Trends in Educational Assortative Marriage from 1940 to 2003." *Demography* 42:621–46.

Seidman, Steven. 1991. *Romantic Longings: Love in America.* New York: Routledge.

Shaw, Chris. 1999. "1996-Based Population Projections by Legal Marital Status for England and Wales." *Population Trends* 95:23–32.

Sherkat, Darren E., and Christopher G. Ellison. 1999. "Recent Developments and Current Controversies in the Sociology of Religion." *Annual Review of Sociology* 25:363–94.

Siegel, Reva B. 1996. " 'The Rule of Love': Wife Beating as Prerogative and Privacy." *Yale Law Journal* 105:2117–207.

Smart, Carol. 2000. "Divorce in England 1950–2000: A Moral Tale." Pp. 363–85 in *Cross Currents: Family Law and Policy in the United States and England,* edited by Sanford N. Katz, John Eekelaar, and Mavis Maclean. Oxford: Oxford University Press.

Smock, Pamela J. 2000. "Cohabitation in the United States: An Appraisal of Research Themes, Findings, and Implications." *Annual Review of Sociology* 26:1–20.

Smock, Pamela J., and Wendy D. Manning. 2004. "Living Together Unmarried in the United States: Demographic Perspectives and Implications for Family Policy." *Law and Policy* 26:87–117.

Smock, Pamela J., Wendy D. Manning, and Meredith Porter. 2005. " 'Everything's There Except Money': How Money Shapes Decisions to Marry Among Cohabitors." *Journal of Marriage and Family* 67:680–96.

Speth, Linda E. 1982. "The Married Women's Property Acts, 1839–1865: Reform, Reaction, or Revolution?" Pp. 69–91 in *Women and the Law: A Social Historical Perspective,* vol. 2, edited by D. K. Weisberg. Cambridge, MA: Schenkman.

Stacey, Judith. 2006. "Gay Parenthood and the Decline of Paternity as We Knew It." *Sexualities* 9:27–55.

Stark, Rodney, and Roger Finke. 2000. *Acts of Faith: Explaining the Human Side of Religion.* Berkeley: University of California Press.

Starr, Paul. 2004. *The Creation of the Media: Political Origins of Modern Communications.* New York: Basic Books.

Statistics Canada. 1997. "Common-Law Unions in Canada at the End of the 20th Century." Catalogue no. 91-209-XPE. Ottawa.

Stone, Lawrence. 1990. *Road to Divorce: England, 1530–1987.* Oxford: Oxford University Press.

Struck, Doug. 2004. "High Court in Canada Backs Gay Marriage." *Washington Post,* December 10.

Swidler, Ann. 1986. "Culture in Action: Symbols and Strategies." *American Sociological Review* 51:273–86.

———. 2001. *Talk of Love: How Culture Matters.* Chicago: University of Chicago Press.

Symonds, William C. 2005. "Earthly Empires: How Evangelical Churches Are Borrowing from the Business Playbook." *BusinessWeek,* May 23.

Tamney, Joseph B. 2002. *The Resilience of Conservative Religion: The Case of Popular, Conservative, and Protestant Congregations.* Cambridge: Cambridge University Press.

Teitelbaum, Michael S., and Jay M. Winter. 1985. *The Fear of Population Decline.* Orlando, FL: Academic Press.

Thomas, William Isaac. 1923. *The Unadjusted Girl.* Boston: Little, Brown.

Thomson, Elizabeth, and Jan M. Hoem. 1998. "Couple Childbearing Plans and Births in Sweden." *Demography* 35:315–22.

Thornton, Arland. 2005. *Reading History Sideways: The Fallacy and Enduring Impact of the Developmental Paradigm on Family Life.* Chicago: University of Chicago Press.

Thornton, Arland, and Linda Young-DeMarco. 2001. "Four Decades of Trends in Attitudes Toward Family Issues in the United States: The 1960s Through the 1990s." *Journal of Marriage and Family* 63:1009–37.

Tiger, Lionel, and Robin Fox. 1971. *The Imperial Animal.* New York: Holt, Rinehart, and Winston.

Tocqueville, Alexis de. 1994. *Democracy in America.* New York: Knopf.

Uhlenberg, Peter. 1980. "Death and the Family." *Journal of Family History* 5:313–20.

U.S. Bureau of Labor. 2007. "Tomorrow's Jobs"; retrieved April 26, 2008, from http://www.bls.gov/oco/oco2003.htm.

U.S. Bureau of the Census. 1975. "Historical Statistics of the United States, Colonial Times to 1970." U.S. Government Printing Office, Washington, DC.

———. 2003. *Married-Couple and Unmarried-Partner Households: 2000.* Census 2000 Special Reports, CENSR-5. Washington, DC: U.S. Government Printing Office.

———. 2004. "Educational Attainment in the United States, 2003." *Current Population Reports,* Series P20-550; retrieved November 23, 2005, from http://www.census.gov/prod/2004pubs/p20–550.pdf.

———. 2005a. "Indicators of Marriage and Fertility in the United States from the American Community Survey: 2000 to 2003"; retrieved November 22, 2005, from http://www.census.gov/population/www/socdemo/fertility/mar-fert-slides.html.

———. 2005b. "Statistical Abstract of the United States, 2004–2005"; retrieved November 1, 2005, from http://www.census.gov/statab/www/minihs.html.

———. 2005c. *Statistical Abstract of the United States: 2006.* Washington, DC: U.S. Government Printing Office.

————. 2006a. "Educational Attainment of the Population 15 Years and Over, by Age, Sex, Race, and Hispanic Origin: 2005"; retrieved July 5, 2007, from http://www.census.gov/population/www/socdemo/education/cps2005.html.

————. 2006b. "A Half Century of Learning: Historical Statistics on Educational Attainment in the United States, 1940 to 2000"; retrieved January 6, 2008, from http://www.census.gov/population/www/socdemo/education/phct41.html.

————. 2007. "Statistical Abstract of the United States, 2007"; retrieved December 16, 2006, and July 1, 2007, from http://www.census.gov/compendia/statab/2007 edition.html.

van de Velde, Theodor H. 1930. *Ideal Marriage: Its Physiology and Technique.* New York: Random House.

Vasoli, Robert H. 1998. *What God Has Joined Together: The Annulment Crisis in American Catholicism.* New York: Oxford University Press.

Waite, Linda J., and Maggie Gallagher. 2000. *The Case for Marriage: Why Married People Are Happier, Healthier and Better Off Financially.* New York: Doubleday.

Wallerstein, Judith S., Julia M. Lewis, and Sandra Blakeslee. 2000. *The Unexpected Legacy of Divorce.* New York: Hyperion.

Warren, Rick. 2002. *The Purpose Driven Life.* Grand Rapids, MI: Zondervan.

Weber, Max. (1904) 2002. *The Protestant Ethic and the Spirit of Capitalism.* London: Routledge.

Weeks, Jeffrey, Brian Heaphy, and Catherine Donovan. 2001. *Same Sex Intimacies: Families of Choice and Other Life Experiments.* London: Routledge.

Weiss, Jessica. 2000. *To Have and to Hold: Marriage, the Baby Boom, and Social Change.* Chicago: University of Chicago Press.

Welch, Cheryl B. 2001. *De Tocqueville.* Oxford: Oxford University Press.

Westoff, Charles F., and Elise F. Jones. 1979. "The End of 'Catholic' Fertility." *Demography* 16:209–17.

Whitehead, Barbara Dafoe. 1997. *The Divorce Culture.* New York: Knopf.

Whitehead, Barbara Dafoe, and David Popenoe. 2001. "Who Wants to Marry a Soul Mate?" Pp. 6–16 in *The State of Our Unions, 2001,* edited by National Marriage Project; retrieved February 12, 2004, from http://marriage.rutgers.edu/Publications/SOOU/NMPAR2001.pdf.

Whyte, Martin King. 1990. *Dating, Mating, and Marriage.* New York: Aldine de Gruyter.

Wilcox, W. Bradford. 2002. "For the Sake of the Children: Family-Related Discourse and Practice in the Mainline." Pp. 287–316 in *The Quiet Hand of God: Faith-Based Activism and the Public Role of Mainline Protestantism,* edited by R. Wuthnow and J. H. Evans. Berkeley: University of California Press.

————. 2004. *Soft Patriarchs, New Men: How Christianity Shapes Fathers and Husbands.* Chicago: University of Chicago Press.

Wilde, Melissa J. 2001. "From Excommunication to Nullification: Testing and Extending Supply-Side." *Journal for the Scientific Study of Religion* 40:235–50.

Wilson, Robin Fretwell. 2006. *Reconceiving the Family: Critique on the American Law Institute's Principles of the Law of Family Dissolution.* New York: Cambridge University Press.

Wilson, William Julius. 1987. *The Truly Disadvantaged: The Inner City, the Underclass, and Public Policy.* Chicago: University of Chicago Press.

Witte, John Jr. 1997. *From Sacrament to Contract: Marriage, Religion, and Law in the Western Tradition.* Louisville: Westminster John Knox Press.

Wolfe, Alan. 1998. *One Nation, After All.* New York: Viking.

———. 2001. *Moral Freedom: The Search for Virtue in a World of Choice.* New York: W. W. Norton.

———. 2003. *The Transformation of American Religion: How We Actually Live Our Faith.* New York: Free Press.

Woodberry, Robert D., and Christian S. Smith. 1998. "Fundamentalism et al.: Conservative Protestants in America." *Annual Review of Sociology* 24:25–56.

Woodward, Lianne, David M. Fergusson, and L. John Horwood. 2001. "Risk Factors and Life Processes Associated with Teenage Pregnancy: Results from a Prospective Study from Birth to 20 Years." *Journal of Marriage and Family* 63:1170–84.

Wu, Lawrence L., and Brian C. Martinson. 1993. "Family Structure and the Risk of Premarital Birth." *American Sociological Review* 59:210–32.

Wu, Lawrence L., and Elizabeth Thomson. 2001. "Race Differences in Family Experience and Early Sexual Initiation: Dynamic Models of Family Structure and Family Change." *Journal of Marriage and Family* 63:682–96.

Wuthnow, Robert. 1988. *The Restructuring of American Religion: Society and Faith Since World War II.* Princeton, NJ: Princeton University Press.

———. 1998. *After Heaven: Spirituality in America Since the 1950s.* Berkeley: University of California Press.

Wyatt, Edward. 2006. "Religious Broadcaster Gets Rich Contract for Next Book." *New York Times,* March 15.

Index

A Note on the Type

The text of this book was set in Simoncini Garamond, a modern version by Francesco Simoncini of the type attributed to the famous Parisian type cutter Claude Garamond (ca. 1480–1561). Garamond was a pupil of Geoffroy Tory and is believed to have based his letters on the Venetian models, although he introduced a number of important differences, and it is to him we owe the letter that we know as old style. He gave to his letters a certain elegance and feeling of movement that won for their creator an immediate reputation and the patronage of Francis I of France.

Composed by North Market Street Graphics
Lancaster, Pennsylvania

Printed and bound by Berryville Graphics
Berryville, Virginia

Designed by M. Kristen Bearse